Teaching Teachers

Teaching Teachers

Changing Paths and Enduring Debates

JAMES W. FRASER *and* LAUREN LEFTY

Foreword by ARTHUR LEVINE

Johns Hopkins University Press

Baltimore

© 2018 Johns Hopkins University Press
All rights reserved. Published 2018
Printed in the United States of America on acid-free paper
9 8 7 6 5 4 3 2 1

Johns Hopkins University Press
2715 North Charles Street
Baltimore, Maryland 21218-4363
www.press.jhu.edu

Library of Congress Cataloging-in-Publication Data

Names: Fraser, James W., 1944– author. | Lefty, Lauren, 1987– author.
Title: Teaching teachers : changing paths and enduring debates / James W.
    Fraser and Lauren Lefty ; Foreword by Arthur Levine.
Description: Baltimore, Maryland : Johns Hopkins University Press, 2018. |
    Includes bibliographical references and index.
Identifiers: LCCN 2017058443 | ISBN 9781421426358 (hardcover : alk. paper) |
    ISBN 1421426358 (hardcover : alk. paper) | ISBN 9781421426365 (electronic)
    | ISBN 1421426366 (electronic)
Subjects: LCSH: Teachers—Training of. | Alternative education. | Educational change.
Classification: LCC LB1707 .F74 2018 | DDC 370.71/1—dc23
    LC record available at https://lccn.loc.gov/2017058443

A catalog record for this book is available from the British Library.

*Special discounts are available for bulk purchases of this book. For more information,
please contact Special Sales at 410-516-6936 or specialsales@press.jhu.edu.*

Johns Hopkins University Press uses environmentally friendly book materials, including
recycled text paper that is composed of at least 30 percent post-consumer waste, whenever
possible.

CONTENTS

FOREWORD

I was honored to be invited to write the foreword to this volume for a host of reasons. First, Jim Fraser is a colleague and friend of long standing, and I deeply admire his work. Jim is one of the most knowledgeable, thoughtful, and creative thinkers on teacher education in the country. He brings a very rare, perhaps unique perspective to the topic. He is a scholar who studies the historical roots of contemporary teacher education and a practitioner who has served as a dean and professor and led major teacher education reform initiatives at universities around the country. He also has extensive experience working on teacher education with school districts and policymakers at the local, state, and national levels.

Second, Jim Fraser is a superb talent scout, and I wanted to be able to say I wrote the foreword to Lauren Lefty's first book.

Third, the field of teacher education is undergoing profound change—the rhetoric is heated; the data scarce; and the future uncertain. We live at a time when the United States is making a transition from a national, analog, industrial economy to a global, digital, information economy. Our social institutions—education, government, media, health care, and the rest—were created for the former economy. They work less well than they once did and appear to be broken. The fact is that change in our social institutions mirrors that of the general society, but lags behind. These institutions need to be refitted for a new world. This can happen in two ways. The existing institutions can be repaired and updated, or they can be replaced. Repair is the more common remedy in not-for-profits, while replacement prevails in for-profits.

Today, both repair and replace are occurring in teacher education, as this book documents. We can see this same pattern if we look back in history to the industrial revolution, when higher education was transformed and the classical college—established for a local, agrarian society—became the modern industrial-era system of higher education. The phases by which that occurred are familiar. In antebellum America, there was criticism from policymakers, media, and the public that higher education was too expensive and out of touch with the times. The response from the nation's colleges was, at many institutions, rejection of the charges and, at others, efforts at reform. In the post–Civil War era, as industrialization accelerated and deepened, the transformation of higher education followed in earnest. New types of institutions were created: universities, technical institutes, land-grant colleges that straddled the old and emerging worlds, and junior colleges (not yet named community colleges). The practices of these institutions were adopted in hurly-burly fashion around the country, with individual institutions giving their own twist to the innovative new practices. The result was something akin to the disorder of the Wild West. With time came standardization of practice through newly created accrediting associations and the adoption of common standards, such as the Carnegie Unit. Integration of the various forms of higher education followed, culminating in the California Master Plan of 1960.

Institutional change in higher education during the nineteenth century and the first half of the twentieth was a messy process in which all of these things occurred simultaneously, more resembling a three-ring circus than a well-staged theater production. Emotions ran high, divisions were wide, the landscape of change seemed incomprehensible, and the ultimate result was unknowable.

In a very real sense, this is the state of teacher education today. The criticism, the rejection, and the experimentation surround us. The new and the old exist side by side. Advocacy, anger, and panaceas bombard us. We cling to the past, and we embrace the future. Teacher education is being transformed. We are once again at the Wild West stage of change. What is certain is that standardization and integration will follow. What is uncertain is what will emerge at the conclusion.

These days, I often feel like Rip Van Winkle from Washington Irving's 1819 short story. It's the tale of a man who sleeps for twenty years but wakes up believing he has slept for a single night. He walks through the village in which he has lived his entire life and does not recognize the homes, the businesses, the names on the doors, or the people. Nearly mad, he screams, "Everything's changed, and I'm changed, and I can't tell what's my name, or who I am." The story has been described as a metaphor for the industrial revolution. So rapid and profound was the transformation that it seemed possible to sleep a single night but wake up the next day and feel as if twenty years of change had occurred.

I have spent the past quarter century studying, administering, and working to strengthen teacher education. The world I knew is disappearing, and a new world, less recognizable, is growing up around me.

In his 1953 novel *The Go-Between*, British author L. P. Hartley wrote "The past is a foreign country: they do things differently there." When I visit a new country, I always buy a guidebook.

This volume is that guidebook. It is a gift. I have been waiting for it for years. It compellingly explains where teacher education is and how it got here. It comprehensively describes the landscape of teacher education today—the types of changes that are occurring and the driving forces they embody. It dispassionately describes and evaluates the changes through case studies of the best-known initiatives of each type. It offers a commonsense set of recommendations to guide the future.

This book should be required reading for the policymakers and practitioners who have the capacity to shape the future of teacher education. It is a must-read for those who hire teachers, who are teachers, who plan to become teachers, or who educate teachers. It is a book that has to be read by those who fund teacher education, who report on teacher education, and who care about the future of teacher education. This is one of those truly exceptional books that enables readers to see the world in new, clearer, and actionable ways. I thank Jim Fraser and Lauren Lefty for writing it.

Arthur Levine

ACKNOWLEDGMENTS

This book has had a long gestation, perhaps far longer than the authors anticipated when the process started. As a result, many debts have been accumulated for which the appearance of this volume is a small partial payment.

James W. Fraser attended a fast-track teacher preparation program at New York University (NYU) and began teaching elementary school in New York City in 1968. The program did not prepare him for what he found at P.S. 76 Manhattan. His next serious encounter with the world of teacher education came in 1987, when Robert Schwartz, then education adviser to Governor Michael Dukakis, asked him to serve as the staff director to the Massachusetts Joint Task Force on Teacher Preparation. This task force was a commission of the state Board of Education and the Board of Regents of Higher Education that was committed to bringing some of the recommendations of the Holmes Group (see Introduction) into the state's public policy.

In 1993, Jack Curry, president of Northeastern University, and Robert Lowndes, then dean of Arts & Sciences, and invited Fraser to be the director of the university's new Center for Innovation in Urban Education with a mandate to lead an effort to rethink the way the university offered teacher education. The result was the creation of the School of Education at Northeastern, with a deep link to the faculty of arts and sciences, a heavy emphasis on content knowledge, and a clearly practice-oriented and community-based approach to the preparation of teachers for city schools.

In 2004, Mary Brabeck, dean of the Steinhardt School of Culture, Education and Human Development at NYU, and several faculty colleagues invited Fraser to come to NYU as a visiting professor. Two years later, the NYU appointment became permanent, and he has spent the last decade splitting time between research and teaching in the history of education and an effort at NYU to fundamentally rethink the preparation of teachers.

In 2008, Arthur Levine invited Fraser to become senior vice president of the Woodrow National Fellowship Foundation just as the foundation, under Levine's leadership, was shifting the heart of its work to providing fellowships for aspiring teachers and working with education schools to radically improve the programs they offered to Woodrow Wilson Teaching Fellows. Fraser happily spent the next four years visiting schools of education, seeing extremely creative efforts on many campuses to rethink the preparation of teachers, and getting to know a generation of terrific teachers who taught him much about their commitments and aspirations.

Fraser owes a great debt to Bob Schwartz for enlisting him in what became part of his life's work; to Bob Lowndes and Jack Curry and their successors, Jim Stellar and Richard Freeland; to his early colleagues at Northeastern, Angels Irving and Peter Murrell; and to many colleagues at NYU, including Mary Brabeck, Rene Arcilla, Jon Zimmerman, Robby Cohen, Joe McDonald, and Diana Turk, as well as current colleagues and students in the Department of Allied Statistics, Social Science, and Humanities, especially department administrative manager Letizia La Rosa for making NYU such a fertile intellectual home for his work in the history of teacher preparation. He has spent many hours discussing this project with many colleagues but owes a special debt to Arthur Levine of the Woodrow Wilson Foundation; Ken Zeichner of the University of Washington, whose detailed comments have made this a much better book; Mary Brabeck of NYU; Bob Bain of the University of Michigan; Audra Watson and Bethany Rogers of the Woodrow Wilson Foundation; and his terrific coauthor, Lauren Lefty. As with every project, he could not have done this without the support of his beloved wife, Katherine.

Lauren Lefty likewise began her career in education through a fast-track teacher preparation program: Teach for America. Similarly frustrated with its meager five-week training but forever altered by the experience of teaching and learning alongside her middle and high school students and adult colleagues on the Texas–Mexico border and in Brooklyn, New York, she has since dedicated her professional life to improving educational equity and justice. Before beginning doctoral work in the history of education at NYU, Lefty worked in education policy with the New York City Department of Education. All of these experiences, from teaching to policy work, led to a firm conviction in the complexity of educational debates, ranging from teacher education policy to school choice to racial segregation, and the need for a critical socio-historical approach to understanding these issues.

As an early career scholar, Lefty is deeply indebted to her coauthor, James Fraser, for the opportunity to research and cowrite this book, a joy-filled process of surprising research finds, thought-provoking discussions, and good-natured debate. She is forever grateful to the intellectual mentorship of the faculty members at NYU, particularly her advisor, Jonathan Zimmerman, and her doctoral cohort. The process of cowriting a book while simultaneously writing a dissertation could not have occurred without the support of friends, a wonderful life and thought partner, and the ever-loving Lefty family.

Many people have contributed to Fraser and Lefty's thinking and research as they have written this book. At the risk of failing to mention some, they want to acknowledge the help and ideas they have received along the way from Tim Knowles of the University of Chicago; Rachel Lotan; Linda Darling-Hammond and Lee Shulman of Stanford University; Deborah Balogh of the University of Indianapolis; Norman Atkins at the Relay Graduate School of Education; and Fran Peterman, Robert Mendenhall, Scott Pulsipher, and their many colleagues at Western Governors University. They also benefited from several conversations with Marisa Bier of the Seattle Teacher Residency, Deborah Hirsch at the Woodrow Wilson Academy, and Larry Rosenstock and his colleagues, including Ady Kayrouz and Kelly Wilson, at High Tech High School.

Funding as well as intellectual support for this project has come from many sources. The authors give special thanks to the Woodrow Wilson Foundation for its support of this effort; to the Annenberg Foundation, which funded some of the initial research on which this book is based through a grant to the Woodrow Wilson Foundation; to the Spencer Foundation, whose support made the case studies of many different programs possible; and to the Steinhardt School of Culture, Education, and Human Development at NYU, which has provided both a stimulating intellectual climate and tangible support toward the completion of this book.

Of course, none of those who supported this research are responsible for the conclusions the authors have reached. They are sure that all of those with whom they talked will find things with which they both agree and sharply disagree. The authors hope that this effort furthers additional conversations that help all involved in teacher preparation learn, reach new understandings, and develop new policies.

Teaching Teachers

Considering the Future of Teacher Preparation in Light of the Past

A S RECENTLY AS 1990, if a person wanted to become a public school teacher in most parts of the United States, they needed to attend a university, either in an undergraduate education program or, if they already had a college degree, in a stand-alone master's degree program. There were, of course exceptions, individuals who were hired on temporary licenses or who had the regular requirements waived, but from the mid-1950s to the late 1980s, the route into teaching was clear and exceptions rare.

Less than three decades later the variety of routes into teaching is staggering. Since 1986, some schools of education and states have implemented selected recommendations from the many reports proposing wide-ranging reforms of teacher education, including the Holmes Group's report, which was the best known of those that appeared in the 1980s. But other schools did not implement any recommendations and, indeed, many actively resisted calls for change.

At the same time that education schools were debating the many reform recommendations, other reformers implemented an extraordinary range of new alternative programs, most of which involved moving teacher education out of universities altogether. Many of these new programs began with substantial government and foundation support. In some school districts and charter schools, superintendents started their own teacher preparation programs—sometimes in collaboration with universities or alternative providers, but sometimes not. Teach for America (TFA), which sometimes operates fully independently and sometimes in partnership with others, is the best known of the many independent teacher preparation programs that emerged in these years, but it is not the only such program.

Other teacher educators designed new blended programs—creating new forms of collaboration between university teacher education programs and other parts of the university, borrowing innovations, linking with school districts and independent providers, and creating a range of novel options.

Today, few people can keep track of the range and variety of alternatives in teacher education. In this book, we explore a series of case studies that exemplify all of these efforts.

There are as many different definitions of the term "alternative providers" as there are options for aspiring teachers. Some people would define everything but the traditional four-year undergraduate program with an education major to be an alternative program. With this definition, even university-based MA and MAT programs are considered alternative routes. Others would include blended programs in which a university and a school district collaborate in the development of a new approach. Yet others insist that only programs with no university connection truly belong in the alternative category. This diversity in definitions is one of the reasons that exact numbers of participants in alternative versus traditional programs are so hard to find. In this book, we include traditional campus-based graduate programs in the definition of traditional programs but generally look at online or district-based programs as alternative routes to teaching, unless a university has the primary role in offering the program.

The latest federal numbers from the 2009–2010 school year show approximately 80% of teachers graduating from university-based education schools, plus another 8% coming from university-based alternative programs, while 12% come from teacher education programs with no university connection. A decade earlier, in 2000–2001, almost 90% of new teachers were education school graduates. By some estimates today, the total number of new teachers coming from alternative routes has grown to somewhere between 30% and 40% of new teachers, though all such numbers are but best guesses, in large part because the definitions are so slippery.[1]

Among university teacher educators there have been intense debates about the best course of action. Some defend the traditional education major with a sprinkling of courses in the disciplines. Some within universities and state agencies call for an arts and sciences major for all new teachers, including elementary. Some call for significantly more time in student teaching or other school-based clinical experiences, while others resent the time away from discipline-based and methods-related courses demanded by such experiences. Some, like the longtime advocate of professionalization in teacher preparation Linda Darling-Hammond and the leaders of the new (2014) teacher accreditation organization Council for the Accreditation of Educator Preparation (CAEP), argue that admission and program quality standards must be raised dramatically and that those schools that fail to measure up should cease to prepare teachers. Others argue that CAEP's standards are too cumbersome, rigid, and expensive and that a greater tolerance for programmatic variety must be fostered, especially in light of the great difficulty in measuring any program's actual quality.[2] To say that there is no agreement about the best system of teacher preparation, even within university schools of education, is a drastic understatement.

Today's alternative providers also debate intensely about the best way to prepare teachers—through short-term summer preparation followed by a deep-dive into the profession, through online programs, through school-based residency arrangements, or through courses offered outside of traditional universities—even as each route seeks its market share.

In the midst of these debates, many different programs have arisen, each claiming to be the best route into teaching. For teacher educators, funders, public officials charged with monitoring the quality of teacher education, participants at national and international conferences seeking a new definition of excellence in teacher preparation, and, perhaps most of all, principals and superintendents who hire teachers and those who seek to enter the profession, what was once a simple straight line has become a confusing range of often mutually hostile options.[3]

Kenneth Zeichner, who has spent as much time as any other contemporary scholar studying teacher education, has described three, perhaps four, competing reform agendas that often collide with one another, but all of which call for change in today's university-based teacher education programs. There is what he calls the "professionalism agenda," which seeks to improve the quality of teacher preparation by creating tough and enforceable national standards enforced by strong accreditation systems like CAEP. There is the "deregulation agenda," which is espoused by some of those who are highly skeptical of any national standards and who seek to support multiple avenues into teaching—outside as well as inside of universities—leaving those who hire teachers responsible for the quality of those placed in the classroom. There is a "social justice agenda"—subject to intense debate even among its adherents—that seeks to transform public schools by transforming teaching education so that a new generation of teachers can help level the playing field in U.S. schools. Finally, there is what Marilyn Cochran-Smith calls an "overregulation agenda," in which some states officials seek to improve the field by micromanaging every aspect of teacher education even as they foster alternative routes.[4]

No one of these agendas is dominant, and directives from state agencies, accrediting bodies, and critical evaluators often reflect conflicting and contradictory directives. No wonder teacher educators feel buffeted. Some of this criticism and some of these demands on us are reasonable. Some are not. Many contradict each other. Taken together they do not give much room to maneuver, innovate, and engage in creative new approaches to the preparation of teachers rather than merely complying with rules and policies set by others.

The purpose of this study is not to take sides in this sometimes overwrought debate among advocates of different approaches to the preparation of teachers, but rather to cast some light on the historical and social forces that led to a sea change in the ways teachers are prepared in the United States in the years since the mid-1980s. How did we come to have the current extraordinary diversity of teacher preparation programs? How did such wide variety appear so quickly? Why is this topic so contentious?

Whenever we tell friends or colleagues about the focus of our study, the immediate question is always the same: "So what is the answer to your question? Why did so many alternative routes to teaching emerge so quickly at the end of the twentieth century and the beginning of the twenty-first?" That question is, indeed, at the core of this book. After looking carefully at this history, we have come to believe that there is no one answer to our core question about why so many alternative routes have emerged in the past thirty years. We have come to see any single answer to this question as inevitably flawed. Indeed, the quest for a single answer seems to be a diversion from getting a clear understanding of what has happened and why. By contrast, multiple answers may provide some clarity that the effort to find one answer never can.

Answering the Question, Why Have So Many Different Routes to Teaching Emerged Since 1980?

In trying to understand the significant developments and changes in teacher education of the last thirty-five or so years, we focus on three broad answers, which taken together explain our history more than any one answer might.

1. As many in traditional education schools charge, it is certainly true that the increasing power of market forces to decide education policy, rather than state or other standards, has fostered the growth of alternative providers and has often led to significant reallocation of resources to these alternative providers.
2. The complaint by advocates of alternative programs that many

education schools are just not that good, and certainly not very interested in change, is also true. While it is unfair to paint all education schools with the same brush—many have gone to extraordinary lengths to improve their programs—some schools have dismissed calls for change as some sort of unholy plot and have remained surprisingly static in their programs and standards.

3. Finally, superintendents have taken a more active role in teacher education. In 1980, nearly all superintendents simply accepted the teachers that education schools produced, even if they sometimes grumbled about the quality of their preparation. Around 2000, superintendents in some districts began to look at the growing diversity in teacher education programs and asked, "Why not us?" The result was that more and more public school districts, as well as many charter school networks, began preparing their own teachers.

At first look, these answers could not be more different. They look at different data, blame different people, and look to different solutions. However, having spent the last two years looking at this history, we have come to the surprising (to ourselves) conclusion that perhaps all three are right—or at least right enough that they need to be taken seriously. Viewing a contentious time through the prism of the discipline of history allows one to embrace the complexity and contingency of historical developments and move beyond simplistic good versus bad value judgments. One can then begin to understand the historical context that shaped developments as well as unforeseen outcomes that had their own impact. Further, while both the positive and negative responses to the rise of alternative teacher preparation providers may point to important truths, neither position alone is sufficient. In this book we explore the developments that, taken together, may help us understand the changes that have taken place since 1986. Let us then look further at each of the three answers and the complaints that are behind them.

Education Schools' Complaints about the Role of Market Forces

If one asks many—perhaps most—members of the faculty of education schools why so many alternative providers have emerged in the past few decades, the answer may well come down to "It's part of a larger effort to privatize public education" or "It is part of an effort to let market forces dominate all aspects of American education." When asked to elaborate, many will say that there is some sort of "evil plot" that is being led by conservative forces in foundations and state houses to overturn many of the educational gains of the last half century. Certainly part of the change in teacher education is due to a growing fascination with letting market forces solve all problems. This dependence on market forces may be traced to the ideas of Milton Friedman in the 1950s; it formed a large part of the so-called Reagan Revolution in the 1980s and has remained strong ever since.[5] If one looks at the federal education budget under recent administrations, both Democratic and Republican, or at the major giving of the nation's largest foundations, the conclusion is inescapable—the floor has been tilted. Alternative teacher preparation providers are the favored children. University programs are denied essential funds by state legislatures, Congress, and private foundations that support innovation in teacher education, while many alternative providers find their funding to be somewhere between adequate and lavish. If the growth in alternative providers represents the power of market forces in educational decision making, then it is also true that market forces have a powerful influence on teacher education. There are all-too-many examples of alternative providers actively campaigning to limit the funds available to those seeking to improve university programs, even without the kind of evidence that the alternative programs work that is often demanded of the defenders of university-based programs.

Many faculty in education schools further complain that the new alternative models of teacher education represent a kind of "quick and dirty" approach that simply does not provide the needed skills or the sophisticated understanding of child and adolescent development essential for today's classrooms. Trusting market forces, they argue, means dramatically lowering the standards for new teachers and, in the end, undercuts the education of the students taught by new teachers. This is especially a problem, they note, when graduates of alternative routes teach in public or charter schools serving poor children and children of color, where the need to understand and be able to respond to complexity is especially great.

As the respected psychologist and educational researcher Lee Shulman said some time ago, "Teaching is impossible. If we simply add together all that is expected of a typical teacher and take note of the circumstances under which those activities are to be carried out, the sum makes greater demands than any individual can possibly fulfill."[6] At the very least, those from within the university say, we owe those who are entering this impossible field the most robust possible preparation—in human development, in pedagogy, in subject-matter content, and in foundations courses that explore the meaning, purpose, and history of education, along with intensive and well-supervised student teaching. To short circuit any aspect of a preparation program is to assume that teaching is easy, that "any smart person can do it," which is simply not true.

Many university-based educators worry about teacher preparation programs that violate their sense that preparing an effective, professional expert teacher is a complex process that requires more time and a more sophisticated preparation program than that offered by most alternative routes. They are concerned that market forces will allow the "quick and dirty" programs to drive programs with higher standards and expectations out of the market. While alternative routes often focus on a list of competencies and strategies, like those promulgated by Doug Lemov, most university-based teacher educators would probably agree with Linda Darling-Hammond that "teachers need to understand how children learn and how to make material accessible to a wide range of students to be successful," and that the kinds of courses offered in a university program of reasonable length are essential for this understanding. In an exhaustive study of the impact of teachers in Houston, Texas, on student achievement, Darling-Hammond and colleagues found, "Although some have suggested that perhaps bright college graduates like those who join TFA may not require professional preparation for teaching, we found no instance where uncertified Teach for America teachers performed as well as standard certified teachers of comparable experience levels teaching in similar settings."[7] The only exception the Darling-Hammond research team reported were TFA teachers who subsequently completed more traditional certification requirements in a university program. Such evidence, these researchers argue, proves the importance of a university teacher certification program. Most university-based teacher educators agree.[8]

Visit the meetings of the American Association of Colleges for Teacher Education or spend much time with university teacher education faculty, and you will hear some version of a second common complaint about alternative approaches to teacher preparation. As Angus Shiva Mungal of the School of Education at the University of Texas at El Paso states:

The marketization of public education means the adoption of market principles such as deregulation, school choice, competition and stratification. A common narrative of market-based reform is that public goods such as education institutions are viewed as bureaucratic monopolies and that deregulation opens the market to more agile, efficient and less costly organizations. This ideological perspective supports the notion that competition from alternative organizations will pressure competitors to be innovative or risk losing consumers. Deregulationists pointed to education schools' teacher preparation programs as ineffectual and aimed to grant full certification to candidates who could pass rigorous tests in lieu of coursework (Brewer, 2006). The deregulationists aim to de-academize coursework allowing potential teachers to bypass courses emphasizing pedagogy. Most importantly the deregulationists seek to expand teacher preparation to outside organizations such as TFA.[9]

Mungal is not alone in making this argument. And for him and many of his colleagues, it is a damning indictment. Deregulation may allow market forces to work well in the world of business, they argue, but in institutions dedicated to the public good, not to private profit, it has no place.

Birth of Alternative Routes

Those being criticized by Darling-Hammond and Mungal are not satisfied with the education schools where these critics sit. The alternative providers give a very different answer to the question of what is wrong with American teacher education and what needs to be fixed. Whether one looks to the best known alternative teacher education program—Teach for America—or to programs like those offered by New Teachers for New Schools, or to independent providers like the Relay Graduate School of Education, or to those who fund these programs, some version of the same answer appears. They argue that traditional university-based teacher education just isn't very good. It relies too much on methods courses and too little on the content that can be provided by a rich arts and sciences major or on the in-depth field experience that a prolonged in-school internship can provide. Going further, many alternative providers and other critics argue that university teacher education programs often have a low bar for student admissions and faculty hiring, are not scholarly places, and, most of all, fail to provide graduates with the practical skills that a beginning teacher needs in order to be successful. Moreover, even at the least expensive state universities, programs are costly and time consuming. Given the sad state of most university programs, the defenders of alternative programs say, it was their duty—to schools and especially to the poor urban and rural kids who often get the least-qualified teachers—to invent something different.

Critics of university-based teacher preparation are not wrong in their complaint about widespread (even if far from universal) mediocrity, even if they too are selective in pointing to exemplars of their complaints. Complaints about university-based teacher education date to the 1950s, just as education schools were beginning to be accepted as the universal route to teaching. The complaints have become especially severe since the mid-1980s. Many superintendents and classroom teachers are angry at a preparation system that they describe as long on theory and short on practice. At the same time, superintendents are often frustrated that education schools do not prepare enough teachers, especially in the high need areas of math, science, special education, and bilingual education. And many teachers and leaders add that the theory taught in university programs does not seem to work well in classrooms.

Education school faculty, like all university faculty, are usually judged primarily on their research. Even at regional schools that give a heavy emphasis to classroom teaching it is hard for a junior professor to justify the time demands involved in visiting schools and working one-on-one with aspiring teachers. What professor seeking tenure or promotion can afford to do so? Some argue that education schools have failed to establish themselves as true centers for the study of and preparation for the practice of the profession of teaching, have tried too hard to emulate more prestigious colleagues in the arts and sciences, have been too concerned with their standing in the university, have modeled their work on their research-oriented peers, and have spent too little time focused on creating informed and critical professional excellence in their students.

Although less often noted, some critics have also complained that most professors in the traditional arts and sciences departments have little interest in or concern with the preparation of future teachers, even in departments like the sciences, mathematics, history, or English, where most future secondary teachers are prepared.[10]

Geraldine Jonçich Clifford and James W. Guthrie's 1988 book *Ed School* describes one essential part of the bind in which university-based schools of education have found themselves:

> Our thesis is that schools of education, particularly those located on the campuses of prestigious research universities, have become ensnared improvidently in the academic and political cultures of their institutions and have neglected their professional allegiances. They are like marginal men, aliens in their own world. They have seldom succeeded in satisfying the scholarly norms of their campus letters and science colleagues, and they are simultaneously estranged from their practicing professional peers. The more forcefully they have rowed toward the shores of scholarly research, the more distant they have become from the public schools they are duty bound to serve. Conversely, systematic efforts at addressing the applied problems of public schools have placed schools of education at risk on their own campuses.[11]

In 1990 John Goodlad wrote in a similar vein about the turn away from an emphasis on teacher preparation within universities and even within schools of education. Looking at changes in university priorities in the 1980s, Goodland concluded, "It appeared that the more successful the school or college of education in advancing faculty research productivity, the less the likelihood of its placing teacher education at the head of its list of priorities. As universities advance in status, we conclude the status of teacher education declines not only within the institution as a whole but also within the school or college of education, which is, in turn, of rather lowly status on most campuses."[12] As Goodlad noted, even within education schools, teacher education has often found itself the least respected of activities. The "serious scholars" engage in research on public policy or on child development and learning theories. They may study teachers but don't often work directly on their preparation. Only less "serious" and certainly less respected faculty—many of them clinical professors and adjuncts— find themselves in a department of teacher education. As Goodlad put it bluntly, faculty who focus on teacher education seem to "suffer from congenital prestige deprivation."[13] Judith Lanier, who founded what became the Holmes Group, and her colleague Judith Warren Little said it succinctly: "There is an inverse relationship between professorial prestige and the intensity of involvement with the formal education of teachers."[14]

Ever the careful observer as well as an advocate for change, Goodlad noted an additional issue beyond "prestige deprivation" that made life in teacher preparation programs difficult for the faculty there. Writing in 1990, he criticized university leaders for failing to stand up to the over-regulation of teacher education by state agencies, something he noted they would never tolerate in more prestigious fields. Thus, he said that while states do have a basic responsibility to ensure minimal competence in those licensed to teach, "States endanger quality and make a mock of professionalism when they take it on themselves to specify the curricula to be followed. College and university boards of trustees, administrators, and faculty members are derelict in their responsibilities when they sit idly by—as they usually do when teacher education programs are being savaged by state edict—while institutional autonomy is seriously eroded."[15] Goodlad expressed a complaint we have heard multiple times almost thirty years later. The level of mandates from states and accrediting bodies fosters an attitude of unthinking compliance and deadens creativity in teacher education programs. No wonder some find education schools difficult places to work and others want to create independent alternative routes.

While Lanier, Goodlad, Clifford, and Guthrie are respected voices in our field, few institutional leaders or faculty members have paid sufficient heed to their warnings. The result is that education schools continue to be marginalized within universities and teacher education programs continue to be marginalized within education schools while being tightly regulated by agencies outside of higher education. Those of us who commit a portion of our professional lives to the teaching of teachers are often seen as "lightweights" by our academic peers, no matter what the quality of our actual research. And all of this is happening in a national context in which university-based teacher education receives all too little respect from those in government, teacher organizations, schools, or the foundations that fund much of the current experimentation in education. Perhaps David Labaree said it best: "Institutionally, the ed school is the Rodney Dangerfield of higher education: it don't get no respect."[16] He might have added, teacher preparation is the Rodney Dangerfield of education schools.

Perhaps it is not surprising that education schools are sometimes slow to change. For professors who feel the push and pull of widely differing university demands and school system demands, who know that their status in institutions of higher education is insecure, and who also have to deal with state and private accreditation agency rules, asking for curricular and programmatic creativity seems unfair. Nevertheless, the slow pace of programmatic change has fueled alternatives of many forms.

There is a widespread desire in the United States to get the "best and brightest" people into the classroom—something that TFA has been brilliant at doing—even if too many of their corps members don't have sufficient preparation for the job and don't stay in teaching positions after their initial commitment. There is a strong sense that traditional education schools don't attract nearly as able a group of students as alternative programs do (whether or not there is sufficient evidence to back up that claim). And there is a desire on the part of many policymakers to focus more on "what works" in the preparation of tomorrow's teachers than on what should work in an ideal world that does not exist or on providing teachers with a theoretical understanding of their work—especially in a way that is far less expensive than traditional university-based teacher preparation programs. Some education schools, including those documented in this study, have taken these complaints to heart and fundamentally rethought the way they do business.[17] Far too many schools, however, have reacted defensively to the criticism without engaging in the hard, self-critical work that would create a different kind of education school.

As we explore in subsequent chapters, a new generation of reformers decided to do more than complain about the problems with schools of education and the hostility to change that they saw on many campuses in the late 1980s. They essentially said, "it is time to give up on education schools. They can't be reformed." These reformers instead embraced a market-based approach to teacher preparation.

In the early 1980s, authorities in New Jersey created what they called an "alternative route" to teaching that allowed—indeed encouraged—people who otherwise seemed qualified to bypass traditional university programs. The New Jersey example, novel at the time, received widespread publicity and was quickly copied. Then, in 1990, a Princeton University senior, Wendy Kopp, wrote a senior thesis proposing a new organization—Teach for America—that would enlist top-flight seniors in a two-year commitment to teaching after a summer of preparation. Today TFA is one of the largest preparers of teachers in the United States.

Both ideas—state-approved alternatives and independent recruitment and preparation programs like TFA—spread rapidly. Programs modeled on TFA, with perhaps lower standards, have sprung up; states and districts all over the country offer alternative routes and teacher fellows programs; and at least a half dozen cities have teacher residency programs. Other providers have gotten into the act with online teacher education. The University of Phoenix, a private, for-profit university, is one of the largest providers of teachers in the nation, even though many on both sides of the teacher preparation debate question the quality of its programs. Recently some states have simply eliminated the requirement that a teacher be licensed and allow principals to hire whom they want, at least in certain high needs fields; sometimes these candidates are required to pass a state exam, sometimes not.

By one estimate as many as 40% of new teachers who entered the field in the fall of 2016 were from alternative routes, though that figure depends on the definition of an alternative route. One wonders whether it is possible to have any resolution in the intense debates about teacher preparation or to set consistent standards for both on-campus and alternative programs so that excellence in outcomes will matter more than the provider. Certainly the answer is "not yet."

Revolt of the Superintendents

There may also be a third answer to the why question about recent changes in teacher preparation. In his book *The Trouble with Ed Schools* and in a series of articles, the historian David Labaree has argued—correctly we think—that there is a huge split between the core ideologies of the teacher education faculty at most schools or departments of education and the beliefs of most school superintendents. As Labaree describes it, education school faculty are the proud heirs of two strands of the progressive education movement: the child-centered and social justice strands. A look at many education course syllabi or a visit to most education school conferences will reveal that John Dewey is still revered and that much discussion focuses on the diverse individual needs of children and on the need for educators to be leaders in the quest for social justice, as found in the work of Jonathan Kozol and other authors.[18] However, Labaree says, most school superintendents focus on other strands that were once as important to progressive educators (though they seldom call themselves progressives any more)—the need for school leaders to be free to set the priorities and curriculum of their schools and systems and to administer schools as they see fit with teachers following the lead of the superintendents rather than challenging them, and the belief that "scientific" testing will allow educators to judge their work and sort students by their basic abilities. Of course, it is important to note that while Labaree's judgments probably apply to a significant majority of the faculty in teacher education programs, some leaders in the field of education research are much closer to the superintendents' position than Labaree acknowledges.[19]

Writing about the larger field of educational research, historian Ellen Lagemann quipped, "Dewey lost and Thorndike won." The model of research advocated by Edward Thorndike, highly quantitative and behavioristic, replaced Dewey's more philosophical and child-centered approach.[20] Yet while that may be true in much of educational research, especially in education policy programs and in all fields of psychology, Dewey remains dominant in teacher preparation programs, and Thorndike and those who followed in his steps are virtually irrelevant.[21]

Nevertheless if Labaree's analysis is mostly right—and we think that for teacher education programs in education schools he is—we also ask, is it also possible that the emergence of alternative routes to teaching can be traced to a revolt of superintendents who got tired of retraining education school graduates to fit into the needs of a top-down, data and test score–driven school system and decided—one could say logically—that it was better to run their own teacher preparation programs than to spend the time, money, and effort to retrain teachers who had graduated from traditional education schools and entered teaching with a very different ideological focus? Many superintendents will cite the deficits that education school graduates seem to have—a lack of attention in their preparation to classroom management, a lack of understanding of or respect for urban bureaucracies, or a lack of knowledge about the realities of the specific school districts where novice teachers begin their work. Many superintendents also reflect the anger of teachers in their districts, who often feel that they are being treated as second-class players when they work with university teacher education faculty. They may say so less often, but many superintendents are also troubled by what they see as a tendency in many young teachers to question the policy limitations and indeed the leadership decisions of superintendents themselves.

In February 2004, Thomas Payzant, then the superintendent of the Boston Public Schools, spoke to a large audience of teacher educators at a plenary session of the American Association of Colleges for Teacher Education. The focus of his talk was the question: *Should teacher preparation take place at colleges and universities?* The deans of three of the university-based education schools in Boston sat in the front row of the audience. Payzant's conclusion was clear. He told the deans and the rest of his audience that he was not optimistic that college and university programs could do the job.

Superintendent Payzant began his speech with an analysis of the difficulty of teaching in an urban school system like that in Boston, which requires a complex mix of skills, knowledge, and good judgment in order to succeed. He went on to make it clear that he was dissatisfied with the graduates of the area's college and university programs and not optimistic that the education schools could make the kinds of changes needed to produce effective teachers for a school system like his. Finally, he announced that the Boston schools planned to create their own district-based pre-service program to compete with the university programs and, he hoped, better meet the needs of the Boston Public Schools students. In response to a later question, the superintendent admitted that he did not really know much about the curriculum or practices of the university-based education schools that were in partnership with the district, but he stuck by his judgments of them based on his experience with their graduates who taught in Boston.[22]

Jesse Solomon, who served as the first leader of the Boston Teacher Residency program—the program that Payzant announced in the 2004 speech—provided more background information on its inception. In 2003, a private foundation had approached Superintendent Payzant with a question: "What is a problem you are unable to fix with the resources you have?" As Solomon recounted it, Payzant responded that "the pipeline of teachers into the BPS was not filling the district's needs." There was no overall shortage of teachers, but there was the usual shortage of teachers for mathematics, science, special education and English language learners. In addition, the available pool of teachers was too white, too many—half—left within three years, and too many new teachers came to Boston schools with too little knowledge of the specific needs and cultural norms of the district. According to Solomon, "Dr. Payzant wanted to build the capacity within the district to recruit, prepare, and induct its own teachers, and thus yield greater control of its teacher pipeline." The result was the first teacher residency program in the nation.[23]

In both Payzant's AACTE speech and in the story Solomon tells, the superintendent had many reasons for dissatisfaction, including the large attrition rate—which strongly implied a mismatch between the programs at universities preparing teachers for the city's schools and the realities of Boston's classrooms—but there is also the intriguing note that "Dr. Payzant wanted . . . greater control of its teacher pipeline."[24] One wonders whether that control was a means to produce more effective teachers or teachers with different values.

As we noted earlier, David Labaree has outlined a core split that has existed for decades between the values and beliefs of most university education school professors and the superintendents in most of the nation's school districts. Based on our study of many alternative teacher preparation programs, and in some cases university programs that were redesigned in close collaboration with school districts, there is strong evidence for the conclusion that many of Payzant's fellow superintendents were dissatisfied with university-based programs not only because of issues with their quality and ability to graduate "classroom-ready" teachers for the specific schools of the district, although those were real problems, but also because of a deep mismatch in values. Many superintendents wanted greater control of the teacher preparation pipeline in order to create a generation of teachers who would be willing to defer to district policies and administrator authority and who valued data-driven approaches to their understanding of effective classroom instruction.

Certainly in the case of many charter schools and charter networks, there was the same sense that the superintendents seemed to have—that university education schools were not preparing graduates who shared either the values or the deeply embedded specific knowledge of the school districts needed to succeed in the classroom. As a result, charter schools and networks from New York to San Diego have developed their own teacher preparation programs, which we will explore later in this volume.

If our view of the importance of superintendents in the radical changes in the shape of teacher preparation between 1986 and the present is correct, then an over-emphasis on Teach for America as the normative alternative program is a mistake. Although TFA does indeed develop contractual partnerships with many of the nation's largest school districts, it is an independent program. On the other hand, programs like the Boston Teacher Residency and a dozen other residencies that have developed across the country, as well as other city- and district-level teaching fellows programs, are under the control of the host school districts and the management of their superintendents. Certainly many of the charter school–based teacher education programs are under the direct control of the charter networks that sponsor them and reflect the same values as the specific network. As we will show in subsequent chapters, these district-led programs more closely mirror the values that Labaree saw as belonging to the superintendents than the values of the majority of university education school faculty.

There may be yet other answers to the core question of this book, but these three answers, when taken together, certainly explain much about not only what has happened in the field of teacher preparation since 1980, but also why it has happened. Teacher preparation programs are shaped by history. We need to understand that history in order to understand current reality as well as how to shape the future. Of course, the history of teacher preparation did not start in 1980. In order to understand the context in which our story rests, we need to take a quick look back farther in the history of teacher preparation in the United States.

A Short History of Teacher Preparation

One of the most overlooked realities in teacher preparation in the United States is that while the route to teaching through a university-based program was the norm—indeed, virtually the exclusive route to teaching—in 1990, that had not been the case for all that long. The university dominance of teacher education really lasted for only thirty years, from 1960 to 1990. During a much longer time period—from the beginnings of what historians call "the common school era" in the 1830s to the late 1950s, a wide range of approaches to teaching flourished in the United States. Most of those who are active in today's debates do not remember much of what happened prior to 1960. Thus, with a kind of generational amnesia, too many act as if the 1960–1990 norm was "the way things have always been," since some time immemorial.[25]

Teacher preparation has been very different at various times in U.S. history. For most of that history, it was characterized by a wide variety of alternative routes to teaching. Prior to the 1830s, the basic approach to teaching was "any smart person can teach." In what Americans now call the colonial era—back when the east coast of the present United States was

British North America—many men taught school, and nearly all of those who did taught for a short period of time before going on to a "real" profession (usually law or ministry). If one had successfully completed school, it was argued, one had sufficient preparation to teach. Then, in the 1830s, schooling expanded rapidly. Whereas most (free white) young people had previously had just a few months or perhaps a couple of years of schooling, they now attended school for four to eight years. Urban centers created grade-leveled schools as students moved in formation from one grade to the next. Rural communities, where most Americans still lived, maintained the one-room schoolhouse, but even there, people attended for more time and on a more regular schedule than ever before.

With the rapid growth of schooling, the teaching profession was pried open by a generation of women, like Catharine Beecher, who insisted that they were at least as well suited to teaching as men were. In fact, Beecher argued, women were better suited to teaching because it called on their maternal instincts and because, with few other options, they were willing to accept far less pay to teach than men demanded.

Reformers argued not only for an extended school year for women teachers, but also for teacher preparation. They created normal schools—state schools that started out offering a few months of preparation for graduates of common (or elementary) schools. These normal schools eventually expanded into mini-colleges. Some states also offered short-term teacher's institutes at which teachers could take summer or winter courses to improve their skills. Reformers also created the high school "normal program" in which high schools prepared elementary teachers; such programs were the single largest producer of elementary teachers in the nineteenth century. Then, late in the nineteenth century, they started creating university teacher preparation programs, although it was well into the twentieth century before a majority of teachers took advantage of these programs and after the middle of the century before most teachers earned a baccalaureate degree. The reformers also started state exams. For much of the nineteenth and early twentieth centuries, anyone who passed the relatively easy state exam could teach, regardless of their preparation. Individuals mixed and matched among the available options, and school boards hired whomever they could find.

Then, in the mid-twentieth century, at least three developments led to increased standards for teachers. The Great Depression of the 1930s allowed school boards to be much more selective than they could have been in the past, so they were able to hire only the best candidates. This was the era in which schools began to demand a college degree of anyone entering teaching. By the end of the 1930s, most high school teachers held a college degree, as did a growing number of elementary teachers. But the degree may or may not have been from a university-based education program. In the years immediately after World War II, the GI Bill—among other developments in the United States—made it possible for more citizens, including aspiring teachers, to attend college. Finally, after the Soviet Union launched Sputnik in 1957, the Cold War led to great fears about undereducated citizens and to an effort to do something about the problem by improving the education of all Americans, including teachers.

By the 1950s, states began requiring a college degree—often with an education major—to be a teacher. Old normal schools were transformed first into state teachers colleges which awarded a baccalaureate degree after four years of post-secondary study, and then into branch campuses of state universities. By 1960 every state required a bachelor's degree for primary and secondary teaching. And, with rare exceptions, that was that . . . for thirty years.[26]

Many colleges and universities welcomed the challenge of educating teachers. While there were often some faculty members—larger numbers on more elite campuses, smaller numbers on others—who thought preparing people for such a low-status profession as teaching was beneath them, university administrators and many faculty were glad to include teacher preparation in their institutions. The embrace of teacher education across higher education was in part a recognition that universities needed to serve public needs and that the need for well-educated teachers was very real. Embracing teacher preparation also served a pressing university need for more students, especially as the large numbers of students funded by the GI Bill began to complete their college programs in the early to mid-1950s. As Elizabeth Green has said in her popular work, *Building a Better Teacher*, "the subject [of education] had to be offered; simple economics demanded it." After all, universities always need more revenue and, as Green points out, "In 1890 total enrollment in US elementary and secondary schools stood at just under thirteen million. By 1920, the number was more than twenty million. . . . By . . . 1948, the number of teachers alone was nearing one million. For a university the calculation was clear; training teachers made financial sense whether there was something to teach them or not."[27] So universities welcomed teacher education "whether there was something [that a university could do well] to teach them or not." The actual education that aspiring teachers needed was something that many thought they could figure out later.

From its beginning, the university-based education school had its critics.

In 1953 Arthur Bestor published *Educational Wastelands: The Retreat from Learning in Our Public Schools*. He blamed education schools for becoming detached from the academy, turning into mere vocational training enterprises. Bestor blamed the education faculty for creating an unholy alliance with school administrators—whom they would not criticize in spite of the problems in the schools—and state agencies, which guaranteed "substantial course work in pedagogy." Thus, Bestor charged, "protected behind state requirements which no department but itself can satisfy, the department is able to defy, or even to wage aggressive warfare against, the academic standards of the university."[28]

A decade later, other critics—James D. Koerner and former Harvard president James Bryant Conant, among them—said essentially the same thing. Koerner was as harsh as Bestor. Though Conant used more gentle language, both he and Koerner added the newly organized accrediting agency, National Council for Accreditation of Teacher Education (NCATE), to their list of those standing in the way of meaningful reform in teacher preparation. Conant also included the arts and sciences faculty in his critique, noting that all too often "the faculties of arts and sciences had shown little interest in school problems. . . . With few exceptions, college professors turned their backs on the problems of mass secondary education."[29] The former college president made it clear that he was not happy with what he considered irresponsible behavior across the campus.

In every decade since, some version of this criticism has emerged: the curriculum of education schools has too many methods courses and too little rigorous study of the basic arts and sciences disciplines that teachers actually teach, but also too little time actually spent in school classrooms where novice teachers can observe, test their wings under careful supervision, and learn not only the "tricks of the trade" but also the actual strategies of excellent master teachers.

In the 1980s a new generation of critics of university-based teacher preparation, many of them within the university-based education schools, emerged, and new calls for significant reform of American education appeared. In the spring of 1986 two reports were released that focused specifically on improving the way teachers were prepared in the United States. Many, but certainly not all, faculty and administrators in schools of education got serious about reform or at least acknowledged that they needed to pay attention to a range of issues, from raising admission standards, to providing much more school-based "clinical" time for students, to fundamentally rethinking what was taught and how it was taught to their students.

In the spring of 1986 *A Nation Prepared*, from the Carnegie Forum on

Education and the Economy, and *Tomorrow's Teachers*, the first of three reports from the Holmes Group of Education Deans [leaders of some of the nation's most prestigious education schools], appeared almost simultaneously. These reports, when taken together—as they almost always were—sought to redefine teacher education in the United States. The reports had surprisingly similar recommendations. Carnegie recommended creating a National Board for Professional Teaching Standards to establish high standards for what the best teachers needed to know and be able to do. Both reports recommended restructuring public schools to provide a professional environment for teaching and introducing a hierarchy within teaching supervised by "lead teachers," with a large number of "professional teachers" supported by aides and interns. Both reports also recommended requiring a bachelor's degree in the arts and sciences for all teachers so that all teachers would have solid content knowledge, developing a new professional curriculum in graduate schools of education leading to a Master in Teaching (MT) degree based on systematic knowledge of teaching, and including internships and residencies in schools.[30]

These reports and the national dialogue and debate that they inspired did change the landscape in teacher education. The Carnegie Corporation of New York launched the National Board for Professional Teaching Standards, which remains important in defining what good teaching looks like. The Board has now granted "professional certification" to thousands of teachers who represent a kind of elite in the profession. Some states demanded increased admission standards for teacher education, and some states have begun requiring that teachers have an arts and sciences degree. In 2013, the accrediting body for university education schools demanded a dramatic increase in admission standards in the next decade. Some states revised their regulations, while many schools of education launched a top-to-bottom rethinking of their curriculum, often with the result that aspiring teachers focused more on content—often taught in the arts and sciences—and spent far more time in actual school settings, while taking fewer education courses in methods and foundations compared to what had been in place earlier.

On the other hand, there was also widespread resistance to these recommendations. School districts and superintendents remained remarkably unwilling to implement any changes to the structures of teaching or to create a differentiated profession. In spite of their often-voiced critique of education schools, school districts also showed surprisingly little interest in creating room for student interns or loaning some of their faculty on a short-term basis to teach in education schools, even as some larger districts have created their own teacher preparation and induction programs independent of universities.

Many in education schools also resisted. While there was growth in graduate programs, the undergraduate teacher preparation program remained—and remains—strong in most places, and the complaint about too many methods courses remains relevant thirty years after the reports. Far too many education faculty members took an attitude of "this too shall pass" and simply ignored the whole reform enterprise. A decade after the reports were issued, Oxford University professor Harry Judge looked back at the work of the Holmes Group, for which he had been a consultant, and wrote, "The effort stalled (which is not to say terminated) when the colleges and schools of education had to think seriously about reforming themselves. They will change only when they really wish to, and not enough yet do."[31] Judge's sad epilogue to these reports remains as true today as when he wrote it in 1998.

Given the reality that Judge accurately described—that not enough education school faculty or their colleagues in other parts of the university really want to change—it is no wonder that many people are giving up on university-based teacher preparation. If we follow the money—from the federal government, state legislatures, and some of the nation's most prestigious foundations—the track leads to alternative routes into teaching, be they TFA, residency programs, or new providers, such as the rapidly growing Relay Graduate School of Education. Whether one looks to the U.S. Department of Education, Congress, or major foundations, it is hard to find a program funding university-based teacher preparation in any substantial way.

Surprisingly little has changed in the general critique of education schools, from Bestor's complaint in the 1950s to the reformers in state legislatures and major foundations in the second decade of the twenty-first century, although the volume of the critique has grown in the last few decades. But administrators and faculty in education schools have had their own complaints about the complainers—complaints that those who criticize teacher education programs simply do not understand the complexity of the work and, as we have seen, that critics have an ulterior agenda, to privatize American education.

For most of the middle decades of the twentieth century, the complaints about education schools remained just that—complaints. Many people asked the schools to get better. Reformers tried to improve the curriculum. In the 1980s, national reports demanded change. But the focus remained on schools of education. Then, in the late 1980s and early 1990s, the system of teacher education based almost solely in schools of education seemed to come apart. A range of alternative providers appeared on the scene. Critics became innovators who launched new efforts based in school districts or totally independent of both schools and universities. Some education schools responded with dramatic efforts to fundamentally rethink their curriculum, and some did not. As historians, we ask, why did this happen when it did? What were the historical forces that led to such a rapid increase in diversity of models for preparing American teachers at the end of the twentieth century? The case studies offered in the chapters that follow seek to answer that question by providing the historical context for change in many diverse institutional settings. There could be more such case studies, but those we have examined have convinced us that only multiple answers can help us understand our fundamental question about why so much change has come to this field in such a relatively short period of time.

A Concluding Word

In the subsequent chapters of this book, we pursue examples that illustrate all of the causes for change that are outlined in this introduction. There is clear evidence that a shift to a more market-oriented approach to teacher education has had an impact, just as many university-based critics have insisted. There is equally clear evidence that in spite of profound changes in many university-based education schools, there are some schools that are terribly weak—that have low admission standards, coursework that is not well coordinated or relevant to the work of teaching, and too little time for aspiring teachers to actively engage in the work of teaching under close supervision—just as the advocates of independent alternative programs insist. While some education schools have remade their curriculum to offer an impressive content-rich and practice-based blend, others have changed surprisingly little in thirty years.

In this context, we have seen a significant rise in district- and charter school–based teacher education, evidence of a revolt by school superintendents who passionately want to create their own teacher preparation programs to mold the kinds of teachers needed in their schools and who have seen in the rise of a new diversity in teacher preparation the opportunity to finally accomplish their goals. Superintendents in some of the nation's largest school districts, from Boston to Seattle, have started their own district-based programs, sometimes in close cooperation with universities and sometimes not, designed to prepare teachers who will fit in from the moment they begin their careers.

One certainly sees the same sort of development in the case of charter schools and charter school networks. Charter schools often have a unique philosophy or educational approach, and their leaders want to be sure they hire teachers who subscribe to that approach. They believe that preparing future teachers themselves is the best way to assure a steady supply of teachers with the "right" values and skills.

We have happily come to one other conclusion in this historical overview of the last thirty years of teacher preparation in the United States. Despite the complexity of these developments, despite the intense rancor that many of the actors feel for each other, the period from 1986 to the present has been one of extraordinary creativity and improvement in the way teachers are prepared for students of the twenty-first century. As has been the case at many other times in the history of American higher education, some of the greatest accomplishments have not been the result of cool and thoughtful deliberation on the part of all parties involved, but rather the result of rancor and frustration. Out of intense deliberations have emerged new programs, like the teacher residencies in Chicago and Seattle, the partnerships that Teach for America has built with some universities, and other we will explore, in which the best of what universities bring to teacher education has been mixed with the wisdom of practice that current teachers and their leaders bring to the conversation. On rarer occasions we have even seen the kinds of collaboration with parents and communities that, difficult as they are, only strengthen the preparation of tomorrow's teachers. The history recounted in this volume is not an easy or always a happy one, but it is one of energy, creativity, and—on some occasions—bursts of excellence.

CHAPTER ONE

The Emergence of Alternative Routes to Teaching

In 1983, when the federal government published *A Nation at Risk*, only eight states offered some form of alternative certification program, affecting 0.06% of teachers nation-wide. By 2016, alternative certification laws existed in forty-seven states, and somewhere between 20% and 40% of American teachers entered the profession through nontraditional routes. In places such as Texas, that number was much higher, hovering around 60%.[1] How did this dizzying array of preparation options come about over a thirty-year period? And what does it mean for teacher education today?

In this chapter, we attempt to dig deeper into the alternative certification debates by providing a brief history of the emergence of alternative certification and offering four case studies on some of the most significant players in the field. The opening study involves New Jersey, where the first state-level alternative certification program began in 1983. From this case emerges many of the major themes that would animate licensure debates for years to come: What do teachers need to know? Who should teach? And how can programs attract better candidates? The second case examines the rise of Teach for America (TFA) and its subsequent impact on the field of teacher education, from policy to public imagination to the rise of similarly organized teaching fellows programs across the country. As the TFA model begs us to consider, Is five weeks of training and a can-do attitude enough to close the achievement gap? The third study considers the Relay Graduate School of Education, which reflects a more recent and extreme rejection of the traditional preparation model with its emphasis on technical skills and entrepreneurial methods. We conclude the chapter by charting the rise of the phoenix—the University of Phoenix, that is—the major for-profit provider of teaching degrees in the nation, raising the issue of the proper place of markets and profit in the business of teacher training. Together, these cases track the rise of alternate routes from the early 1980s to their heyday at the turn of the millennium to the year 2016, and they consider the major themes, developments, and challenges we face as we move forward in the twenty-first century.

The Rise of Alternative Certification

Although our study of the recent history of teacher preparation begins in the early 1980s, movements for alternative certification outside the university setting started much earlier as critics from the left and right sought new ways to educate teachers and, in many cases, find ways around the schools of education they found resistant to change.

Some early alternative route programs grew from the civil rights and community control battles of the 1960s and 1970s, for example, as communities of color became increasingly frustrated with the lack of quality education in their public schools and the low expectations placed on black, Latinx, and Asian children from a predominately white professionalized teaching force.[2] Paraprofessional programs attempted to bring parents and community members into the classroom to combat this problem, bypassing the traditional education school-to-classroom pipeline.[3] Some parents started independent schools to circumvent teacher training and certification laws entirely,[4] while others applied for War on Poverty funds to train teachers in cultural competencies themselves, recognizing a gap in university teacher training curricula. Bilingual education advocates likewise lobbied for licensure reforms that would bring more Spanish-speaking teachers with similar cultural backgrounds as students into classrooms without having to secure an expensive and onerous teaching degree and pass an arduous, arguably biased test.[5] The education school route, many of these parent advocates argued, simply wasn't providing a diverse and competent teaching pool for the nation's increasingly diverse schools.

Programs like the federal government's 1960s Peace Corps-inspired National Teacher Corps also brought idealistic, young, mostly white teachers into low-income schools through an alternative preparation route, reflecting a belief that education schools and professional educators were more part of the problem than part of the solution.[6] Foreshadowing TFA but with a sixties liberal flavor, Teacher Corps trainees, considered "the best and the brightest," bypassed undergraduate teaching degrees and instead attended what was meant to be an innovative summer institute before taking the lead in some of the nation's most struggling urban and rural schools. As historian Bethany Rogers explains, "According to the reformers' thinking, existing teachers lacked the qualities of innovation, dedication, and social and political engagement required to teach students in America's low-income communities. In response, they called for a new breed of teacher, with attributes and characteristics distinct from those of conventional educators, as well as a new approach to teacher training."[7] Many of these arguments would resurface in the 1990s, simply with another era's political rhetoric.[8]

The sixties-era liberal origins of alternative certification often receive short shrift in the literature on teacher education, while the right-leaning, neoliberal origins more often claim the spotlight.[9] By the 1970s and early 1980s, ideas about the power of markets to solve social problems and increase efficiency started gaining prominence, with economists such as Milton Friedman and Chester Finn Jr. proliferating ideas about how to improve the nation's public schools through competition and private choice—rather than through more state intervention or professional expertise. "Markets work in education," Friedman and his peers argued in numerous published manifestos, academic journals, and popular television and magazine articles, and more and more Americans came to agree.[10] An important part of the story, however, is that both right-wing intellectuals *and* left-leaning communities of color and their white allies agreed by the end of the 1960s and into the 1970s that the university monopoly was a problem.

The growing distrust of university-based teacher preparation in the 1960s should not come as a surprise. Universities as a whole were objects of great distrust, especially from the left, as evidenced by student demonstrations at the University of California, Columbia, Harvard, and hundreds of other schools across the country. In *Tinkering toward Utopia*, historians David Tyack and Larry Cuban argue that in the 1960s Americans lost faith in public schools (and, we would argue, by extension in the institutions that prepared public school teachers) as part of their loss of faith in government and large-scale institutions more broadly. "Opinions about advance or decline in education reflect general confidence in American institutions," Tyack and Cuban note.[11] Thus, in the immediate aftermath of World War II, public support for schools proved strong. As a result of the Vietnam War, Watergate, civil rights backlash, and other government debacles, however, people felt less sure about the ability of the state to educate their children.

This mistrust likewise translated to conversations on how to improve the quality of the teaching force, which was seen then, as today, as a major contributing factor to raising the quality of K–12 education. Liberal and New Left advocates saw solutions in alternative programs and community-led teacher training. Friedman, Finn, and like-minded conservatives argued in the language of business that education schools held a monopoly on teacher preparation, with no incentive to provide a quality product or improve, and that credentials and licensure only served as barriers to entry for talented individuals. In his ten-part 1980 television series *Free to Choose*, Friedman promoted a vision of a pro-market, free choice–driven society and turned to a successful, independently funded school in Harlem to prove his theories in the realm of education. In relation to teaching, he was quick to note that at the Harlem school, "many of the teachers didn't have the right pieces of paper to qualify for employment in public schools. That didn't stop them from doing a good job here."[12] With comments like these, Friedman joined a growing bipartisan chorus insisting that teaching credentials presented too many roadblocks for passionate and intelligent individuals to enter the classroom.

By the early 1980s, as the movement for standards and accountability emerged, proponents pushed for reforms in teacher education as part of a broader platform. Reformers advocated a move away from theory and methods courses to an embrace of subject matter and liberal arts training in order to increase the academic quality of potential teachers, the implementation of competency tests, and the provision of more alternative routes into teaching. When *A Nation at Risk* was published in 1983, it served as a clarion call for this agenda, stating, "the teacher preparation curriculum is weighted heavily with courses in 'educational methods' at the expense of courses in subjects to be taught," and recommending that barriers be lowered for talented individuals to enter the field.[13] By the end of 1983 almost all fifty states held education summits to revamp their education systems, with nearly half considering changing their rules on how teachers could enter the classroom.[14]

While the left and right brought very different rationales to their criticisms of traditional teacher training, both sides could agree by the 1980s that easing entry into the classroom for higher quality, better qualified candidates— whether that be defined by academic success or cultural competency—was ultimately a positive goal, and alternative certification appeared as an appealing strategy to achieve it.

Other factors contributed to the rise of alternative certification as well.[15] Developments within universities aided this process (a topic that will be discussed at length in the next section), as education schools found themselves under fire from within and without. Administrators and many faculty based in other parts of the university doubted the quality and academic standards of the education faculty, and the media increasingly painted education schools as low-quality, non-rigorous, and drawing on the bottom of the barrel for their student bodies. The Carnegie and Holmes reports were among the many publications that forcefully criticized education schools, only fueling these concerns. School-based leaders faced with teaching shortages also welcomed new alternative programs that offered to provide both enough teachers and better ones to help overcome emergency licensure problems. Calls for greater diversity and quality in the teaching workforce, from people of color to military veterans to late-in-life career changers, also gave alternative certification an appealing air. As alternative certification became a non-partisan issue, local, state, and federal leaders on both sides of the aisle could embrace reforms in teacher preparation programs. President Ronald Reagan gave the New Jersey alternative route program a ringing endorsement in the early 1980s, as did both Republican and Democratic governors.[16] Those within education schools, along with the increasingly villainized teachers unions, seemed to be the lone voices against alternative routes as the twentieth century came to a close.[17]

Reports of states changing their certification and licensure laws came to fill the pages of newspapers throughout the 1980s and 1990s, as states implemented alternative route programs in domino-like fashion, with New Jersey first and Texas, California, South Carolina, Virginia, Florida, and others quickly following suit.[18] As early as 1986 an *Education Week* story titled "Alternative Licensing Prevalent" noted that half of the states were allowing alternative certification in some form or another.[19]

Teach for America arose out of this late 1980s zeitgeist, as Princeton University graduate Wendy Kopp turned her senior thesis into what became the most public face of alternative certification. With TFA's first corps heading out to classrooms in 1990, its controversial, highly influential program became a significant player in the alternative route scene. Its army of reform-minded alumni and staff then went on to create a policy atmosphere conducive to TFA's pro-alternative certification mission. Some argue that TFA's policy footprint remains its most significant legacy.

Even some teacher educators themselves, frustrated with their field, came to support alternative certification. Martin Haberman, a teacher educator and critic of education schools, argued in the early 1980s, "Better people will be attracted and offered a more practical preparation if they can avoid the piffle of traditional teacher ed programs."[20] Throughout the 1990s, research from academics and think tanks alike came out in favor of alternate routes, leading more philanthropies to jump on board.[21] Presidents George H. W. Bush and Bill Clinton both seemed to support the policy, along with an onslaught of pro-education reform governors who used alternative certification as a low-hanging fruit politically palatable to the right, left, and seemingly everyone in between, save the education establishment.

By the early 2000s, alternative certification became thoroughly embedded in the "reform" agenda and received broad political, philanthropic, and public backing in the United States. A coalition of educators, activists, politicians, and philanthropic and business leaders embraced the idea that past academic success, boot camp–style skills training, and the right can-do spirit—rather than theory and coursework—were the necessary ingredients to create high-quality teachers.[22] Once the recession hit in 2008, TFA experienced record application numbers, as bright young college graduates and mid-career professionals found themselves in need of jobs. TFA and its highly selective teaching fellows peer programs also managed to bypass the low-status, feminized taint of the education school degree by amassing a high level of social capital. In 2011, nearly a quarter of Harvard's graduating class applied to TFA; only 16% of those applicants got in.

Programs in highly deregulated states, such as Texas, often modeled themselves on TFA but with significantly lower admissions standards and even more limited preparation than the TFA summer program. These "TFA-light" programs offered only a minimum level of low-quality training to anyone willing to pay the price for the credential, ushering in an era of Wild West–style, stand-alone alternative providers. For-profit providers started entering the fray as well, attempting to cash in on the significant amount of federal, state, and individual dollars being directed toward teacher education yearly and made available through new certification pathway laws, as exemplified by the University of Phoenix.

Even pro-alternative certification advocates such as Chester Finn Jr. and Kate Walsh expressed concern about some alternative programs. While Finn worried that education schools, for which he had little respect, were themselves becoming major players in offering fast-track or other alternative programs, he and his colleagues also called attention to the prevalence of low standards in "true alternative" programs. Looking at a 2007 study conducted among forty-nine alternative route programs in eleven states, they admitted, "Two-thirds of the programs . . . accept half or more of their applicants. One-quarter accept virtually everyone who applies. Only four in ten programs require a college GPA of 2.75 or above—no lofty standard in this age of grade inflation. . . . As for intense mentoring by an experienced teacher or administrator—long considered the hallmark of great alternate routes—only one-third of surveyed programs report providing it at least once a week during a rookie teacher's first semester."[23]

Alternative certification 2.0 programs cropped up in the first two decades of the new millennium. These included the Relay Graduate School of Education, the charter-based Match Residency, and the myriad teaching fellows programs run by The New Teacher Project (TNTP). Even teachers unions thought they could do a better job than education schools; in 2002 the Chicago Teachers Union opened their own degree-granting master's program to provide leadership degrees to teachers. Other unions followed.[24] "Let a thousand flowers bloom" seemed to be the mindset, particularly with the rise of Silicon Valley and its entrepreneurial ethos. Educational entrepreneurs set out from all corners of the tech world to offer new solutions and "disruptive models" to teacher preparation.

Although traditional programs continued to prepare the majority of K–12 educators in the United States, and still do in the second decade of the twenty-first century, from 1980 onward alternative routes made an indelible mark on the teacher education landscape. And they continue to grow through the support of philanthropic dollars, public policy, and student demand.

Certification: The Debate

The verdict is still out on the overall efficacy of alternative certification routes, however, making it a highly controversial and often acrimonious issue. Proponents cite a number of positive attributes. For example, many alternative programs succeed in keeping costs low, unlike traditional teaching degrees that often leave low-paid teachers in debt. These programs also have the potential to draw a more diverse group of candidates into the teaching workforce, one of the goals of the community-based movements of the 1960s and 1970s and a continuing problem today. While many initially criticized TFA for being predominantly white and upper middle class, TFA now boasts that around half of its 2016 corps were people of color, with greater numbers from working class and immigrant backgrounds than ever before.[25] Conversely, with the implementation of the new Council for the Accreditation of Educator Preparation (CAEP) standards, the number of Black and Latinx teachers are actually expected to go *down* in traditional university-based routes.

Alternative certification boosters also laud the ability of such programs to serve as incubators of creativity and innovation, and celebrate that they put pressure on traditional programs to improve—a "competitive threat" to the lethargic monopoly. Some of those who usually defend the value of schools of education concede that just as there are many types of teacher candidates, there should also be many types of preparation programs; no "one best system" will fit everyone.

Opponents of alternative routes, meanwhile, counter with a long list of complaints. The rapid proliferation of such programs—some not-for-profit and some for-profit—means that there is a wide range of quality. While some are strong, far too many offer little to no preparation and simply provide a credential. Other critics argue that quick-prep crash courses, even when elite, overemphasize the technical aspects of teaching while downplaying the necessary subject matter competency, pedagogical theory, and other fields of learning that constitute a real professional education in teaching, a line of thinking most ardently defended by Stanford education professor Linda Darling-Hammond.[26] Doug Lemov's *Teach Like a Champion: 49 Techniques that Put Students on the Path to College*, used by many alternative certification providers, is one prominent example of the kind of technocratic vision of teaching that receives significant criticism, as it boils the job down to a list of skills that critics say de-professionalizes the field and demeans the art and science of teaching.[27] According to critics, not only does a technical preparation not adequately prepare teachers to serve children well, but it also depoliticizes the teaching force by rendering teachers less able and apt to organize for their labor rights and to engage in policy and leadership debates.

Other critics argue that these alternate programs disproportionately experiment on low-income students of color, as they are the most likely to receive teachers with this type of crash-course training, while middle and upper income students are still largely taught by education school–trained professionals. Indeed, it is one of the great ironies of the last three decades that alternative route programs have led to a situation in which many poor children and children of color in urban and rural districts are taught by TFA fellows or other teachers from an upper-middle-class background and elite universities, while many middle- and upper-class children are taught by teachers of moderate or working-class backgrounds who entered the profession through traditional university pathways, the largest of which are often based in regional campuses serving less well-to-do college students. Such a dichotomy, critics charge, only furthers the othering of poor children of color and makes "urban education" something akin to missionary work, while not addressing the status and professionalization issues of teachers or achieving the end goal of equity in the American education system.

Research on program route efficacy, however, is simply inconclusive. We do not know for sure if alternative certification leads to greater levels of student achievement; researchers have found it a particularly difficult phenomenon to measure. Moreover, there is little agreement on what should be measured; the test scores that some use to show strengths for one program or another are often themselves the subject of intense disagreement. Studies exist to support both sides of the debate. These studies are often conducted by researchers who are fierce partisans of one type of program even before they begin their research, rendering research-based argumentation all the more challenging on this issue. For example, in 2003, then U.S. Secretary of Education Rod Paige cited research that showed that "in mathematics, students of new Teacher for America recruits finished 12 percent of a standard deviation higher than students of other teachers." Paige agreed with the researchers that "if you were choosing between two math teachers and the only thing you knew about them was that one was a TFA member and one was not, you would choose the TFA member."[28]

Not surprisingly Linda Darling-Hammond challenged the research that Paige cited, noting that it compared TFA graduates with all teachers in a district—some of who may have come to teaching through less rigorous alternative routes—and not with those who had completed a full university program. Given that Paige and the researchers he cited had a long track record of favoring TFA and that Darling-Hammond was a long-time critic, both judgments were hard to trust.[29]

To complicate matters further, researchers working at the respected organization Mathematica conducted their own study and found surprisingly little difference in the impact of TFA teachers as compared to other teachers, including regularly certified teachers, in the same schools and districts.[30] Based on this study, some concluded that there really was no difference and therefore districts should hire whomever they wanted. Linda Darling-Hammond, however, pointed out that the real conclusion of the Mathematica study was that in the districts analyzed, none of the teachers made much of an impact on student learning whatever their preparation—a sad commentary on all forms of teacher preparation.[31]

Nearly twenty years into the twenty-first century, the preparation pathway debate rages on. Some continue to argue that alternative routes be shut down across the board, while others contend that schools of education cannot be salvaged and that the majority of teachers need to be prepared in new ways. Still others are simply trying to increase standards for all programs and to dissuade teacher candidates from choosing "irresponsible" preparation pathways, irrespective of route. In an era when nearly everyone recognizes the significant impact of teacher quality on student learning outcomes, stakeholders in U.S. education continue to debate not only the best pathway but also the best curriculum and evaluation requirements to prepare teachers for a new millennium—in short, the very definition of a good teacher and how to measure good teaching.

Sowing the Seeds of Alternative Certification: New Jersey's Teacher Preparation Battles

A front-page article in the *Newark Star-Ledger* introduced readers to three "brilliant," talented women who wanted to teach science in New Jersey's public schools. They held degrees from prominent universities and possessed meaningful real-world work experience. Yet there was one thing preventing these women from fulfilling their teaching dreams: they lacked the necessary education courses to gain certification.[32] This article also introduced readers to a relatively new but growing idea that would come to shape the course of teacher education in New Jersey and the nation in the 1980s and onward—the idea that talented individuals wishing to teach should not be hindered by requirements to take non-rigorous and non-essential pedagogy courses in colleges of education.

In the early 1980s New Jersey became the first state to propose and implement an alternative certification program based on this premise, allowing teacher candidates to bypass a traditional education degree in favor of a fast-track route into the classroom. While other states quickly followed suit, the *Wall Street Journal* and other observers were quick to note that the debate about what teachers needed to know in order to teach—the question at the very heart of debates over teacher education—was "nowhere hotter than in New Jersey."[33]

Many forget that before there was Teach for America there was New Jersey Alternative Certification. It is perhaps no coincidence that Princeton University senior Wendy Kopp devised her proposal at a time and in a state where the teacher education wars were raging. In fact, many of the very premises that we now associate with TFA—that we need to bring better quality candidates into public school classrooms, that tenacity coupled with quick-prep based on key competencies is enough, and that most of what happens in education schools is unnecessary fluff—are the arguments that fueled the advocates of New Jersey's alternative certification route six years before Kopp published her thesis.[34]

Proposed in September 1983 and approved in September 1984 after a year of rancorous debate, the New Jersey program was in many ways a game changer. While previous law required teachers to complete a degree in education or a required number of education courses at one of the twenty-six state-approved programs, the new route allowed liberal arts majors to gain certification after passing a subject-matter test, fulfilling just twenty hours of pre-service training, and completing a year-long mentored internship in a school while serving as the lead teacher of record.[35]

Passage of such a ground-breaking proposal grew from both national and local forces. *A Nation at Risk*, the report that spurred a nation-wide debate about "the rising tide of mediocrity" that plagued American schools was published in the same year that the New Jersey program was proposed.[36] In regards to teacher preparation, the report echoed earlier criticisms by Bestor and Conant, noting, "the teacher preparation curriculum is weighted heavily with courses in 'educational methods' at the expense of courses in the subjects to be taught."[37] Newspaper and magazine articles, radio spots, and television segments helped bring the matter to national attention, leading popular sentiment to favor action. The setting was therefore ripe for an era of "education governors" to step in and capitalize on the political potential of school reform. A number of state leaders throughout the 1980s and 1990s ran on platforms that spotlighted education. Lamar Alexander, in his 1985 bid for the governor's seat of Tennessee, went as far as to say he would spend "80 percent of [his] waking hours" promoting education reform.[38] James M. Souby, executive director of the Council of State Planning Agencies noted in the same year, "Almost every Governor in the country has run on a platform of job creation and its link to the educational system."[39] Governors from both sides of the political aisle, such as Bill Clinton (D) in Arkansas, George W. Bush (R) in Texas, and James Hunt (D) in North Carolina, continued to take a similar course throughout the 1990s. Tom Kean, Republican governor of New Jersey from 1982 to 1990 and a former member of the National Task Force on Education for Economic Growth was no exception, and he eventually gained national prestige for his efforts.

Kean addressed teacher preparation within a larger bundle of reforms that reflected the reigning wisdom of what came to be known as the standards and accountability movement. Based on a belief that high standards, evaluation, and market-based competition would solve many of the problems facing American public schools, Kean proposed a tougher graduation exam for high school students, a merit-pay program for master teachers, new standardized tests for third- and sixth-grade students, a greater emphasis on discipline in the classroom, and an English proficiency exam, even for bilingual students. The hallmark of his wide-ranging reform package, however, was a plan for bringing liberal arts majors and passionate career-changers into classrooms through changes in state teacher licensing procedures.[40]

The impetus for change in certification also came from—perhaps surprisingly—the very higher education institutions that housed teacher preparation programs. New Jersey's normal schools and teachers colleges followed national trends and transformed from stand-alone teacher preparation entities into comprehensive four-year colleges and universities in the 1960s and 1970s. Along with these moves came status anxiety among many of the now much more disciplinarily diverse faculty who did not want to be tagged with the low esteem in which teachers colleges had often been held. Worries over quality and rigor among college leaders and the public led the New Jersey legislature to create a commission that would examine teacher preparation and quality statewide. The subsequent 1978 study concluded that the quality of education programs and their candidates was indeed very low, bolstering a decades-long public perception of education schools as warehouses for the low-achieving student and anti-intellectual professor.[41] The social movements and racial upheaval of the late 1960s and early 1970s also hurt the reputation of education schools and teachers in many urban communities of color, as education school–prepared teachers, who were mostly white, often opposed community control and greater parental involvement in schools, two movements championed by Black and Latinx parents in New Jersey cities like Newark and Camden.[42]

Yet while the media often portrayed teachers as incompetent or pilloried them as the bottom of the barrel academically, politicians also knew they needed the support of teachers and their unions to pull off any major reforms. In New Jersey, teachers therefore started to assume the role of victim in political and media rhetoric; instead of incompetent, they became underpaid, under-appreciated and, most of all, ill-prepared. Like teachers in many states, New Jersey teachers complained loudly about the quality of their preparation. The result was that teacher educators, and not their students, began to bear the brunt of public and political ire. It was *ed schools*, reformers and the media claimed, with all their fluffy classes and low prestige, that were preventing better candidates from entering the field and the classroom. It did not help that as this debate unfolded, a former state education commissioner was caught with a plagiarized dissertation from a doctoral program in education, rendering the field all the more suspicious in the public eye.[43]

The time seemed ripe for alternative certification. In a rare joint session of the New Jersey state legislature in September 1983, State Education Commissioner Saul Cooperman, with the support of Governor Kean, introduced the details of a bold new plan for certification: reform teacher preparation by making changes in traditional routes and add an alternative pathway into the classroom that would allow high-quality candidates to bypass pedagogy and theory courses. Cooperman made his case based on a couple key arguments. First, he stressed that "there [was] a crisis of quality in our educational enterprise," as some of the least academically gifted students were being recruited into teacher preparation programs.[44] He cited low comparative SAT and ACT scores and middling grade point averages for education majors. Second, he criticized the quality and relevance of many of the courses that students were receiving in education schools, courses he viewed as trivial excesses, explaining, "despite continued and extensive research, none has been able to establish the existence of a systematic relationship between theoretical courses, including pedagogical courses, and effective teaching practice."[45] He stressed the importance of subject mastery in a liberal arts major and skills such as lesson planning and behavior management.

Alternative certification, Cooperman explained, would serve the function of recruiting high-quality candidates who are usually deterred by having to take education courses and getting them into the classroom where students need them. "We will move from a system that will certify people of limited ability," Cooperman proclaimed, "to a system that will deny those people admittance to the profession. We will move from a system that systematically discourages talented people to a system that will make it possible for them to teach."[46] Cooperman also drummed up concern over certification by detailing the issue of emergency certification, which already granted teaching licenses to those without the legally required coursework if there were vacancies that principals could not fill with certified candidates. He said this practice, rampant with patronage, would only worsen in the next decade.

Before coming to the state commissioner's job, Cooperman had been superintendent in Madison, New Jersey. Looking back on his years as a local school superintendent, he was proud of his efforts to raise the standards for teachers in his town. He insisted that it was the duty of a superintendent to ask, "'What's essential for beginning teachers to know?' The key word is 'essential.'" He was also clear on what not to do: "I wouldn't let the education deans get control of teacher certification and load people up with certification courses on pedagogy, so to speak."[47] Perhaps Cooperman was an early example of a trend that became much stronger in the twenty-first century: the "revolt of the superintendents" against not only the courses but also the reigning philosophy of most schools of education.

Reaction to the proposal across the state was immediate and mixed. Cooperman and Kean successfully gained the endorsement of a number of key organizations, including the state's Chancellor of Higher Education, the New Jersey School Boards Association, the Principals and Supervisors Association, the state's major newspapers, and a number of state legislators. In December 1983, President Reagan even gave his blessing to the proposal, saying in a speech, "In New Jersey, Governor Tom Kean has a proposal that deserves wide support. Under his plan, the New Jersey Board of Education would allow successful mathematicians, scientists, linguists, and journalists to pass a competency test in their subjects, then go into the classroom as paid teaching interns."[48] An aggressive public relations tour, coupled with supportive news articles at the state and national level, also helped Cooperman and Kean gain strong public approval. In November 1983, pro-alternative certification advocates received another major boost when a study entitled "What's Wrong with Teacher Education," also known as the Thornburn Study, was released to the public. Much to the horror of the education school world and the delight of critics, the study detailed the experience of a man who enrolled in an unnamed New Jersey education school under the alias William Thornburn. He found incompetence and neglect on the part of teacher educators, as well as a weak and irrelevant curriculum. A sensational report, even if based on just one person's experience, it garnered even more public backing for the idea that education schools were superfluous.[49]

Ardent opposition to the proposal also formed, mostly from two expected places: schools of education and teachers unions. The New Jersey Education Association (NJEA), the state's largest union for K–12 teachers; the New Jersey Federation of Teachers (NJFT), a union mainly for state college faculty; and the New Jersey Association of Colleges for Teacher Education (NJACTE), all released statements opposing the plan. All of these groups saw the proposal as a means to undermine their professional statuses by implying that anyone off the street could do what they did, whether that be K–12 teaching or teacher preparation. They did not take too well to the public perception that they represented a body of academically weak ne'er-do-wells, either. Calling the proposal a "sham and a delusion," representatives from NJEA noted that Cooperman's plan would allow people with no professional training to experiment on the state's children like guinea pigs.[50] Some prominent education professors released analyses that critiqued the data in the report. A number of state assemblymen likewise expressed worries that the proposal would let anyone off the street into classrooms and would attract people who failed at other professions.[51] Most of these legislators also had campuses in their districts and felt a need to defend them as loyal constituents, at least at first.

The most vocal opposition, however, came from the teacher education establishment housed in colleges of education, who had been cast as the real villains in the proposal and in public debate. They objected to the idea that what they taught—the theory and methods courses that were being castigated—were irrelevant. They believed, as Rider College Associate Dean of Education William Guthrie expressed, that there was, in fact, a "body of knowledge—a legitimate type learned in college—[that] is necessary before teaching" and that "successful clinical experience is necessary before you take over the classroom."[52] They also expressed concern that the commissioner and governor did not consult them in drafting the proposal. Ken Carlson, then Associate Dean of Education and Teacher Certification at Rutgers and an outspoken opponent of the plan, noted, "The vehemence of their [education deans and professors] response to the proposal when it was officially released was in part conditioned by the fact that their expertise had been treated as a *disqualification* for participation in the policymaking."[53]

It was true that Cooperman, Kean, and Leo Klagholz, another leading architect of the proposal, did not believe that teacher educators had any insight on reforming their own field of teacher education. As a reflection of this belief, their proposal also entailed the creation of two blue-ribbon commissions that would be charged with determining the core body of knowledge that teachers *did* need to know and what the internship experience would look like. No teacher educators were appointed to either panel.

The first commission, officially titled the Panel on the Preparation of Beginning Teachers but referred to as the Boyer Panel, was charged with answering two major questions at the heart of teacher preparation debates: What is essential for beginning teachers to know? How do effective teachers teach? Ernest L. Boyer, former U.S. Commissioner of Education under the Carter administration and then president of the Carnegie Foundation for the Advancement of Teaching, led the panel. The other members included education professors from across the country, mostly dominated by educational psychologists, and representatives from education policy think tanks. The panel met for two days in January 1984, after a fall of bitter debate. By February 28, the panel members announced their findings, concluding that beginning teachers needed to know quite a bit: about curriculum development, teaching strategies, materials selection, human development, assessment of pupils, classroom management, and the sociology of schooling (knowledge of history and philosophies of education would be desirable, but not essential for a beginning teacher). On the question of how, they discussed the need for strong ethics and having clear goals and organizational skills. The panel attempted to avoid getting mixed up in the political fray by publishing a rather aloof report that remained unspecific in its recommendations about implementation. Some teacher educators breathed a sigh of relief that the panel at least agreed that teachers needed to know something and did not render what they did entirely irrelevant. But although the panel members expressed the conviction that if teaching were to become a reputable profession, it needed to maintain ties with colleges and universities, they ultimately concluded that teacher preparation could occur in a variety of institutional settings and did not need to entail an undergraduate education degree or take place in a college of education at all.[54]

The panel charged with determining recommendations for the internship component was more diverse, comprising education professors, principals, superintendents, teachers, business representatives, and parents. Harry Jaroslaw, superintendent of the Tenafly Public Schools, served as chairman and lent his name to what became known as the Jaroslaw Commission. Again to the relief of the teachers unions and teacher educators, the panel concluded that the originally proposed five days of pre-service training was insufficient and instead recommended a twenty-day training period before the school year began. They also concluded that these trainings could be offered by existing education schools, private consultants, or the districts themselves.[55] While the commission therefore encouraged partnerships with education schools, they did not require alternative programs to establish them. One panel member, Marcantonio Lacatena, issued a minority report that would require college participation and college courses before, during, and after the internship year; in so doing, he became a champion for the opposition coalition. But the majority of the members of the commission, including Superintendent Jaroslaw, were quite happy to allow programs under the management and control of individual school districts to do this work.

After the commissions released their panel reports, heated debate picked back up in the months leading to the State Board hearing that was to be held the following September. This time, national figures entered the fray. University of Cincinnati Dean of Education Hendrick Gideonse wrote a long and scathing analysis of the New Jersey proposal. David Imig, executive director of the nation-wide American Association of Colleges for Teacher Education (AACTE), offered $5,000 in financial assistance for the opposition campaign and provided coverage of the issue in AACTE briefs. Jere Brophy, co-director of the Institute for Research on Teaching at Michigan State University; Wilma Longstreet, dean of the College of Education at University of New Orleans; Charles Myers, chairperson of the Department of Teaching and Learning at Vanderbilt; David Tyack, Vida Jacks Professor of Education at Stanford University; and others also made their qualms with the proposal known to the public. In May, the Council of New Jersey State College Locals sent hundreds of copies of a booklet entitled "Educational Reform: The New Jersey Experience" to education stakeholders across the state and country. The pamphlet contained an overview of the year's events and suggested actions if people thought such a proposal was harming the teaching profession. They received phone calls from fifteen education deans around the country and fifteen more written responses, all in agreement that the proposal was a problem.[56]

In perhaps a last-ditch effort to stop or at least significantly alter the plan, leaders of the opposition campaign held a conference in July 1984. They invited education establishment leaders such as Myron Atkin, dean of the highly-regarded Stanford School of Education, and American Federation of Teachers (AFT) president and nationally known figure Albert Shanker. As Carlson reported, Atkin "assailed the notion that teaching can be learned through an apprenticeship in the same way as bricklaying or soldering. Teaching, he said, requires more than imitation of a journeyman or master; it involves the understanding of underlying principles." Atkin also critiqued the twenty-day preparation course as anti-intellectual because it did not have teacher candidates discuss such issues as vouchers, merit pay, or other then-current controversies and would therefore keep teachers from understanding the profession and playing a role in policy. Atkin tied the current debate to a long-standing American tradition of "education school bashing." Shanker criticized both sides for being anti-intellectual and critiqued the courses he received at Columbia's Teachers College. Yet he also called the New Jersey Plan "hare-brained" and listed a number of things a teacher should know before entering the classroom as a professional.[57]

Despite these efforts, when the vote came before the State Board of Education in September 1984, it passed unanimously.[58] The final proposal required changes to existing undergraduate education programs as well as offering the new alternative path, a key ingredient to the plan's success, according to Klagholz. Those seeking the traditional route would have to major in a liberal arts subject while also fulfilling a limited number of education coursework requirements, complete student teaching, and then pass a competency test. Those in the alternative pathway would also need to hold a bachelor's degree in the subject area to be taught, demonstrate subject competency through a standardized test, and acquire and demonstrate teaching skills by completing twenty days of pre-service training, continued coursework throughout the year, and a school-based mentorship during the first "internship" year. Although the original plan required alternative certification programs to first seek partnerships with colleges of education, they were not required to do so, and the state established regional training centers where alternative certification candidates could complete their mandated coursework.

In the end, the NJEA and the remaining skeptical assemblymen endorsed the proposal after the extension of pre-service training and a more intensive, though still sparse, mentorship component, leaving the education college deans and professors as some of the last voices of opposition.[59] The pro-proposal advocates framed this criticism as self-interest, and the public largely agreed. Throughout 1984, more than twenty other states had also begun similar discussions and embarked on the process of changing their state laws in favor of alternative pathways into the classroom. By the mid-1980s, alternative certification was having its moment.[60]

In the following years, many hailed New Jersey's alternative certification pathway as a success. Governor Kean, a highly popular governor with both Republicans and Democrats, received praise from Presidents Reagan and Bush for his leadership on education reform and served as a mentor to other governors by sharing his experiences with teacher preparation policy. He also became an active national voice in education reform by participating in education task forces, and news articles and discussions regarding state-level alternative certification almost always cited Kean and the New Jersey experiment.

Kean, Cooperman, and Klagholz could also claim success in the following decade based on follow-up reports of the program. These reports cited studies that showed the superior quality of alternative certification candidates based on SAT scores, GPAs, and results on the basic skills assessment tests required of teachers in the following years. They also boasted that alternative pathways succeeded in recruiting a more racially diverse teaching force.[61] The program enjoyed significant demand, particularly after the 2008 recession when more people needed jobs and found something with a social mission appealing. The media added to this positive review, offering glowing portrayals of the program in local and national newspapers and magazines, and state officials could brag that their state, unlike many others, had solved the problem of teacher shortages.[62] Programs like Teach for America also brought prestige to this route into teaching and greater support for alternative certification as a policy. By 2010, around one third of new teachers in New Jersey entered through the alternative pathway, second only to Texas, which followed and then expanded on New Jersey's lead.[63]

After two decades of alternative certification and the rise of TFA, however, criticisms began to mount. The camp critical of standards, accountability, market competition, and fast-track teacher preparation programs grew. According to critics, the reform movement not only failed to deliver on its promises but in many cases heightened inequality, de-professionalized the teaching field, threatened democracy, and narrowed the K–12 curriculum.[64] Many TFA and alternative route teachers testified that crash courses did not prepare them adequately for work in the classroom, particularly in high-needs urban districts. If the testimony of education school deans was easy to ignore because of their perceived self-interest, the testimony of teachers claiming not to be well prepared was much harder to set aside. Principals and superintendents were mixed on their opinions about whether they liked to hire alternative-route candidates.[65] While some praised alternative-route teachers' passion and quality, others lamented their lack of classroom management skills or their high burnout and turnover rates. Some New Jersey alternative providers started reforming themselves throughout the early 2000s in response to graduate feedback that school-based mentoring and twenty days of pre-service coursework were not enough.[66] By the 2010s more research had also been published regarding the efficacy of various preparation pathways, with many researchers citing the desirability of professional coursework and year-long clinical experiences that allowed teachers to assume control of classrooms more gradually while simultaneously exploring pedagogical theory and methods.[67] When the Obama administration's 2010 Race to the Top grant competition rewarded state proposals that embraced teacher education reform, particularly through teacher evaluations, discussion on teacher preparation opened again in New Jersey, as elsewhere.

About thirty years after the original proposal, New Jersey passed legislation reforming its alternative pathway program once again, this time to reflect a greater faith in education coursework and practice teaching. In 2015, the State Board of Education announced new, tougher requirements for both traditional and alternative route candidates. Starting in September 2017, alternative route candidates needed to complete a year-long clinical teaching experience in an approved learning setting prior to receiving a Certificate of Eligibility to serve as lead classroom teacher, significantly altering the original alternative pathway plan. Traditional candidates likewise experienced changes in their current student teaching requirements to something more akin to clinical residency rounds for medical patients. Now alternative candidates also need to complete additional instructional hours during their clinical training as well as in their first year as a provisionally licensed teacher, adding more education coursework back into certification requirements. Moreover, the new rules provide higher standards for teacher candidate quality, including mandated passage of a tougher basic skills test, a 3.0 undergraduate GPA (up from 2.75), and a new evaluation process that includes a performance assessment. State officials explained that these reforms came after deliberations with prospective and former teacher candidates, principals, researchers, parents, and teacher educators, and were also based on recent research on teacher education and federal recommendations.[68]

While some debate regarding these changes arose, the most heated aspect of this round of New Jersey teacher preparation reform seems to have shifted from how much professional training a teacher needs before entering the classroom—more, most sides conclude—to how teachers will be evaluated after their training, a shift in thinking from "inputs" to "outputs." At the writing of this book, Governor Chris Christie and the teachers unions were engaged in an ugly, protracted battle over the nature of these evaluations, with the former wanting to take student achievement data into account and the latter adamantly opposing that idea. Christie also favored charter schools being allowed to control their own teacher preparation requirements, another controversial proposal, but one that exists in many states already.[69]

What hasn't changed, however, is the continued focus on the quality of education schools and teacher candidates. In response to federal recommendations, New Jersey started evaluating and ranking college- and university-based teacher preparation programs with the intent of incentivizing them to improve and to give prospective teacher candidate "consumers" more knowledge about which programs they should choose. Education schools have vocally criticized such rankings and the evaluation metrics, while tougher entrance requirements clearly signal a desire to strengthen the academic quality of the teaching pool.

A few decades after the original contentious proposal for a state-wide alternative pathway into public school teaching, one thing seems to be clear: both alternative pathways and traditional routes seem here to stay. Debate has shifted from inputs to outputs, with the general assumption that it matters less where, institutionally, preparation takes place as long as quality preparation occurs and the teachers are performing well. What hasn't changed from the 1980s is the desire to attract more high-quality, diverse individuals into the teaching profession; ensure their academic ability; and determine the proper balance among subject-matter knowledge, pedagogical theory, and skill competencies. The debate rages on.

Perhaps it was Ernest Boyer of the Boyer panel who was most prescient. After recommending a moderate-size body of core knowledge a teacher needs to know before his or her first year—somewhere in between the die-hard deregulation and the professional agenda crowds—he also noted, "With respect to the issue of where professional knowledge can best be presented, there is no single answer, no one arrangement that is always best. The college setting offers obvious advantages . . . There are non-collegiate 'laboratory' settings that also may be appropriate for conveying knowledge and skills to prospective teachers . . . Perhaps the best approach is to join the learning places, to build partnerships or coalitions among the separate institutions interested in teacher preparation with new organizational arrangements to help educators carry on their work."[70] He mused that the ideal program would probably be something like a one-year post-baccalaureate program that would combine formal learning through seminars and practical experience with a professional mentor, something that looks closer to the 2015 reforms than to the 1984 ones. "As a personal opinion," he confessed after the report of his panel was released, "I think frankly that just a couple of days or a few weeks (of pre-internship training) would be unacceptable." At that point in time, however, a new and rising generation of reformers did not seem to agree.

One Day All Teachers: Teach for America and Quick-Prep Fellows Programs

The origin story of Teach for America is by now well known. In 1989 Princeton University senior Wendy Kopp published her senior thesis project, *An Argument and Plan for the Creation of the Teacher Corps*. Despite her advisor telling her the idea was "quite evidently deranged," Kopp turned her project into an education reform behemoth, a successful multibillion-dollar organization, and a household name.[71] TFA now sends nearly 5,000 teachers into high-needs urban and rural classrooms every year, operates on a $35 million yearly budget, and maintains an alumni base of 46,000 strong.[72] Yet the verdict is still out on whether TFA has been a force for good in teacher education or a painful episode from which to recover. On whichever side of the debate one falls, it is hard to disagree that the organization shifted the conversation surrounding American teacher preparation, bringing significant public attention to the question of *who* should teach in the nation's most struggling schools and *how* those teachers should be trained.

TFA combined strains of the 1960s Teacher Corps with the ideology of the 1980s Me Generation. The idea was to send the best and brightest college graduates into the nation's highest needs schools to teach for two years, something akin to the Peace Corps, to solve what Kopp and others saw as the greatest civil rights issue of their time: closing the racial academic achievement gap. As Kopp explains in her book *One Day All Children*, through sheer grit, a lean in–style confidence, and a stellar education at one of the nation's most elite universities, she was able to turn her project into reality—an experience corps members were then supposed to replicate in the nation's most struggling schools with high-needs children.[73] Yet unlike many involved in the 1960s Teacher Corps, who believed in the ability of communities to contribute to their own development and were involved in a larger structural critique of poverty, TFA architects—generally well-to-do individuals trained in some of the nation's most elite baccalaureate institutions—believed in the power of competition, the salubrious impact of Wall Street and the private sector, data-driven standards and account-ability, and the ability of education—"what happened in the four walls of the classroom"—to solve problems of inequality. Education researcher and journalist Donna Foote, who spent a year following TFA teachers in their classrooms, described the organization as bringing together a "swing in civil sensibilities of America's young elite" and a "federally backed move toward outcome-based instruction."[74]

The guiding beliefs behind Kopp's proposal were also many of the same arguments that fueled the New Jersey certification debates—that high-achieving college grads will be more effective than traditional teachers, that a quick-prep program would address dire teacher shortages, and that what happened in schools of education was largely unnecessary in the business of creating high-quality teachers. Moreover, as a component of the TFA plan, Kopp expected that corps teachers would move on after their two years of service into influential positions in policy and the professions to spur change at the structural level, including allowing more high-quality teacher candidates to enter through alternative routes, but also to build support for a range of education reforms from whatever career they eventually found themselves pursuing.[75]

Kopp's inspiration to start the project grew in part from her own experience trying to become a teacher in New York City public schools and in part from a conference on the teacher shortage crisis she attended as an undergraduate student in 1988. As Kopp set off on the job market at the end of her college years, applying to a number of high-power consulting, advertising, and Wall Street financial firms, she also considered dipping her toes into something more service-oriented until she decided which of those career paths she wanted to take. Encouraged by the decade's *Nation at Risk* discourse, she turned to teaching as one way she could make a positive difference. Yet Kopp soon realized that, just like the teachers featured on the front page of the *Newark Star Ledger* in 1983, she would have to complete multiple pedagogy courses before entering the classroom, a requirement she thought was unnecessary and onerous. She started researching the issue and decided that licensure regulations were preventing talented individuals like herself who did not study education during their undergraduate years from teaching in the country's most high-needs schools. Her senior thesis sought to solve these problems by building on an idea already underway in New Jersey: bypass education schools to get bright students into classrooms immediately.[76]

After graduating, Kopp and two colleagues, also recent Ivy League graduates who would later become influential education reformers, set up shop in donated office space from Union Carbide and worked around the clock soliciting donations from private companies such as Mobil, Merck, Chrysler, and Hertz to get the project off the ground. Their work, and Kopp's connections and Princeton credentials, eventually paid off. The first TFA corps convened in Los Angeles in the summer of 1990 for the inaugural TFA institute. Notably, when Kopp ran this institute, she and her colleagues had never taught in a classroom or taken a single course on pedagogy. Tales from that first summer are legendary. Corps members complained of inadequate planning and training, and issues involving race and class bubbled up from the recruits while Kopp holed herself up in her dorm room. Nonetheless, 489 corps members made their way into classrooms that first fall, and the rest is non-profit startup history. From an original network of a few hundred teachers in six regions, TFA now trains around 5,000 corps members per year in fifty-two regions, making it one of the largest suppliers of teachers in the nation, particularly in high-needs districts.[77] In New Orleans, for example, TFA doubled its corps following Hurricane Katrina, displacing many veteran teachers of color with roots in the community and currently comprising a significant percentage of the overall teaching force.[78]

Kopp and her colleagues caught a couple of big breaks in the early years as they gained the trust and financial backing of people in high places. Morgan Stanley became a major funder in the early 1990s, among other big-name banks, foundations, and Fortune 500 companies. President Clinton's newly established AmeriCorps program also served as a major boon for the organization. By 1996 AmeriCorps supplied 20% of TFA's budget, and the federal government gave the organization another $2 million in other forms of support.[79] As TFA grew, it also became highly adept at public relations and lobbying, earning a prestigious reputation among elite college students and employers, not to mention philanthropies, individual donors, and influential figures on Capitol Hill—quite a contrast with the much-

FIGURE 1. The first Teach for America Corps at their summer institute in Houston, Texas, in the summer of 1990. *Source:* Courtesy of Teach for America.

maligned education schools. Every U.S. president from Clinton to Obama has endorsed TFA and lent it federal financial and policy support.

Although some things have changed over the years at TFA, others have stayed constant. The recruitment process was and still is highly rigorous and selective, aided by a 1999 McKinsey-devised selection regimen.[80] Candidates, many from elite universities, usually go through two rounds of phone interviews. If they pass through the phone interviews, they attend an all-day, in-person interview that includes one-on-one questioning, whole-group simulations, role-play scenarios, pen-and-paper tests, and a five-minute lesson plan demonstration. Chosen corps members then attend a five-week summer institute during which they teach a summer school class and receive crash-course training from TFA's teacher educators, many of whom only taught two years as corps members themselves, according to the TFA-designed Teaching as Learning (TAL) rubric. The TAL curriculum, first implemented in 2001, is based on a set of actions, or competencies, inspired by TFA's most successful teachers (notably not the research produced by professional teacher educators) and organized around six categories that

The Emergence of Alternative Routes to Teaching   47

are hammered home to corps members from day one: set big goals, plan purposefully, execute effectively, continuously increase effectiveness, and work relentlessly. The summer institute acts as part training, part initiation, and part hazing, as corps members are pushed to work long hours day in and day out, learning TFA jargon and organizational culture, even operating on "TFA time"—the official time set by the organization, which serves as one of many in-house rituals that critics deem "cultish" and proponents describe as community-building. After attending the summer institute, corps members find jobs at either traditional public schools or charter schools, and they begin work as teachers of record in the fall. TFA is adamant that internships or other slower entry programs are unacceptable; the TFA fellow must be in charge of their own classroom. Professional development then continues throughout the first and second years, as corps members gain certification either through a partnership with a local university or an alternative certification provider, and in some regions a master's degree in education.

TFA is important for its impact on schools, no doubt, but also for proliferating a number of underlying assumptions related to teacher education that have taken hold far beyond the TFA arena. One assumption is that if you are smart, hardworking, and tenacious, you can be a good teacher after a boot camp–style training. "I remember the whole auditorium full of kids, you know, chanting 'best and brightest!,'" recalled Brent Lyles, an alumnus of the original 1990 corps, in an interview with historian Bethany Rogers.[81] Although this idea first surfaced in the 1960s Teacher Corps, it has become one of TFA's best-known attributes—and a major source of criticism. As early as 1994, just four years into the experiment, Darling-Hammond published a now famous article in *Phi Delta Kappan* critiquing TFA and this mentality, calling it an arrogant missionary organization that was a quickfix at best, but ultimately harmful to students in need of the *most*, not least, qualified teachers.[82]

Also among TFA's major assumptions are that abolishing the achievement gap is *the* way to solve problems of inequality in the United States and that education is *the* ticket out for a low-income child. These assumptions meant pushing an agenda that ignored out-of-school factors, such as access to quality health care and jobs, and structural racism in various realms, like the criminal justice system. Critics charged that TFA raised a whole generation of influential education reformers and students on the idea that education alone can solve poverty, as opposed to education serving as one key lever in a multifaceted approach to poverty alleviation. As one former corps member complained, "Idealism is insufficient to dismantle structural inequality. TFA's hero narrative calls for CMs [corps members] to overcome the obstacles of structural oppression, institutional racism, and historic inequity through their individual hard work and caring, and in doing so, it minimizes the need for systemic change."[83] Another alum noted, "You go in there thinking . . . [that] goodwill will change the world and you leave realizing that that's necessary but not sufficient. . . . That's a valuable lesson."[84]

TFA also promotes the idea that by making the program competitive, elite students concerned with prestige and resume building will want to join, making education an appealing field for the talented, ambitious, and well connected. This has proved to be somewhat true. By the turn of the twenty-first century, education reform had become a highly respected career path for an Ivy League graduate, male or female. Kopp and TFA alums such as Michelle Rhee graced the cover of *Time* and *Newsweek*. Even indie band Vampire Weekend's front man Ezra Koeing, a Columbia University graduate, is a TFA alum. One corps member recalled, "You know, [the idea that] this is the 'best and brightest' and you're going to go out there and fix all of America's public schools, [that] appealed to my vanity."[85] Rather than raising the prestige of the teaching profession generally, however, TFA arguably created a bifurcated system of cultural capital. A corps member at a cocktail party, for example, would likely slip in that she was a *TFA* teacher, not just any old education school graduate.

Whether one supports the program or not, it did aid in bringing the term "achievement gap" into common parlance and the idea that "all children can learn" into mainstream thought, particularly among those in powerful positions. (Though to be fair, civil rights activists had been arguing this all along.) And many bright, service-oriented young Americans have gone into the field of education instead of consulting or investment banking, at least for a while. While most corps members do not stay in teaching after their two-year commitments, as critics of TFA never fail to note, many have stayed in education in some form or another, or stay committed to educational equity while pursuing careers in other fields. TFA estimates that while only 32% of their teachers stay in classrooms after two years, 78% stay in jobs that affect education in some way.[86]

In fact, TFA's most lasting legacy may not exist in the many classrooms run by TFA teachers, but rather in the post-TFA lives of its thousands of alumni who now occupy powerful positions in the public and private sectors. TFA alums fill a number of important positions across the nation, from school administration to board of education seats to state senator offices, all the way to lobbying and staffer positions on Capitol Hill. "We think of TFA as a farm system of leaders," admitted Keven Hall, a former TFA staff member who is now chief operating officer of the Broad Education Foundation.[87] Jim Shelton of the Gates Foundation agrees that TFA seeds the education reform landscape with high-caliber human capital and thinks it is one of the most important organizations shaping education today.[88] The number of TFA alumni on staff in major city departments of education is staggering.

TFA as an organization has also proved highly influential in changing the policy landscape in support of a broader education reform agenda, but also in relation to alternative certification law specifically. In 2010, TFA spent $573,952 on lobbying.[89] Politico called TFA a "political powerhouse," noting its ability to shape prominent legislation at all levels, including the way "highly qualified" was defined in the No Child Left Behind (NCLB) Act and what types of teacher education reforms were valued by the Obama administration, particularly in its Race to the Top initiative.[90] Not surprisingly, creating more alternative certification routes was considered a positive attribute in state Race to the Top grant applications. There are also those who have charged that TFA's substantial lobbying efforts essentially closed the spigot on government and foundation funds reaching reformers within university schools of education.

TFA's 501c4 political arm, Leadership for Educational Equity (LEE), also acts as a major political tool, providing start-up cash to alumni to launch advocacy groups, spending hundreds of thousands of dollars on lobbying, and providing fellowships aimed at grooming alums for posts as state cabinet secretaries and superintendents, as well as for interns for senators, representatives, and members of the House Education and Workforce Committee. LEE also throws its weight behind pro-reform alumni running for office, as when it spent $20,000 to help elect two former corps members to the board of education in Nevada, where TFA sought to expand but faced legislative resistance.[91]

TFA's structural influence also extends to the world of charter schools, as TFA has proved highly successful in graduating a devoted cadre of pro-charter school teachers, administrators, and backers. Over half of America's largest charter school networks maintain ties with TFA, either through formal partnerships or through their leadership teams.[92] TFA alum Dave Levin's KIPP Academy charter network is perhaps the most famous TFA offshoot, but other examples include charter chains such as Uncommon Schools, YES Prep, and IDEA Public Schools. Many of these charter schools hire TFA or alternatively certified teachers. Moreover, in many states charter schools do not have to abide by the same certification and licensure laws as traditional public schools, meaning TFA-fueled charter chains are also fueling the pipeline of alternatively certified teachers into America's publicly funded classrooms.

TFA also inspired many similar teaching fellows programs across the country. The New Teacher Project (TNTP), founded in 1997 by controversial TFA alumnus and former District of Columbia Schools Chancellor Michelle Rhee, aimed to bring high-quality alternative certification programs to an even wider audience. By partnering with districts and states, TNTP helped launch teaching fellows programs in New York City, Baltimore, the District of Columbia, New Orleans, and Nashville, among other cities. Aiming to get rid of "senseless" barriers of entry into the classroom, TNTP conducted a similar recruitment, application, and training model as TFA, targeted at career-changers and centered on a rigorous selection process with a five-week summer training before fellows began teaching. As TNTP grew as on organization in the early 2000s, it also began offering consulting services to districts, encouraging more districts to implement and favor alternative certification programs. It published influential reports on teacher education that supported the pro-alternative route philosophy and later took up such issues as teacher evaluations, support, and retention in addition to certification pathway. Today, TNTP offers services and partners with over 200 school districts across the country, and TNTP teaching fellows programs operate in six states as well as cities across the nation.[93]

TFA also decided that its innovative approach to teacher and school leadership training deserved a wider audience, and in 2007 Wendy Kopp resigned from her position to start Teach for All, a separate non-profit organization that brings the TFA model to countries around the world. As of this writing, Teach for All operates in forty-six nations.[94]

From Darling-Hammond's critical 1994 article, however, TFA has occupied the role of lightning rod in education reform and teacher education circles. Being pro- or anti-TFA often signals which sort of reforms one favors and how one self-identifies politically. From its very beginning, many have critiqued TFA for its elite tinge and blatant disregard for professional teacher training—and even for professional teachers themselves. Others have called it out for its arrogant, arguably missionary ethos, which told young, mostly white twentysomethings that they could waltz into poor communities of color as savior figures. Teach for All has only heightened these anti-imperial critiques, as TFA expands on a global scale. Still others have highlighted the organization's influence in furthering a privatizing, anti-union, neoliberal reform agenda under the guise of being apolitical. "We're a leadership organization, not a political organization. . . . We have no ideological positions on issues," former TFA CEO Matt Kramer has stated publicly.[95] Critics disagree. "TFA seems to be training their corps to believe a simple narrative: that public schools are irreparably damaged. Bad teachers and bureaucracy are to blame, and our only salvation is by diminishing the union, innovating and creating systems of choice and competition," former TFA teacher Beth Sondel, currently an education professor at North Carolina State University who writes against neoliberal reform, told NPR.[96]

Sondel is not the only less-than-satisfied alum. Beginning in the 1990s and increasing in the early 2000s, criticism has poured in from other corps members, as alumni have submitted horror stories and critiques of the organization to major publications (much to the dismay of TFA's mighty public relations wing), and have shared their qualms about the program with their social networks. They have charged that TFA does not train its corps members well enough and that it proliferates an unhealthy ideology that places blame for not raising student achievement on individual corps members, rather than on a difficult and complex system. It likewise does not encourage its members to stay in the classroom, even though teacher turnover is a serious challenge facing high-poverty schools. The TAL rubric that TFA uses as the basis of its summer preparation program and TFA's entire pedagogical philosophy, others have argued, is based on raising test scores. This philosophy promotes a narrow vision of the purpose of education and leads to a limited style of pedagogy that hinders critical thinking and prizes test scores and data-driven competition. Darling-Hammond and others also have continued to critique TFA for de-professionalizing the field of teaching and encouraging districts to kick out higher-paid veteran teachers in favor of lower-paid novices. Many who were sympathetic to the mission have agreed that while TFA was serving a need when it first started to address teacher shortages, after ten or fifteen years of existence it outgrew that original purpose and took jobs away from trained and committed professionals.

By the 2010s, critiques of crash-course style teacher preparation reverberated from a variety of voices, not just defenders of education schools. A 2012 *Onion* article with the headline "Can We Please, Just Once, Have a Real Teacher?" popularized the rancor with a satirical exchange between a young, white, female TFA teacher who "was certain [she] wanted to make a difference in the world" and a young Latino boy. The fictional boy lamented, "Just once, it would be nice to walk into a classroom and see a teacher who has a real, honest-to-God degree in education and not a twentysomething English graduate trying to bolster a middling GPA and a sparse law school application. I don't think it's too much to ask for a qualified educator who has experience standing up in front of a classroom and isn't desperately trying to prove to herself that she's a good person. I'm not some sort of stepping stone to a larger career, okay? I'm an actual child with a single working mother, and I need to be educated by someone who actually wants to be a teacher, actually comprehends the mechanics of teaching, and won't get completely eaten alive by a classroom full of 10-year-olds within the first two months on the job."[97] The boy's rant captured the growing critiques of TFA and struck a nerve with many corps members who wrote back in response.

A widely read 2013 *Slate* article also spread awareness of a movement bubbling up among college professors not to write recommendation letters for any student applying to TFA. Professor Catherine Michna of Tulane University wrote,

> Every year, TFA installs thousands of unprepared 22-year-olds, the majority of whom are from economically and culturally privileged backgrounds, into disadvantaged public schools. They are given a class of their own after only five to six weeks of training and a scant number of hours co-teaching summer school (in a different city, frequently in a different subject, and with students in a different age group than the one they end up teaching in the fall). College and university faculty allow these well-meaning young people to become pawns in a massive game to de-professionalize teaching. TFA may look good on their resumés and allow them to attain social capital for their bright futures in consulting firms, law schools, and graduate schools. But in exchange for this social capital, our students have to take part in essentially privatizing public schools.[98]

By 2014, criticisms of TFA were so rampant that a #ResistTFA hashtag surfaced on social media, led by two teacher candidates who headed the grassroots group Students United for Public Education. Stephanie Rivera and Hannah Nguyen explained in a press release, "The overwhelming response to the #ResistTFA hashtag proves that there is an enormous concern among students, teachers, parents and citizens across the country regarding Teach for America's disproportionate influence on public education. We are encouraged to see this massive outpouring on Twitter, and we look forward to continuing this important discussion about Teach for America on campuses across the country."[99]

In 2016, TFA received perhaps the toughest blow. While staff and corps members argue that they are working tirelessly on behalf of disadvantaged communities of color, the Black Lives Matter (BLM) movement published a K–12 reform platform that called for an end to "corporate backed reformer programs such as Teach for America" and the many charter schools run and staffed by current and former members.[100] BLM activist DeRay Mckesson's mayoral run in Baltimore came under scrutiny for his close ties with TFA, garnering such headlines in local media as "Promotion from TFA, Shade From Local Organizers," referencing the community's skeptical attitude toward the organization.[101]

Yet while criticism of TFA has mounted over the years, the organization has maintained support and popularity with some in the education policy world and many in the broader political and corporate establishment. TFA has continued to receive large donations from major philanthropies and private donors, particularly from the financial sector, as well as significant funding from government at many levels. Moreover, while alumni critics abound, there are also many former corps members who have not joined in the backlash but rather have supported TFA whole-heartedly. An outpouring of TFA defenses came in the wake of the *Onion* article. One impassioned corps member argued that she was, in fact, a "real" teacher and that her dedication and results with her students should be recognized: "My world revolves around my students," she wrote:

> They fill my head every evening and weekend, and invade my dreams. I am thinking about them when I read the news, when I talk to friends, when I'm at the grocery store. I am working for them when I arrive at school an hour early to make copies, when my car is the last one in the teacher parking lot in the evening, when I agree to chaperone dances and arrange guest speakers and write recommendation letters. Most importantly, I am working for my students when veteran teachers raise their eyebrows at my lessons on tolerance, explicit teachings of problem-solving, discussions about integrity, and pep talks on goal-setting.[102]

Though this statement in itself reflects many corps members' tendencies to look down on career teachers, many commentators concede that TFA has produced a number of inspiring teachers who have stayed in classrooms, often serving as devoted members of their school and local communities. Other proponents argue that while the summer institute only lasts five weeks, corps members receive professional development throughout their two years, and in some regions receive a master's degree, which can be more meaningful as they can relate coursework to practice in real time rather than thinking about theory before ever teaching themselves.

School district leaders have also remained satisfied enough to keep hiring corps members in many schools. Despite some districts ending their relationships with TFA amid principals citing high turnover and trouble with classroom management, other districts remain anxious to continue hiring corps members. Defenders in districts and beyond have pointed out that concerns with teacher turnover and behavior management apply equally—or more so—to traditionally trained rookie teachers.[103] The revolt of the superintendents, and principals, has largely remained a rejection of poor preparation, agnostic to the certification pathway.

Research on TFA corps members' effectiveness remains disputed, leading the debate to reflect more politics than substance. Both sides can cite studies that back their claims that TFA teachers are either better or worse than traditionally trained teachers. Yet, as University of Washington economist Dan Goldhaber and many others have concluded, "The weight of the evidence suggests that TFA teachers as a whole are at least as effective as other teachers in the schools they end up in."[104] This conclusion gives credence to the argument that while TFA may not be perfect, education schools are also not getting the job done, so why not bring dedicated young teachers into the classroom from other routes? Writing in the *Daily Beast*, education reporter Conor P. Williams noted, "These are (mostly) 22-year-old kids with five weeks of formal preparation stepping into some of the toughest classrooms in the U.S. That they do about as well as their traditionally trained peers isn't so much a TFA success story as a national scandal for our traditional teacher prep programs, which prepare 80 percent of American teachers."[105] Earlier in these debates, Frederick (Rick) Hess, an American Enterprise Institute scholar known for his generally conservative views on education policy, asked policymakers to suspend restrictions on the acceptable methods of teacher preparation until more conclusive evidence could be found that certain routes were, in fact, better than others. In the meantime, Hess and colleagues argued, it was best to try multiple methods of teacher preparation, from TFA to traditional education schools, while seeking the kind of solid evidence that could, in fact, be useful in creating meaningful policy.[106]

Moreover, in response to some of the criticism—especially that from alumni—Teach for America has made some significant changes in its programming. When Wendy Kopp moved on to focus on the international arm of Teach for All, two new co-CEOS, Matt Kramer and Elisa Villanueva, took the helm (though Kramer stepped down two years later, leaving Villanueva as the lone CEO). Under the new leadership, TFA did some soul-searching and began reforming from within. The organization has made significant strides on the diversity front, for example. While only 27% of corps members identified as people of color in 2005, that number rose to nearly 40% in 2017, and the organization has launched campaigns to specifically recruit immigrants or children of immigrants and African American men. They likewise now recruit at a variety of colleges and universities, not just elite ones, including many historically black colleges and universities (HBCUs). (Critics, however, are quick to point out that overall TFA has displaced many teachers of color in urban districts, particularly black teachers, as corps members often take jobs in "turnaround" schools and in new charters that replace district schools, a phenomenon that is particularly pronounced in cities like Chicago, New Orleans, Philadelphia, and Washington, DC.[107]) TFA is also trying to encourage its corps members to stay longer than two years, departing from its original emphasis on teaching as a stepping stone to another career and is experimenting with altering TFA's pedagogical philosophy so that the initial summer curriculum and ongoing professional development of TFA teachers would focus more on culturally responsive teaching and less on data-driven achievement. Perhaps most promising, in 2014 the organization launched a pilot program that would recruit college students in their junior year, so that their senior year included a year-long internship in a classroom and some coursework in education theory and methods. That way corps members would experience far more classroom time and training than what is possible in a stand-alone five-week institute.[108]

Kramer and many TFA supporters also argue that their critics represent a small percentage of alumni, amplified by such figures as Darling-Hammond and education historian turned anti-reform crusader Diane Ravitch. At the organization's twenty-fifth anniversary celebration, held in 2015 in Washington, DC, and attended by 15,000 current and former corps members, the guest list contained a veritable who's who of political and education reform leaders, including U.S. Education Secretary John King, former New York City Schools Chancellor Joel Klein, and DC Schools Chancellor Kaya Henderson, to name just a few prominent, if not controversial, reformers. President Barack Obama delivered a video message, expressing praise for the organization and highlighting the ways in which the 50,000-strong alumni base influences the education world from the classroom to political offices. "There are even TFA alumni working for me in the White House," he said to the crowd.[109] TFA enthusiasts could even pick up TFA t-shirts at their local J. Crew stores.[110]

As TFA continues to mature, it faces an uphill battle to regain its image as the altruistic education darling. Recruitment numbers were down for the second year in a row in 2016, and in major TFA regions across the country, corps are shrinking. In 2016, the New York City corps was the smallest it had been in eleven years; while 400 corps members entered New York City public schools in 2014, only 200 did so for the 2016–2017 school year.[111] Josh Starr, CEO of PDK International, an organization of professional teachers, reflected, "As the 25-year-old program ages, college students may be less willing to accept the narrative that they can 'change the world' with just weeks of training before stepping into the country's neediest schools."[112]

Teach for America cannot take all the credit (or blame) for advancing the alternative certification agenda, but its legacy remains important in terms of the ideas it raised and proliferated. It is also the symbol of the larger alternative route movement. TFA popularized the debate over American teacher education in a way that no other actor did during an era when the most dramatic changes in certification laws were taking place—as the country transitioned from an education school monopoly to the reopening of the field to a wide variety of pathways into the profession. While only around 0.2% of teachers nation-wide are current or former TFA corps members, the organization's impact remains much larger because of its symbolic importance, as well as the vast alumni network that still shapes the education system and will continue to do so into the future. Part of TFA's impact is also linked to the fact that it has inspired so many others to try alternative approaches to the education of teachers, including the Relay Graduate School of Education and other similar offshoots.

Entrepreneurs Take on Teacher Prep:
The Relay Graduate School of Education

There are no textbooks. No mention of Dewey or Pestalozzi, Freire or Kozol. No campus, at least not in the traditional sense. One could argue whether there are even professors. Yet according to the State of New York, Relay is a degree-granting graduate school of education, as well as a model of non-university-based teacher preparation in the spirit of the alternative certification movement. Embracing "a fast-paced, continuously evolving start-up culture," its founders represent a camp of teacher educators, like Kopp and her allies, who lost faith in the ability of universities to adequately train teachers and therefore started their own approach, with only a few similarities to earlier models.[113] The Relay Graduate School of Education (Relay GSE) currently trains 3,000 teacher candidates in fifteen cities across the nation, embracing a skills- and performance-based approach that has garnered praise from philanthropic foundations and the White House, but also intense criticism from many education experts.[114] Whether one believes Relay GSE is the exciting new frontier of teacher preparation or an affront to the art and profession of teaching, many can at least agree it is a lightning rod in this debate.

Relay GSE grew out of an initiative called Teacher U, which was created in 2007 by TFA alums and leaders of three prominent charter school net-works: KIPP, Uncommon Schools, and Achievement First. Teacher U's two primary founders, Dave Levin, co-founder of KIPP, and Norman Atkins, a "serial entrepreneur" who started the Robin Hood Foundation, Uncommon Schools, and North Star Prep Newark Charter School, both came to the same conclusion after they found their charter networks competing for talent: they needed more and better teachers, and they could do a better job training them than education schools could.[115] Levin and Atkins reasoned that if they based their curriculum on proven strategies developed by master teachers, and not on the "Ivory Tower" theory that too many teachers spent time studying in traditional university programs, they could produce a pipeline of high-quality educators ready to effectively serve the most high-needs students in like-minded charter schools across the country.

In 2007, Levin and Atkins set off to find a home for their new teacher preparation institution. They began by soliciting partnerships with thirteen New York City area schools of education, but only five even considered the idea. Eventually, David Steiner, then dean of Hunter College's School of Education, welcomed them with open arms.[116] Originally serving around three dozen graduate students, Teacher U eventually grew into a master's degree program that reflected the growing national sentiment, propelled by TFA and other alternative providers, that an entrepreneurial spirit, thought-ful planning akin to a well-run startup, and the right candidates could pro-duce stellar teachers with equally stellar results in the classroom. Reflecting this ethos, Atkins explained in a 2010 *Wall Street Journal* op-ed column that urban districts and teacher preparation institutions "must act like Silicon Valley, not the car industry."[117] Atkins's op-ed also reflected the growing belief that the problem with public education stemmed from bad teachers and that good teaching meant mastery of teaching strategies, execution, and high test scores, not academic training.

While Hunter proved a supportive home for Teacher U's incubation years, by 2011 Atkins and Levin decided they needed even more freedom from university bureaucracy and set off on their own. They applied to the New York Regents for a charter for their own standalone graduate school and received approval after review by a state-appointed team of university educators—though the board insisted that they include some sort of sus-tained effort at producing academic scholarship to be considered a graduate school. While advocates celebrated, and former Teachers College President Arthur Levine declared Relay "the future of teacher education," not all were convinced.[118] The office of the City University of New York's (CUNY) chan-cellor wrote a formal objection to the state, arguing that Relay "is essentially a similar educational model as the existing Teacher U/Hunter College partnership program, except that it would lack the depth of educational and other resources that a university brings to a partnership."[119] Diane Ravitch criticized the school for not offering any courses that should be part of a teacher's rigorous professional education, such as child psychology, cognitive development, and the history and sociology of education.[120] Others, such as sociologist Pedro Noguera, critiqued programs like Relay GSE and its "no excuses" pedagogy for promoting a boot camp style of discipline enforced mainly on poor minority children by mostly white and upper-middle-class teachers, reflecting low expectations and a classroom environment that few wealthy white parents would subject their own children to.[121]

These debates reflected a larger set of questions central to the teacher preparation wars, which reached a boiling point by 2010: Is teaching an art or a science? A profession or a vocation? Studied or mastered? Relay GSE, it seems, chose the side of the latter three answers. The two-year curriculum builds off charter school favorite Doug Lemov's forty-nine teaching strategies distilled in his popular yet controversial book *Teach Like a Champion*. Instructional practices such as "Right is Right" and "Precise Praise" make up Relay's fifty modules—units that form the curriculum in lieu of courses. While teacher candidates concentrate on the basics of how to build relationships with students, write a lesson, and manage a classroom in their first year, the second year emphasizes unit planning and incorporating literacy across different content areas. But, as its critics note, little to no theory, no history, and no psychology can be found in the units. "To make a crude analogy," Relay's senior manager for teaching and learning told the *New York Times*, "if I am learning to become a blacksmith, I also don't learn how to be a pipefitter. I also don't read a ton of books about how to shoe a horse. What I do is I show up and shoe horses."[122]

Much of Relay's instruction occurs online, while the rest happens through in-person interaction with master teachers and interactive handouts. The content component is then combined with intense clinical field work in partner charter schools—something akin to a nursing or doctor's residency—where teacher candidates observe expert teachers, practice themselves, and receive coaching and feedback from live observations and video recordings. The approach attempts to provide a "gradual, supportive on-ramp to the teaching profession," as students start by working in classrooms with mentor teachers, teach one period a day by the spring of their first year, and then become lead teachers the next.[123] At the end of the program, graduates automatically receive a job at a partner charter school. Costs run around the same price as a traditional university-based master's program—$35,000 for two years, though candidates are eligible for an Urban Teacher scholarship.[124]

Relay's other prized innovation, and perhaps its most controversial, is that graduation is tied to actual classroom performance based on student test scores. In order for a Relay trainee to become a certified teacher with a master's degree, he or she needs to demonstrate in their first year of lead teaching that students averaged a full year's growth in learning at the elementary level, or that on average students display 70% mastery of a subject at the middle and secondary level. By creating a "feedback loop" between individual student data and the teacher, and tying graduation to achievement numbers, Relay hopes to serve as a vanguard in the way data-driven instruction can work in practice. This approach was praised by former Secretary of Education Arne Duncan and is now being experimented with by other teacher preparation programs, both in and out of universities.

Some, however, remain skeptical of Relay's model. University of Washington teacher education researcher Ken Zeichner and Connecticut College's Lauren Anderson noted that Relay has expanded from one to thirteen campuses "despite no credible evidence to suggest it has met its goal of preparing teachers who can raise student achievement in urban districts."[125] Zeichner and Anderson therefore caution against overinvestment in independent "alternative certification 2.0" programs that overemphasize student test data, like Relay, and create a system where students in poverty are increasingly taught by alternatively certified teachers. They wrote,

> Policymakers should not accept the argument made by two of these five [independent teacher education] programs (MTR and Relay) that the ability to raise standardized test scores is in and of itself an indicator of teacher and program quality. Teacher education program quality needs to be determined from an analysis of the costs and benefits of a fuller set of outcomes associated with particular programs. The defunding of the public universities where most U.S. teachers are still prepared by states, and a loss of opportunities for philanthropic resources for innovation in college and university programs contributes to creating a situation in the U.S. where teachers for students in high poverty communities will be prepared by non-university programs while teachers in more economically advantaged middle class communities will continue to be prepared by colleges and universities. This bifurcation of the public school system in the U.S. is likely to widen the opportunity for learning gaps that currently exist.[126]

In Relay's first few years, it has, in fact, expanded very rapidly beyond its initial geographic domain of New York and Newark (NJ). It now serves around 3,000 teachers in Baton Rouge (LA), Chicago (IL), Connecticut, Dallas-Fort Worth (TX), Delaware, Denver (CO), Houston (TX), Memphis (TN), Nashville (TN), New Orleans (LA), Philadelphia (PA), Camden (NJ), and Washington, DC.[127] Atkins is on record saying he would like that number to reach 5,000.[128] Part of this expansion is due to funding from states and philanthropies, and in part due to Relay's significant partnership with Teach for America. TFA corps members make up roughly 55% of current Relay teacher candidates, exemplifying the TFA effect on the larger teacher education terrain.[129] In this case, TFA uses Relay to certify TFA corps members and offer them graduate-level classes as they complete their two-year commitment. The TFA candidates, however, bypass the clinical practice year required for Relay GSE candidates and enter the classroom as lead instructors after the traditional institute experience. Moreover, in addition to its two-year program, Relay GSE offers one-year certification programs that do not lead to a master's degree, including a mid-career certificate, and a new National Principals Academy, a year-long fellowship experience for current principals to "push their instructional leadership to new heights," based on Uncommon Schools CEO Paul Bambrick's leadership philosophy.[130]

Relay's self-proclaimed revolutionary approach to teacher education has received significant support from private philanthropies, government agencies, and backers of the "corporate reform agenda," including the Gates Foundation, the Walton Family Foundation, and Credit Suisse, as well as the more moderate Carnegie Corporation of New York.[131] The U.S. Department of Education cited Relay as a model of innovation in its 2015 plan to strengthen teacher preparation as part of the Every Student Succeeds Act (ESSA); the Department of Education's proposal took many ideas from the Relay playbook, while Relay's founders were influential in the drafting of ESSA. The ideas adopted by the Department of Education included requiring data reporting at the program level, supporting states in developing systems that differentiate programs by performance on student outcomes, providing feedback to programs about graduates' performance and satisfaction, holding programs accountable for how well they prepare teachers to succeed throughout their careers, and providing Title II dollars for new teacher preparation "academies" meant to spur innovation. The U.S. Department of Education's press release announcing the 2016 regulations also cited Relay as a model of data-driven innovation.[132]

While Atkins has been quoted saying his model of teacher education is "beyond ideology," Relay epitomizes what has become, at heart, an ideological debate, one that has raged throughout American educational history but reached new heights at the turn of the twenty-first century.[133] What does it mean to be an educator? Does education mean training children for success on standardized tests, preparing them for a job, or cultivating a life of critical thought and self-reflection? Do teachers educate citizens for a democracy or workers in a global marketplace? Do teachers build knowledge together to confront social injustice? Instill values of cultural pride? Build a competent work force?

Relay reflects a certain vision of teaching and of education, one that embraces the entrepreneurial ethos and market-based ideology of its neoliberal and millennial moment. Wherever one comes down on these questions, we should at least ask, should teacher training give space to educators to confront these very questions? Because at the moment, Relay does not.

From the Ashes of the University Monopoly: The University of Phoenix and the Rise of For-Profit Teacher Preparation

"Ten years ago the idea of advertising in a newspaper by an institution of education was almost a cardinal sin," Jim Miklich, vice president of the University of Phoenix told the *Los Angeles Times* in 1985. But education had changed "from a seller's market to a buyer's market," he explained: "Universities found they could no longer sit back and students would come to them because they were there."[134] This notion—that students were consumers in an education marketplace in which universities no longer had the monopoly—took root in the 1980s and shaped the course of K–12 and higher education, not to mention teacher preparation, for the following three decades. Rather than just marketization, the harnessing of competition to spur innovation and efficiency, full-out *privatization* also began to occur. For-profit colleges and universities entered the degree-granting game as funding for and faith in public universities began to erode and certification laws loosened around the country allowing them to enter the fray.

The for-profit, mostly online University of Phoenix in many ways exemplifies the extremes of this shift, but as the largest education-degree granting institution in the country, it is by no means an insignificant outlier in the teacher education landscape. For-profit teacher preparation is a large and growing industry, of which policymakers, teacher educators, and the public need to take heed.[135] The story of the University of Phoenix begs us to consider the question, Is there something fundamentally wrong with a private company offering teacher education degrees, or is it simply providing a valuable service to students that traditional colleges and universities ignore? Put another way, is there something fundamentally wrong with traditional teacher education that would necessitate private, for-profit companies entering the field?

John G. Sperling, the controversial and quixotic founder of the University of Phoenix, would urge you to choose the latter assessment. In his autobiography, *Rebel with a Cause*, he describes the rise of the University of Phoenix in sensational terms, with himself cast in the role of David and the entrenched and self-interested higher education world as Goliath.[136] According to his account, Sperling is a social justice hero and a business maverick who brought degrees to the underserved world of working adults. Innovators like him became targets of the higher education and media establishments, who did all in their power to discredit, "harass," and thwart him and his plans. Yet due to his smarts, determination, and three self-identified skills of success—"opportunism, indifference to the advice of experts, and lack of concern for what peers and authority figures think of me," he won the war.[137] Now the University of Phoenix is a publicly traded, multibillion-dollar corporation that enrolls nearly 500,000 students across the country, including over 6,000 teacher candidates each year, making it one of the largest teacher preparation programs in the country.[138]

Critics see a different story, one centered around a power-hungry entrepreneur who found a lucrative market and, in so doing, changed the landscape of higher education in general and teacher preparation specifically, both for the worse. As a profit-seeking corporation, opponents claim, the University of Phoenix remains largely unconcerned about the quality of the education it provides. It also unscrupulously targets vulnerable populations while raking in billions of taxpayer dollars through federally subsidized loan programs. Although the University of Phoenix has faced several scandals over corruption, questionable recruiting tactics, and lawsuits by former students and employees, it is allowed to exist because of a well-financed lobbying team and powerful political allies. Those concerned with the continual improvement of professional teacher education are likely to side more with its critics, but Sperling does make a strong point: working adults, who make up the vast majority of the university's students, have been long ignored by traditional colleges and universities, something these programs may want to consider.

Sperling's biography reads as a classic American rags-to-riches, bootstraps tale—or as an insufferable story of an overly confident opportunist, depending on one's perspective. Sperling was born in 1922 in a log cabin in the Ozarks of Missouri to a loving mother but an abusive father. After escaping a life of poverty and joining the armed forces, he climbed his way up the social ladder via education, as a white male of his generation could do, hopping from San Francisco Community College to Reed College to the University of California at Berkeley for a PhD. He fondly recalls his days as a graduate student, writing, "Those days at Berkeley were the most blissful of my life. In the cafes, we honed our academic skills by expounding and arguing theory, fact, and fiction. It was a movable intellectual feast."[139] (This treasured intellectual experience is ironically unavailable to the students of his online University of Phoenix.) After his doctoral work, Sperling found a tenure-track position at San Jose State University teaching the history of economics. As a self-proclaimed left-leaning academic who flirted with Marxism and socialism in his youth (but eventually gave it up), he also gained a reputation as a rabble-rousing union leader who led a strike and sit-in, not afraid to scuffle with the administration or earn adversaries among colleagues. It was only later in life that he turned to business, when "at age 53, I began a new career as an entrepreneur."[140]

The idea for the University of Phoenix was thus born in California, not in the city of its namesake. In the mid-1970s Sperling found himself leading a federally funded program to alleviate problems of juvenile delinquency in a neighboring community, a position given to him because of his reputation as an outsider—and therefore supposed neutral adviser—to the Chicano community with whom he worked. There was also an expectation that as an abrasive leader he could get things done. He devised a strategy to target the adults who served children labeled delinquents, such as police officers, parents, and teachers, and started offering them night courses in the humanities as a way to improve their interactions with struggling youth. As the story goes, these adults enjoyed the courses a great deal and repeatedly expressed to Sperling the desire to earn bachelor's and master's degrees so they could advance their careers. Sperling saw a golden opportunity and seized it: create degree programs for working adults who sought a promotion by gaining an extra credential. He set out to share the plan with university officials.

The road from there to the eventual creation and accreditation of the University of Phoenix was a rocky one. As Sperling describes it, it was a battle between the forces of good—him and his innovative idea—and evil— the self-interested higher education establishment. Others would frame it as higher education officials and policymakers attempting to maintain academic standards and regulate the harmful industry of for-profit colleges. After encountering initial skepticism from San Jose State administrators, Sperling received advice from a friend to take his idea to a struggling institution, as no financially healthy one would accept innovation. Sperling took this advice, and in 1972, with $23,000 in savings, he quit his job as a professor, set up shop in his house to save money on rent, and took his idea to the University of San Francisco, a school he was told was struggling financially and had a president willing to take risks. He found an early ally, perhaps surprisingly, in their education dean, Allen Calvin, who had recently taken the position after working for a private textbook publishing company involved in curriculum development, notably during the Ocean Hill-Brownsville community control standoff in Brooklyn, New York. Calvin was ultimately a business man, not an academic. He liked Sperling's project and encouraged him to establish a for-profit private organization instead of a non-profit to avoid the oversight of a board of directors. (Only much later did the University of Phoenix establish the board of directors that it now has.) Sperling liked the idea of being in total control. He formed the Institute for Professional Development (IDP), which offered two degrees, one of which was a master's in education. Sperling envisioned IDP as a sub-contractor that would partner with existing universities to offer degree programs for adults. In addition to the University of San Francisco, he found a few other takers, mainly small and struggling Catholic universities that also found the adult outreach mission appealing.

During those early years in the mid-1970s, Sperling and a few partners, including his son and some former students, encountered stiff opposition from the California State Department of Education and the Western Association of Schools and Colleges (WASC) as they attempted to gain accreditation, which would allow them to secure not only legitimacy but also federal student loan money. The leader of WASC proved particularly skeptical; Sperling framed him as an "educational reactionary who had established a reign of terror among the small colleges and universities in California" and was particularly bent on taking Sperling down.[141] "It is not an exaggeration to describe that period [1976–1978] as a struggle between the totality of the higher education establishment and an idea," he described in his usual bravado.[142] As the fight grew uglier and the media joined the side of the skeptical, Sperling realized he would have to take his idea out of the jurisdiction of WASC to move forward. A regional accrediting agency housed in Illinois, the North Central Association (NCA), proved a promising bet. Sperling realized he could stay out West but fall under NCA's jurisdiction if he moved shop one state over to the "Valley of the Sun." Arizona maintained a particularly unregulated higher education landscape, and the booming sunbelt city of Phoenix seemed like a perfect location.

The path to accreditation in Arizona also proved treacherous, however. The local media, as in California, published a number of critical stories early on, and the Arizona Regents, officials at the State Board of Education, and the presidents and vice presidents of the three major state universities were highly critical and recommended against accreditation. Legislation was also proposed in the state legislature that would limit "diploma mills" from operating, and even though Sperling and his supporters always denied such a label, the University of Phoenix certainly suffered from the public debate regarding the proposed regulations. Eventually, through intense and costly lobbying, countless meetings, phone calls, letters, and political maneuverings —a process that prompted an FBI investigation based on charges of bribery by Sperling (though nothing was ever confirmed)—the newly named University of Phoenix gained official NCA accreditation in 1979, much to the dismay of many. Both the University of Arizona and Arizona State University initially refused to accept University of Phoenix transfer credits.

The later success of the University of Phoenix was far from a foregone conclusion in the 1980s, despite its newly gained status as an accredited university. The decade was marked by a number of speedbumps, as Sperling quarreled with some of his key partners, many of whom believed he had strayed too far from the original mission. The company faced continued regulation and legislative battles, almost declared bankruptcy twice, and made failed forays into international expansion programs in Manila, Kuala Lumpur, and Hungary. Negative press continued to roll in as well, including stories about the University of Phoenix granting students credit for such "life experiences" as going through a divorce or coaching a Little League team—not untrue stories, but ones that continued to undermine the school's credibility. Many employers also remained skeptical. For example, one manager, quoted in a 1985 *Los Angeles Times* article, admitted, "If I had two candidates apply for a job with equal credentials and one had an MBA from Long Beach State and another from the University of Phoenix, I'd take the Long Beach guy. It's just a better degree."[143] Enrollment miraculously continued to increase, albeit slowly, and by the end of the decade Sperling received two lucky breaks: the growth of the Internet and a national turn to increased educational privatization.

Sperling decided to take his program online starting in 1989, and with it his ambitions went national. He hired a full-time lobbyist in Washington, DC, to work on the university's relationship with the federal Department of Education, attempting to ward off any pesky regulations that would prevent expansion. He also was able to capitalize on the Republican sweep of the 1994 elections, the general pro-market ethos embraced by the Bush and Clinton administrations, enthusiasm by pro-reform governors from both major parties, and the general support of market solutions and entrepreneurial spirit ushered in by the Reagan Revolution. These developments coincided with the rise of the alternative certification movement, as the debates in New Jersey, California, and elsewhere popularized ideas about the failures of traditional institutions of higher learning, particularly schools of education.

The 1990s became the golden era for the University of Phoenix, as more Americans began to own home computers. Online enrollment skyrocketed. Demand was also spurred by an economy where educational credentials could increasingly translate into significant financial returns. Consumerism and privatization in the educational marketplace was on the rise. Writing in the mid-1990s, one Denver journalist described the higher-education credentials rush bluntly: "Like retailers hawking crayons and Levi 501s in pre-Labor Day sales, colleges and universities in the Denver area aggressively are pitching their goods and services to adults looking to upgrade job skills or prepare for a career change."[144] Although the University of Phoenix was still relatively obscure on a national level, by 1994 the company went public under a strategically created parent company called the Apollo Group, and it blossomed from there. For-profit higher education, with the University of Phoenix at the helm, grew tremendously around the turn of the new millennium.

Critics did not disappear, however. "It's kind of like McEducation," Milton Blood, director of accreditation at the American Assembly of Collegiate Schools of Business, which accredits 305 business schools, including Harvard, Yale, and Northwestern, told the *Wall Street Journal* in 1994.[145] "I can't imagine that they could convince one of our committees that their faculty have the appropriate qualifications," he continued.

Similar to other education entrepreneurs, the University of Phoenix saw a large and lucrative market in teacher preparation. With passage of the 2001 NCLB Act, which called for a "highly qualified" teacher in every classroom, the University of Phoenix was right there to market a credential-granting degree to those who sought the "highly qualified" label.[146] The University of Phoenix also appealed to already licensed teachers and administrators who could receive a pay raise if they earned an additional credential, such as a master's or doctoral degree, according to state law or district policy.

While the University of Phoenix always claimed that it valiantly provided degrees to working adults in a way that traditional institutions of higher education failed to do, evidence against its altruistic claims began to mount in the 2000s. Many have called attention to the fact that the university preys on vulnerable demographic categories, like veterans and their spouses, single mothers, and people of color. The university then urges these students to take out federal loans, channeling taxpayer dollars into their profit margins to the tune of $30 billion per year and 90% of their total earnings, while many who enroll drop out or fail out—with thousands of dollars in student debt. For some, this sounds all too familiar: "These schools are marketing machines masquerading as universities," said Steve Eisman, who made billions betting against the housing market before the 2008 financial collapse, as he testified before Congress regarding the for-profit college industry.[147] "I thought there would never again be an opportunity to be involved in the short side of an industry as socially destructive and morally bankrupt as the sub-prime mortgage industry. . . . Unfortunately, I was wrong." A representative from the University of Phoenix argued that this analogy was silly and simplistic, calling attention to the money that Eisman, as a short-seller, can make if the industry goes bust. Yet the comparisons between for-profit higher education and aggressive Wall Street–style opportunism did not end there.

A 2015 lawsuit over the University of Phoenix's "boiler room"–style recruiting tactics didn't help perceptions of the university. In the lawsuit, it was found that the company violated regulations by compensating recruiters based on enrollment numbers; gave prospective students misinformation about costs, loans, credentialing, and employment prospects; and violated regulations about over-recruiting among military personnel and their families.[148] "They misled me the entire way," a student from Missouri stated. "I've just wasted years and money and thousands of dollars on nothing," added a Texas Army wife.[149] Moreover, a 2014 whistleblower lawsuit, the details of which were made public in 2016, included charges that University of Phoenix employees were told to enroll as students so the university could maintain the correct numbers for the 90/10 rule, which stipulates that for-profit colleges can receive no more than 90% of their income from federal sources.[150] Fox News, NBC, and ABC all conducted undercover investigations into the university's practices, exposing stories of unscrupulous recruiters, false promises, and broken dreams. Although the university claims that it has reformed its recruiting strategies and is more concerned with curricular quality than it has been in the past, many still wonder why the University of Phoenix and other for-profit institutions are allowed to operate at all.

Dick Durbin, a Democratic senator from Illinois, offered one answer to this question: the for-profit higher education industry "owns every lobbyist in town."[151] According to David Halperin, journalist, academic, and higher education activist, the for-profits maintain an "army of lobbyists and consultants" in Washington, DC, and in all fifty states, and they spend giant sums of money to ensure that regulatory bills do not live long.[152] (Though to be fair, the not-for-profit higher education establishment also employs lobbyists.) As recently as 2014, President Barack Obama told a group of veterans in a speech in Georgia that for-profit schools are "trying to swindle and hoodwink" them because they only "care about the cash," a claim based on verified predatory tactics by for-profit universities, including the University of Phoenix. In 2014, the University Phoenix enrolled about 9,400 active-duty service members and 24,000 Iraq and Afghanistan war veterans, receiving $20.5 million in revenue from the Department of Defense's tuition assistance program, and it has received $1.2 billion in post-9/11 GI Bill benefits since 2009. Such tactics led to an investigation by the Federal Trade Commission and the attorney general of California, which ended with the university being barred from enrolling active-duty service members and being placed on probation by their accreditors. As one former serviceman commented in an online forum that collected 1,200 complaints about the University of Phoenix, "Just google University of Phoenix and veterans."[153] Other targeted populations include Native Americans, who also qualify for generous tuition assistance from the federal government, and HBCUs, many of which struggle with falling enrollment but traditionally serve student populations that qualify for federally financed loans. As of yet, however, only a few of these institutions seem open to the idea of a partnership.[154]

The Obama administration attempted to put the brakes on the taxpayer bankrolling of the industry—Phoenix is by far the largest recipient of federal Pell Grants in the country—by proposing new regulations in 2014.[155] In the end, however, the bill failed miserably. Lobbying efforts proved fierce, and key Republicans and Democrats were swayed in the University of Phoenix's direction, as many receive generous campaign contributions from the Apollo Group's political action committee, which spent $1.39 billion in 2015 alone, as well as from other for-profit industry backers. Representative John Kline of Minnesota, chairman of the House Committee on Education and the Workforce, helped summarily kill the bill. Kline receives more campaign funds from the Apollo Education Group than does any other member of Congress.[156] Early in the development of the University of Phoenix, Sperling recognized the valuable influence of lobbying money to the longevity of the industry: "Yes, we use money to get their [politicians'] attention—our American system of campaign finance gives us no other alternative. Sadly, it's the only way to do it when you are from out-of-state and the forces against you [the higher education establishment] have money, votes, and even football tickets! In the immortal words of Jess Unruh, '*Money is the Mother's Milk of Politics.*' "[157] While for-profit universities were challenged repeatedly by the Obama administration, the Trump administration now appears willing to let them prosper, signaling alarm bells to those concerned about the industry's rise.

Despite all the negative press and its less-than-stellar reputation, the University of Phoenix still enrolls hundreds of thousands of adults in its programs each year, including thousands of teacher candidates. As one sales manager for a cement company in Riverside, California, put it, "The public schools and better private schools don't provide education to the working guy."[158] The University of Phoenix is convenient and flexible, others explain. And perhaps they have a point. For far too long, traditional institutions of higher learning have not served working adults by providing affordable and accessible programs to meet their needs, particularly in a changing job market where education credentials matter. Traditional colleges and universities—including their education schools—schedule classes at times that do not fit busy working adults' schedules, move with great caution in embracing the Internet, and pride themselves on the numbers of students they can reject. Thus, they arguably set the stage for the emergence of alternative providers of degrees and credentials. Perhaps in time, more traditional universities will expand the programs that some already have that offer strong academic programs to working adults. Until that day comes, too much of the field is left to the unscrupulous.

With the steady rise of alternative certification meant to attract the late-in-life career switchers to the classroom, this point is less relevant to teachers than it is to other professions—something prospective teacher candidates and teacher preparation policymakers should take into consideration. In most states there are a number of flexible, online alternative route teacher preparation programs that do not run on a profit-making model and are much less expensive than the University of Phoenix. The average teacher preparation program through the University of Phoenix still costs upwards of $50,000. This makes the case for its teacher education degrees all the less convincing. Why do so many teacher candidates *really* enroll in the University of Phoenix? The same reason Coca-Cola is the most recognizable global brand, many contend: they know how to market. The university made headlines when it spent $155 million (largely taxpayer dollars) for naming rights to Phoenix's professional football stadium, as companies like U.S. Cellular and Minute Maid have done, although the university fields no sports teams of its own.

As market-based thinking gained prominence and states eased teacher certification requirements in the 1980s and 1990s, the University of Phoenix and other for-profit universities were right there to capitalize on those trends. "The private sector sees teacher education and professional development as a low-cost, high-volume field with the potential for significant profits," Arthur Levine warns, noting the for-profits are ready to jump right in if non-profits do not do a better job and policies do not prevent it.[159] Now, as the University of Phoenix certifies thousands of teachers per year and many more enroll in its programs, education stakeholders must seriously reckon with the idea of for-profit teacher preparation. They must ask themselves whether schools like the University of Phoenix are the inevitable way of the future and what that means for students in American classrooms. Prospective teachers looking for the right program, policymakers with the ability to regulate, and existing traditional university-based programs who could better appeal to working adults all have a role to play in ensuring the profit motive does not continue to shape teacher education.

CHAPTER TWO

Transforming University Programs

A MUCH COMMENTED-UPON *New York Times* op-ed in 2013 opened with the following unattributed aphorism: "Those who can, do. Those who can't, teach. And those who can't teach, teach teaching."[1] The column's author, Bill Keller, went on to assail education schools for their low quality, low selectivity, and complicity in robbing the nation's children of a high-quality education. In doing so he joined a long tradition of education-school bashing, a literary genre unto itself in the American canon. As politically protected "cash cows" and "contented cartels," he argued, teacher education programs within schools of education have little incentive to provide a high-quality product or to ever improve, echoing many sentiments from the early 1980s, and even going back to the 1950s. Did he have a point, thirty years after those same arguments made headway in New Jersey and a 1983 *Newsweek* article called teacher education "perhaps the biggest running joke in higher education," and sixty years after Arthur Bestor blamed educationists for turning public schools into "educational wastelands?"[2] Or were his comments part of a longer, unfounded attempt to discredit teacher education at the university level?

As chapter 1 demonstrated, a number of actors outside of education schools, from progressive community-based groups, to scholars at conservative think tanks, to for- and not-for-profit education entrepreneurs, launched a movement for a wide range of alternative certification programs in the last few decades of the twentieth century. This trend, however, also resulted from forces within the university and education schools themselves. Understanding the rise of alternative certification therefore requires a close examination of teacher education within the university setting, where it enjoyed a near monopoly from the 1960s to 1990. It also requires delving into the difficult questions of whether education schools were under siege from enemies without, as many of their defenders claim, or whether their lack of initiative led to their own demise, or at least to their marginalization and uncertainty.

In this chapter, we turn to a few key case studies to answer these questions, ultimately concluding that the answer is far more complex than any easy effort to blame or absolve university programs. Many teacher education programs did, in fact, suffer from institutional neglect, left to fight a valiant but ultimately losing battle. A few were closed outright. Still others engaged in significant internal reform and found innovative ways to prepare high-quality teachers through rigorous professional, research- and practice-based training. Nevertheless, those that did so often found themselves painted with the same brush by outside reformers as were the programs that made very few changes. And too many schools and departments of education did not take the steps needed to create the kinds of high-quality programs that more and more people were calling for from the 1980s on, rendering them somewhat worthy of the critiques launched by Keller and others at the close of the century.

This chapter's six case studies turn to different moments in this tumultuous history of university-based teacher preparation. The first three consider teacher preparation at elite universities. At the University of Chicago, the education school did not reform and was eventually closed. The work of preparing teachers was then reborn under quite a different institutional model. Harvard is now attempting to revive high-quality, elite teacher preparation as a university-based Teach for America (TFA) alternative after years of internal bickering about the place of teacher education at an Ivy League institution. Stanford maintained a high-quality program throughout the most rancorous decades of the teacher prep wars and continues to do so.

We also explore a former normal school turned regional public state university, New Jersey's Montclair State, which despite its modest overall rankings has maintained its reputation as the "Harvard of teacher education" and prepares more teachers than Harvard, Stanford, and Chicago combined. We then explore a less-elite regional private university, the University of Indianapolis, where administrators and faculty have made concerted efforts to build a high-quality professional program. Finally, we turn to a new model of twenty-first-century higher education, the online Western Governors University, to consider what it means for non-traditional students and working adults to enroll in a program with no campus and no regular faculty in a not-for-profit model.

Teacher Preparation within the University

To explain the fate of university-based teacher education, it is important to understand that such training long suffered from a precarious place within the world of American higher education. Before the mid-twentieth-century, most teacher preparation took place through a variety of pathways.[3] Only after World War II did teacher education become firmly consolidated in schools, departments, and colleges of education located within comprehensive regional state liberal arts colleges (many of which were former normal schools that once prepared only teachers), a wide range of private elite and non-elite institutions of higher learning, and public research universities. By the mid-1960s, the stand-alone teachers college and the range of alternative routes into teaching that had marked the previous decades were things of the past.

At elite universities, the history of teacher preparation often began in the late nineteenth and early twentieth centuries when many of the more prestigious institutions appointed chairs of pedagogy, tasked with preparing students for careers in schools and conducting research on educational matters. What started as isolated examples at places like the University of Michigan and the University of Iowa spread to many flagship state and elite private universities around the country, such as the University of Chicago, Stanford, Harvard, the University of California at Berkeley, and Ohio State University.[4] Beginning about 1900, these individual professorships were then turned into departments of education and eventually schools of education, starting with the School of Pedagogy at New York University and followed quickly by the soon-to-be prestigious Teachers College at Columbia University. Unlike normal schools and teachers colleges, these new schools of education focused on the narrower goal of conducting educational research and training new doctoral students, only credentialing a few administrators and high school teachers in what David Labaree calls "boutique" teacher education programs.[5]

The story was somewhat different at normal schools and teachers colleges, institutions created in the mid- and late nineteenth century to the early twentieth century with the explicit purpose of preparing teachers. By the 1950s and 1960s, when the baby boom generation entered college in far greater numbers than any previous moment in American history, many experts argued in favor of requiring a college degree for all aspiring teachers and for bringing all teacher education into comprehensive universities, under the leadership of doctoral degree–holding professors in a school or college of education. Normal schools and teachers colleges were therefore transformed into regional colleges, often by state law. The education faculty at these new regional state colleges and universities imitated the structure of the more prestigious universities like the University of Michigan and the University of Chicago, and established education schools themselves, a phenomenon aided by philanthropies like the Ford Foundation that saw this as a beneficial move for American educational success, and normal schools' own desire to improve their reputations.[6] This trend is reflected in the history of a school like Northern State University in DeKalb, Illinois, which went from being Northern State Normal School in 1899, to Northern State Teachers College in 1921, to Northern State College in 1955, and eventually Northern State University in 1957, with a standalone college of education created in 1958.[7] Universities known for their teaching programs such as Montclair State in New Jersey and Millersville University in Pennsylvania followed nearly identical patterns, as did public higher education systems from Massachusetts to California, with only slightly differing timelines.

Ironically, as normal schools became part of comprehensive colleges and sought the status of university-based education schools, two things were lost—a specific focus on the preparation of teachers and a close link between content knowledge and pedagogical expertise. Comprehensive colleges and universities, by definition, prepared their students for many different fields of endeavor, creating a potentially rich academic environment but marginalizing an emphasis on excellence in teaching. The loss of curricular integration proved to be a serious consequence of the disappearance of the normal schools and teachers colleges. At many of the older institutions, the same person taught mathematics and the methods of teaching mathematics, while another taught history and the teaching of history. Comprehensive institutions created their own mathematics and history departments; as a result, the education faculty were generally limited to pedagogy courses. In far too many cases this created a deep split between content and pedagogy and, equally serious, a move by the education faculty to capture more of the curriculum that emphasized *how* to teach at the sacrifice of *what* to teach. The roots of much future critique of schools of education was thus laid when the institutions were first created and, given the structure of higher education, became very difficult to eradicate.[8]

The new state regional universities that emerged from the normal schools and teachers colleges often failed to attain the prestige of their already established peers; instead, they gained reputations for low standards and easy entrance requirements. This was exacerbated by the opening of the job market for previously marginalized groups in the 1970s. As many high-achieving women and people of color, for whom teaching had been one of the few available occupations, turned to previously closed-off fields, the quality of the applicant pool for K–12 teachers lowered. Moreover, as the post-war economy spurred the growth of higher paying jobs while teachers' wages remained meager, talented white men likewise turned elsewhere.[9]

Education schools at elite universities faced a similar situation as that of the state regional universities: they did not earn the same respect as their peers in the arts and sciences even as they relinquished their professional commitments to actual K–12 schools. In order to gain the respect of the larger university community, education schools in the post-war period concentrated on producing academic scholarship deemed fit for disciplinary standards in psychology, sociology, anthropology, and other prominent social science fields. Yet even then education researchers, considered too "applied" and tainted by the stigma of feminization, often failed in gaining their peers' respect. Historian of education Jeffrey Mirel called 120th Street, the avenue separating Columbia University from Columbia's Teachers College, "the widest street in the world."[10] Teacher education, deemed low-status even within the field of education, eventually fell by the wayside at many of these institutions. As Labaree explains, teacher education had trouble ridding itself of a threefold legacy of being a high-demand field (and the sense that "anyone can get in"), its association with women and the working or middle class, and its applied rather than theoretical nature.[11]

While teacher education often served as the "cash cow" of larger universities, bringing in significant levels of income while remaining cheap to run, administrators often did not support these programs, leaving teacher educators with a very difficult job.[12] An AACTE study conducted in the late 1970s concluded that while teacher education programs generated 11% of all credit hours earned by university students, administrators only returned around 3% of that income to the schools of education.[13] The leading scholar of teacher education in the 1980s, John Goodlad, noted that while schools of education were considered low status within most universities, even within education schools, the lowest status of all was reserved for the teacher education faculty. Others in the education faulty "consciously distanced themselves from training and serving classroom instructors." Goodland concluded, "that which was honored no longer is, leading to a sense of betrayal and resentment."[14] Thus, while the larger world—of university faculty as well as the general public—was questioning the value of education schools, the faculty of those schools, especially those in teacher education, were often a demoralized group.[15]

Moreover, by the 1970s and 1980s, public consensus converged on the idea that education schools simply were not getting the job done, whether they were considered prestigious by the larger academy or not. School-based personnel—superintendents, principals, and even graduates of these programs who were now teaching—did not clamor to defend education schools as they came under assault. Prospective teachers, as "consumers" in a growing education marketplace, also had no trouble abandoning education schools and looking elsewhere for their teacher training. Why spend time and money on a low-status education degree if you could enter the profession through easier, cheaper, and arguably higher status means?

The conservative ascendency in the 1980s also carried an agenda for teacher education. Think tanks such as the American Enterprise Institute, the Manhattan Institute, and the Thomas B. Fordham Foundation all released influential reports that called for reforms in teacher preparation, including higher standards for teacher candidates, a liberal arts undergraduate degree, and tougher licensure tests, while downplaying the importance of education degrees and methods courses. The Holmes and Carnegie reports of the 1980s and 1990s, among others, also highlighted the low quality of education schools and called for reforms along the lines of the 1910 Flexner Report, which demanded improvements in the nation's medical schools. Writing in 1981, Tom Toch of *Education Week* noted that "in the face of such vexing dilemmas, the future of the education schools does not look particularly bright."[16] This reflection proved prescient.

Critiques continued into the new millennium. In 2005, Arthur Levine, then-president of Columbia's Teachers College, published a scathing critique of education schools and their generally low quality, concluding that teacher preparation programs ranged from "inadequate to appalling."[17] The National Council on Teacher Quality called the programs "an industry of mediocrity."[18]

Some university-based teacher educators did make a powerful case for university-based training, however, winning a fair number of converts to their professionalization agenda and proving their worth through the quality of their teacher graduates. Linda Darling-Hammond, based at Stanford, published a number of academic and public-facing books and articles in the 2000s that outlined the need for a holistic, rigorous, and professional training for the nation's teacher workforce.[19] Marilyn Cochran-Smith, Kenneth Zeichner, and other teacher education researchers also produced important scholarship on the topic, attempting to sift through competing analyses of pathway efficacy and making strong cases for well-rounded, often university-based or university-affiliated preparation.[20] Scholars such as Gloria Ladson-Billings and Sonia Nieto argued that more professional training in culturally responsive pedagogy was necessary for social justice but often did not happen in either university or alternative route programs, though more and better preparation was required from all.[21] Teacher educators such as Bob Bain, Deborah Ball, Magdalene Lampert, and their colleagues at the University of Michigan and Michigan State even argued that proper, university-based teacher education was a matter of ethics; teachers should be "safe to practice" on their first day of their first year of teaching, just as a pilot or a doctor should be on their first days on the job. They further argued that teachers should be prepared to teach all types of children from all backgrounds, whether they be high-poverty students, English language learners, gifted children, or students with special needs.[22] When critiques of alternative certification programs like Teach for America grew in the 2010s, university-based teacher educators sighed a breath of relief as more people began to defend the benefit of at least some theory and research-based training connected to a university.

Other factors have led university programs to reform over the past thirty years as well. Some came from within, and others from without. State and federal legislation have long placed constraints and arguably unfair expectations on schools of education. In the early 1980s, University of Wisconsin's Dean of the School of Education John R. Palmer noted, "More and more we are being told what to teach. We do a lot of responding to state influence."[23] In addition to curriculum mandates imposed throughout the 1980s, 1990s, and 2000s, recent federal legislation has called for states to evaluate and rank teacher training programs. This has led many universities to take proactive steps to help define those criteria themselves and to ensure that their programs make the grade. Other organizations, like the Council for the Accreditation of Educator Preparation (CAEP)—a merger of two older accreditation agencies and composed of university-based professional educators—devised their own standards to define and encourage excellence in the field of teacher preparation. Still other university-based teacher educators merely decried the news without making any significant or proactive changes.

In 1981, Peter L. LoPresti, chairman of the National Teacher Examination Policy Council and professor of education at California State University, Los Angeles, noted, "Ed schools will have to fish or cut bait; the marketplace may very well resolve the problem."[24] Market-based teacher preparation alternatives may not have resolved the problem of teacher education quality, but they certainly challenged education schools in the thirty years that followed. And while some university-based programs indeed put up a fight, others cut bait. The case studies that follow provide examples of each.

School, Department, or Research Center?:
The University of Chicago

In 1895, the University of Chicago stood at the forefront of educational research. With John Dewey at the helm, the Department of Philosophy, Pedagogy, and Psychology and the University Lab School brought together key education reformers and served as the country's epicenter for progressive educational research.[25] Roughly one hundred years later the university closed its education department entirely, much to the shock and dismay of the education world. What led to the demise of such a historically significant center of educational scholarship? And, more importantly, what did it mean for teacher preparation in America's universities?

The roots of the education department's dissolution remain contested, yet most agree that by the mid-1990s it lay in disarray.[26] First founded as an academic department that conducted research, it became linked to an undergraduate teachers college in the first half of the twentieth century. Education as a field then morphed into its own graduate college between 1958 and 1975, graduating a few dozen teachers per cohort in addition to conducting educational research. After the graduate college closed, education as a field migrated back to the social sciences division in the College of Arts and Sciences, embraced a more theoretical focus, and largely eliminated teacher preparation, save for a small master's program in secondary English and Mathematics.[27]

This institutional itinerancy reflected difficulties faced by the field of education in the twentieth-century research university more broadly, particularly in elite institutions, as education struggled to find its place between the push of theoretical work and the pull of practice-oriented applied research. It also reflected the most common tendency of university-based educationists: a move toward theory and away from practice. What often resulted was an attempt to establish academic credibility at the expense of classroom-oriented projects, which were often deemed "low status." Teacher preparation, occupying one of the lowest rungs on the status ladder, fell to the wayside.[28] The University of Chicago, where throughout the mid-1970s and into the 1980s only a very small and poorly regarded teacher education program remained, reflects this broader trend perfectly. By the mid-1990s, the University of Chicago produced a meager twelve to fifteen teachers per year, and the education department did not see teacher preparation as one of its prime responsibilities.

In addition to an uneasy place within the university, the education department faced other problems. In 1980 the department faculty boasted thirty scholars, but by 1995 that number had dropped to fifteen, with an average age of sixty-four, after years of denied funding for new hires. The department's budget likewise decreased significantly due to cuts from university administration, and faculty took little action to secure outside grant support.[29] Richard P. Saller, then-dean of the social sciences division, where the department was housed, called for a departmental review in the fall of 1995, citing concerns over academic quality. He first required a self-study conducted by education faculty, to be followed by an external review by two university professors and two outside education experts. While the former report spoke of the department's integral mission, quality, and significant influence in the field, the latter concluded that the academic work was "uneven," the faculty too aging, the commitment to teaching lacking, and the whole department out of step with the quality of the rest of the division and the university at large. These and other details contained in the external review prompted Saller to make a bold recommendation: the department should close its doors by 2001. The faculty of the social sciences division would be allowed a non-binding vote on Saller's recommendation, but the ultimate decision would lay with university President Hugo Sonnenschein and Provost Geoffrey Stone.[30]

In the aftermath of the recommendation, the faculty and students of the department, along with prominent education researchers and organizations around the country, rallied in support. A graduate student organization sprung up, a petition garnered 145 signatures from prominent faculty and administrators from schools across the nation, and hundreds of letters arrived to the office of Dean Saller and President Sonnenschein calling on the university to reaffirm its long-standing commitment to education.[31] Letters to the editor of the student-run *Chicago Maroon* criticized the recommendation, and both local and national news sources covered the story.[32] The American Education Research Association (AERA) and the National Academy of Education, along with prominent scholars such as Stanford's Lee Shulman (a graduate of the Chicago program), Columbia's Teachers College Dean Karen Zumwalt, and University of Pennsylvania's William Lowe Boyd, wrote passionate letters to the dean and president calling on the university to reconsider and recognize the importance of university support for the field of educational research.[33] A resolution adopted by members of the National Academy of Education in 1996 stated:

> We express our deep concern over the proposal to close the University
> of Chicago's Department of Education. When one of America's greatest

FIGURE 2. A front-page article from the September 23, 1996, edition of the *Chicago Maroon*, the student newspaper of the University of Chicago, is headlined, "Education dept. faces elimination." *Source*: The University of Chicago Library

research universities, especially one with such a long and distinguished record of accomplishments in the field of education, contemplates such a decision, its consequences reverberate throughout the education community and the larger society. At this time in Chicago and in the United States, the need for high quality research on teaching, learning, curriculum, and policy is indisputable. . . . As members of other research universities with a continuing commitment to education, we call on the University of Chicago to reaffirm its long-standing and distinguished commitment to this field.[34]

Those backing the department also criticized the university's decades-long neglect and the opaque review process, arguing that institution-wide financial woes and education's prestige problem were the real sources of the closure recommendation, not low quality in the department. Despite the department's current struggles, they argued, the university should help revitalize, not dismantle, it.[35]

Yet while the education department received an outpouring of support, the majority of that support came from those inside the education research establishment. Little evidence suggests that anyone outside of education schools joined in the outrage. By November 1996, one day before the faculty vote, even the *Maroon* editorial board changed its mind and reluctantly endorsed the dean's recommendation to close the department, concluding that it represented more of a "collection of independent scholars and teachers" than a coherent department and noting that many of its prominent faculty members were about to retire.[36] A campus rally that week drew a paltry twelve people.[37] A Chicago high school teacher wrote a telling op-ed in *Education Week* after the closure decision entitled "The University of Chicago's Education Department Will Not Be Missed," decrying the "immense intellectual distance between classroom teachers and schools and departments of education at elite universities" like the University of Chicago. "When it is cut off from the real world of schools and teachers, educational research becomes arcane, irrelevant, and sometimes downright silly," wrote the teacher.[38] No one from the Chicago Public Schools seemed concerned, either, as they were not benefitting from particularly helpful research or a steady supply of new teachers.

Dean Saller repeatedly stated publicly that academic quality and not financial pressure was the driving concern of the administration and that the university would remain committed to education research through its other departments, such as sociology, economics, and anthropology, and through the Center for Urban Education and the Consortium for Chicago Schools

Research, founded in 1988 and 1990 respectively to conduct research on the city's school reforms.[39] The department, he repeatedly noted in one of his leading arguments, was not even preparing many teachers. Sure enough, on November 13, 1996, the social sciences faculty voted 75 to 41 in favor of closing the department for good.[40] The school stopped accepting graduate students and the few teacher candidates it had been taking in, and eventually started phasing itself out entirely.

As the *New York Times* reported,

> A common version of the events leading to the decision asserted that the money men, the bean counters, had taken over Chicago, found its education department—with its modest-earning alumni—wanting, and chose to kill it off. . . . But in recent months, a more complex discussion has emerged, one which raises questions about the nature of educational research, notably about the links between educational theory and practice, and how they fit into a traditional academic setting. Increasingly, insiders and outsiders are contending that the decline started in the late 70s, when Chicago's education department stopped its day-to-day involvement with teacher training and schools, devoting itself more purely to theory.

University of Chicago professor of psychology and education researcher Bert Cohler even noted, "A department of education which terminates all ties to the real world of schooling and focuses only on statistical manipulation of schooling outcomes is getting itself in trouble. We became more and more ivory-towered in the worst sense."[41] In the 1990s, while scholars like John Goodlad bemoaned the marginalization of teacher education within prestigious education schools, Cohler's comment described the end result of that marginalization: the failure of more prestigious researchers to thrive as they lost contact with the day-to-day concerns and needs of actual schools and teachers. What had been the University of Chicago's education department's greatest strength in John Dewey's day—its close link to education reformers working within the Chicago Public Schools—was long gone from the department before the department itself departed the scene.

In the wake of what appeared to be the death knell for the field of education and teacher preparation at the University of Chicago, education made a powerful resurgence. Under the aegis of the Center for Urban Education (CUE), the Consortium for Chicago School Research (CCSR), a few university-run charter schools, and the newly formed Urban Teacher Education Program (UTEP)—all later grouped under the umbrella organization the Urban Education Institute (UEI)—the University of Chicago again became a leader in the field of applied educational research and urban teacher education in the decade between 2005 and 2015.

The winding road from the education department's closure to the widely hailed UEI initiatives provides some important insights into the teacher education debates. UTEP officially launched in 2003 as an elementary education program with only a small cohort of University of Chicago graduates. It looked to fill the gap left by the closure of the education department and the university's decades-long neglect of the task of teacher preparation. UTEP then grew substantially under the leadership of director Kavita Kapadia Matsko and with support from Anthony S. Bryk, original founder of the CCSR and an influential administrator of the UEI, and Timothy Knowles, director of UEI. In 2007 the program began accepting graduates of other universities in an effort to attract a more diverse cohort, and in 2009 it grew again to prepare math and biology teachers at the secondary level in addition to its elementary program.[42]

UTEP now serves as a national model for teacher preparation. It was the template for the residency program promoted by then-senators Barack Obama and Ted Kennedy in their 2007 education reform bill. It boasts a five-year retention rate of over 90% for its graduates—a number far exceeding the 50% average for urban educators. And it received a 2011 U.S. Department of Education grant that has allowed the program to quadruple its cohort sizes, so that the University of Chicago can educate and mentor roughly 300 teachers for service in Chicago Public Schools per year—a far cry from the twelve to fifteen teacher graduates in the 1980s and 1990s.[43] Outside researchers, news sources, and teacher education experts have lauded the program for its efficacy and ability to bridge the "town–gown" divide. In a statement that would have been unheard of in relation to the University of Chicago in the 1970s through the 1990s, Secretary of Education Arne Duncan encouraged other universities to take a cue from Chicago: "The fact is, you're not an ivory tower in the middle of the city, but you're running some of the best charter schools in the city, and arguably, the country. You're not just thinking theoretically about the problem, but you're putting your resources on the line."[44]

UTEP students participate in a five-year sequence. The first two years consist of coursework and fieldwork blending theory and practice, after which students become certified to teach in city schools. They then receive mentoring and professional development support in their first three years on the job. The program also emphasizes Chicago's unique urban context and includes a "Soul Strand," a space in the curriculum for teacher candidates to engage with questions of identity, race, class, gender, and sexuality.[45]

Despite its great success, the University of Chicago's program has not yet produced the kind of evidence that would convince advocates of alternative routes that they should stop their efforts to create outside-of-university programs or convince more traditional education schools to adopt the Chicago model entirely. Indeed, the national failure to be able to define good teaching or to conduct trustworthy evaluations of teacher education programs remains an issue that plagues all reform efforts within and beyond colleges and universities.

Nevertheless, the rise, fall, and rebirth of education and teacher preparation at the University of Chicago holds significant lessons for those engaging questions of where, exactly, teacher preparation should happen. Under the education department in the 1980s and 1990s, teacher education was pushed aside, considered low status, and practically ignored despite the existence of an academic department devoted to educational studies. After the department was dismantled, educational research and teacher preparation made an unexpected comeback through a university-sponsored research institute where an innovative teacher preparation program grew into a resounding success. Moreover—and somewhat ironically—it was only when teacher education became housed within a research institute, and not an education department or school, that teaching became framed as "intellectual work" by those who ran it, and the applied research of education began to gain more prestige campus- and community-wide.

Now the 300-person, $27 million UEI and its UTEP model are arguably sources of pride for the University of Chicago, exemplars beloved by President Robert Zimmer, who is publicly committed to service and community-oriented scholarship.[46] Undergrads have called on the university to devote even more resources to creating pathways to become public school teachers, and the university announced new grants to encourage pathways into education careers. While John Dewey would expect nothing less of his former institution, few at the university would have likely predicted such a successful turnaround in the nineties. According to Timothy Knowles, former director of the UEI, no other university conducts work on education with such scope, ambition, or coherence as the University of Chicago, including other universities with education schools known for their outreach and high-quality research.[47]

The downfall of the University of Chicago's education department was the result of a number of factors: favoring theory over practice, a lack of support from the university administration, the failure of the education faculty to renew itself and cultivate outside funding sources, and, arguably, a turn away from teacher preparation. Yet the major question this story raises is whether university-based teacher preparation requires a school or department of education at all. That question will be taken up in more depth in chapter 3, on new hybrid models of teacher preparation. Yet the question of "how do we know" about the quality of graduates of any program remains.

The Nurtured STEP Child: Stanford University

Stanford's Teacher Education Program (STEP), housed within Stanford's acclaimed Graduate School of Education, consistently ranks as one of the leading teacher preparation programs in the country. Whereas the demise of the University of Chicago Department of Education and its teacher training represents a tale of institutional neglect and ambivalent faculty, Stanford provides a counter story. From the early 1980s through the present, a steady stream of university presidents and key education faculty members have committed time and resources to teacher education, allowing a once merely tolerated program to grow into a celebrated model for university-based teacher preparation and a source of campus-wide pride.

Much like education departments at other prestigious research universities, Stanford's School of Education did not prioritize teacher preparation in the post-war years. Following a series of faculty appointments in the behavioral and social sciences starting in the mid-1950s, the school dismantled its elementary teacher education program entirely, de-emphasized its commitment to community service, and focused on training more PhDs—ironically following the model of the University of Chicago department. When faculty founded the STEP teacher training program in 1959 with funding from the Ford Foundation, its original mission was more research-oriented and experimental, and less about the conviction that a research university should be in the business of educating teachers. In the 1960s and 1970s, Stanford's School of Education rose in the rankings, and research centers proliferated. The teacher education program, however, remained a small blip on the school's radar, producing only a few secondary-level graduates per year and always facing the specter of closure.[48]

Things were set to change in the following decades. By the late 1970s many in the higher education world—both in and out of Stanford—expressed concern about the growing distance between educational research and real-world schools. Stanford's then-president Donald Kennedy was one of those voices, and he proved to be a key figure in Stanford's renewed commitment to teacher preparation and K–12 education. He exhorted educationists to "get closer to your field" and spearheaded a three-year project entitled "Stanford and the Schools" that brought university-based education researchers together with Bay Area secondary school administrators and teachers.[49] Stanford's provost called for an evaluation of the education school in the summer of 1980 and considered going the way of the University of Chicago and Johns Hopkins University: turning the school into an education department. Instead, the administrators encouraged the education school to gain greater coherence and further reconnect with the K–12 world, allowing them to prove themselves as a valuable asset to both the university and public education before any drastic steps were taken.[50]

Kennedy continued to champion university-based teacher preparation both at Stanford and across the nation throughout the 1980s. In 1983, a few months after the *Nation at Risk* report, which led to the Carnegie Report, Kennedy led an informal conference in Pajaro Dunes, California, with the presidents of six major research universities—Harvard, Columbia, the University of Chicago, the University of Michigan, and the University of California at Berkeley—and the heads of their schools or departments of education. Those in the higher education world noted that it had been twenty-five years since Harvard President James B. Conant led a movement for universities to connect with K–12 concerns. Members of the conference concluded that universities should actively commit themselves to improving public education and partner with local schools to do so. They also offered a ten-point plan for accomplishing these goals, with point number two committing to improve "teacher education programs, including opportunities for helping classroom teachers."[51] According to some attendees, perhaps three or four education schools were saved by this conference (though the University of Chicago's education department was clearly not one of them). Kennedy continued his leadership by pledging financial support for initiatives linked to K–12 schooling. He also spearheaded another conference in 1987 that issued an open letter to 3,300 college presidents, calling on them to devote more resources to improving public education, including reinvigorating the programs on their campuses devoted to preparing better and more professional teachers for service in public schools.[52] While many prominent research universities turned their backs on their education schools in the late 1980s and 1990s, Stanford showed unique leadership in supporting the enterprise. It was this leadership that allowed teacher education advocates to overcome internal difficulties and problems of prestige.

This level of public backing found support from those within the school of education, not surprisingly, and relations between the administration and the education faculty remained fairly positive despite some mild controversies over the Stanford and the Schools Project. Two deans in the 1980s,

J. Myron Atkin—known for his criticism of overly theoretical work at the University of Illinois—and Marshall Smith, both proved influential figures in bringing the department closer to schools, smoothing the theory and practice divide, and in helping to give STEP a central position within the education school itself. When Lee Shulman moved from the University of Michigan to Stanford in 1982, he brought with him a well-established reputation as an educational psychologist who was deeply committed to the education of teachers and to understanding their needs. Soon after coming to Stanford, Shulman coined the term "pedagogical content knowledge," which he defined as both "the most regularly taught topics in one's subject area" and "the ways of representing and formulating the subject that make it comprehensible to others." In other words, Shulman insisted teachers needed to know their subjects very well and be equally expert at making those subjects interesting and comprehensible to their students. A teacher education program needed to produce just such teachers.[53] By 1987, when Dean Smith reported to his colleagues at a faculty meeting about a recent retreat of Stanford administrators, he could gladly note that after a discussion of what the university would look like in the year 2010, "The School of Education came out looking good."[54]

The two subsequent Stanford presidents after Kennedy demonstrated a similar commitment to the field of education and to STEP specifically. Gerhard Casper, president from 1992 to 2000, commissioned an evaluation of STEP in 1997 and supported subsequent reforms that resulted from the report's recommendations, which included the hiring of Linda Darling-Hammond, a teacher education researcher and strong advocate of teacher professionalization.[55] Darling-Hammond took Shulman's old position when he moved on to be the president of the Carnegie Foundation for the Advancement of Teaching. Following the report and Darling-Hammond's hiring, STEP significantly revamped its curriculum and solidified its place as a leading model of teacher education in the country. President John Hennessy, whose tenure ran from 2000 to 2016, likewise demonstrated his commitment to STEP and was considered by foundations and university leaders to be one of the strongest spokespersons in the higher education world for investing in teacher education and working to build the prestige of teaching as a university-based profession.[56]

While the highest rungs of Stanford's university leadership expressed support for teacher preparation from 1980 onward, the education faculty did not sit idly by. The success of STEP also resulted from the proactive efforts of those within the school of education to continuously improve the program and secure funding. In 1987 the faculty reiterated in one of its meetings that "it is crucial that we [The School of Education] continue to commit the resources to ensure that the STEP program be one of the very best, if not the best, fifth year teacher training program in the nation. In terms of faculty we need a way to responsibly meet substantive needs of STEP students in math, science, English, social studies and history, and world languages."[57] And although the evaluation from 1997 cited continued problems with prestige and consistency of mission—Stanford did not completely escape the woes of education school status problems; STEP was often referred to as the "STEP child" of the university, as research was valued over practice—it did note a lot of positive aspects. Strong faculty commitment to teacher preparation, reflected in the large number of tenure-track instructors in STEP; "supportive and critical supervision"; a well-regarded end-of-year portfolio conference; and a year-long student teaching experience all made the program one of the strongest around, despite room for improvement.[58]

Following that evaluation report, the faculty also took proactive steps to put the recommendations into action. In 1998, as mentioned, the school hired Darling-Hammond as the Charles E. Ducommun Professor of Education and faculty director of the Stanford Center of Opportunity in Policy Education. Such a hire was referred to as a "watershed event in STEP's history" and signaled a commitment to teacher education.[59] Darling-Hammond had already made a name for herself in the teacher education world as a vociferous advocate of a professional and high-quality approach to teacher education. In 1999 the school hired Rachel Lotan to direct STEP, a crucial move for the program's success. Lotan was the first director of STEP to have academic standing in the school's academic council and professorial rank. She worked tirelessly on the development of STEP in the early 2000s, and the curriculum changed significantly to reflect what would become the holistic skill- and theory-based residency model outlined in Darling-Hammond and Joan Baratz-Snowden's 2005 teacher education blueprint, *A Good Teacher in Every Classroom*.[60] Lotan and her STEP colleagues also restructured the summer school program in response to student feedback and the report's recommendations, making the practical aspect of the program more beneficial to students and partnering schools. Later, with support from the Annenberg and Woodrow Wilson National Fellowship foundations, STEP also developed a robust three-year post-graduation mentoring program for new teachers who completed their STEP degree.

STEP's twelve-month course of study came to include classes in pedagogical theory, teaching content, social justice in the classroom, and classroom management, along with an intensive clinical practicum experience that placed students in real classrooms beginning in their first week and paired them with a cooperating teacher for an entire school year, a model that many of the best programs throughout the nation would adopt. Lotan, who had taught at Stanford since 1991 while working on teacher education research and equitable pedagogical strategies in the classroom and professional development for teachers, also began tracking evaluation metrics associated with the efficacy of STEP graduates, a rarity in university-based teacher education. This allowed program leaders to target weak spots and demonstrate their effectiveness through data relating to retention rates and student test scores. She and her colleagues also stressed the importance of diversity—a leading concern of the education school faculty and student body since at least the late 1980s, particularly after the graduating STEP class of 1994 voiced loud concerns over the lack of diversity within the program.[61]

In 1999 Ira Lit joined Stanford as associate director, and later director, of the elementary education–focused STEP program, redressing a lack in Stanford's offerings, since elementary education had been dropped from the curriculum in the 1950s. Stanford faculty and administrators also succeeded in securing internal and external resources for the teacher education programs, particularly in the early 2000s. STEP received a prestigious $5 million Teachers for a New Era grant from the Carnegie Corporation of New York in 2003 to continue to improve the program.[62] In 2005 the STEP master's program in elementary education was founded, and in 2004 actor Bill Cosby (pre-scandal) helped raise $1 million for STEP.[63] In 2006 generous alum Judy Avery donated $10 million to the program to help STEP students with loan forgiveness, which President Hennessy matched with another $10 million—in addition to the $125 million of university money he pledged to put toward K–12 research initiatives.[64] By 2009, in the wake of such success and greater student demand for high-quality pathways into teaching, Stanford created a new education minor for its undergraduate population.[65] Though not a certificate-granting teacher preparation program, the minor still encourages students to pursue careers in education, including teaching. STEP also became one of only four programs chosen by the Woodrow Wilson Foundation to receive its first fellows for a program often touted as the "Rhodes Scholarship in teaching."[66]

In 1980 Stanford was educating around thirty future educators. STEP now accepts around 100 teacher candidates per year and is consistently ranked as one of the top programs in the nation. Under Lotan's leadership, the program launched Inquiry into STEP, which encourages visitors from other teacher education programs around the world to come to Stanford and learn more about its efforts.

STEP's success and longevity can be attributed to the decades-long institutional and financial support from university presidents and officials, strong consistent leadership, and an ability among the education school faculty to self-assess, renew, and reinvigorate in response to inside challenges and outside pressures.

Beneath the Dignity of the Ivy League?: Harvard University

In 1966, the *Harvard Crimson* reported on growing student unrest in the Harvard Graduate School of Education (HGSE). In regards to teacher preparation, staff writer F. Andre Favat noted, "Ed School students accept the fact that that HGSE is really not interested in being the purveyor of teachers to the nation. They know that the School may supply teachers—by coincidence—but that it clearly concentrates its energies on preparing its students to achieve positions of leadership in teaching, administration, and scholarship."[67] Nearly fifty years later one could argue this sentiment still rings true. In a 2003 article in *The Atlantic* entitled "Why Isn't Harvard Training More Teachers?," one answer surfaced: "institutional snobbery toward teaching." According to Walter Isaacson, journalist-turned-education policy leader, this mentality—that Harvard is in the business of preparing leaders, not *just teachers*—is rampant; there is a perception that it is "beneath the dignity of an Ivy League school to train teachers."[68]

Yet this mindset is slowly eroding, arguably due to a few decades of effort from HGSE faculty, but perhaps more so from the rising prestige of teaching due to competitive alternative certification programs such as Teach for America. In 2011, over 18% of Harvard College's senior class applied to TFA, and the percentage has remained at or about that level since.[69] Although Harvard education faculty briefly discussed eliminating teacher preparation in 2010, by the fall of 2014 they switched course and launched what is being hailed as a "TFA alternative": an undergraduate fellowship program that attempts to maintain the prestige and competitive acceptance rate of TFA (and Harvard) while "doing it right" in terms of preparation.[70] What can this tell us about university-based teacher education and the teacher education wars?

Education as a field and teacher education specifically have a troubled history at Harvard. Originally an academic department, the field of education was then supplemented by a Graduate School of Education in 1920, with the department officially closing in the late 1950s, leaving only HGSE. Like other university-housed educationists, Harvard's education faculty struggled with institutional misfit and asserting authority from their earliest days in Cambridge. Teacher preparation, as elsewhere, became a poorly regarded pursuit as the school sought more academic and professional credibility. Its former partnership with the all-female Radcliffe College and its status as the first program to grant women degrees only hurt its campus-wide reputation. As a result, the undergraduate preparation of teachers was eliminated at Harvard as early as the 1930s. However, in 1936 Harvard's then-president James Bryant Conant convinced the faculty of arts and sciences, as well as the faculty of education, to offer a MAT (Master of Arts in Teaching degree) to be pursued half in the arts and sciences disciplines and half in the school of education. In time, Harvard's MAT became a highly regarded program, especially in the baby-boom 1950s as school enrollments, and the demand for teachers, ballooned. However, the degree always maintained its internal Harvard detractors, and after much institutional soul-searching in the 1950s and 1960s, the education faculty voted to eliminate the MAT in 1973, a decision later explained as caused by "changes in faculty interest" and the loss of federal funding to support teacher education.[71]

Yet the education fervor of the 1980s, along with the leadership of newly appointed HGSE Dean Patricia Graham and University President Derek Bok, laid some important foundations for reviving teacher preparation at Harvard. Bok and Graham joined Stanford President Donald Kennedy at the 1983 Pajaro Dunes conference in response to increasing concern from the media and politicians regarding the "crisis" in American public education following the *Nation at Risk* report.[72] Over three days spent at a resort in Monterey County in 1983, prominent heads of higher education publicly agreed that universities such as Harvard should take the lead on issues relating to the elementary and secondary grades, including teacher training. According to Geraldine Jonçich Clifford and James Guthrie, the conference was an "extraordinary event which, behind the public rhetoric, was a message from two powerful university presidents to their counterparts to 'lay off' bashing their schools of education."[73]

Building off this public backing from the administration and the work of preceding Dean Paul Ylvisaker, who in a 1979 report recommitted HGSE to issues of schooling, Pat Graham began rebuilding Harvard's links to the K–12 world and teacher education.[74] Dean from 1982 to 1991, Graham initiated a mid-career math and science Master of Arts in Teaching in 1983, the Undergraduate Teacher Education Program (UTEP) in 1985, and other school-based community initiatives throughout the 1980s. In an article that Graham wrote for the *Harvard Crimson* detailing these changes, she explained, "The present public outcry about the schools has focused upon teachers, stressing their academic inadequacies. Beginning in July 1982, we undertook to investigate ways of attracting nontraditional candidates—persons in their middle years who have had experience in technical fields but who have not previously considered teaching, who had mastered their subject matter and were academically strong—to the teaching profession. . . . We believe that such a step is an important one, both actually and symbolically, indicating as it does our renewed commitment to work with both beginning and experienced teachers."[75] Yet despite these victories and a general move back toward practice, UTEP only drew about six students per year, as the program was designed in a way that overwhelmed even a Harvard undergrad; it led to many drop-outs and a mediocre campus-wide reputation.[76] The mid-career master's program also remained relatively small and limited to its math and science focus.

During the 1990s and early 2000s, however, interest among Harvard undergrads for service in public schools heightened dramatically, and many of them did become teachers—just not through Harvard.[77] TFA deserves much of the credit for this change of heart, as do a few other non-traditional alternative certification programs, such as the Boston Teacher Residency (BTR). Despite the controversies around TFA (see chapter 1), its effect on the likelihood of Ivy Leaguers to pursue teaching careers is undeniable. Harvard consistently ranks as one of the leading suppliers of TFA corps members and as the school with the highest percentage of applicants, with just around one-fifth of the entire senior class submitting applications. Some of this interest can be attributed to an increased desire to give back to the community, a supposed trait of the millennial generation. But TFA's brilliant branding strategy is more likely the real culprit. By destigmatizing teaching from its feminine, anti-intellectual, and working-class associations, and creating a highly competitive and career-boosting network, TFA managed to instill teaching with immense cultural capital. Ivy Leaguers and high-achieving students from universities across the country responded in droves, making TFA a household name and a coveted resume booster. Harvard undergrads also attributed their decisions to apply to bleak job prospects following the 2008 recession, as well as to the organization's impressive recruitment strategies. Interviewed in a *Harvard Crimson* article in 2010, one student said she had no intention of applying to TFA at the beginning of the school year, but by the time October rolled around, TFA's recruiting efforts had paid off: "Word of mouth has been very valuable," she said. "I think the numbers will continue to increase."[78] The prestige factor of TFA made teaching something it had never been for Harvard students or for Americans in general: elite.

While TFA and the alternative certification bandwagon were picking up steam, HGSE focused on other realms. Under the leadership of deans Jerome T. Murphy and Ellen Condliffe Lagemann in the 1990s and early 2000s, the school created a number of new master's and doctoral programs, successfully raised $111 million through a capital campaign, revamped the curriculum and organizational structure of the school, and secured key partnerships with the Kennedy School of Government, the arts and sciences faculty, and the Harvard Business School.[79] While this era in HGSE's development was certainly crucial to its success and current standing as one of the leading education schools in the nation, few changes to teacher preparation occurred, despite Lagemann's interest in supporting it. Speaking to a crowd of around 200 in the fall of 2002, she noted, "Unless we can get the support, we cannot improve. It's about status. It's about appreciating teachers and about appreciating education and research in education."[80] In the early 2000s, that status and support had not yet fully accrued to HGSE and its teaching program, housed in one of the poorest and smallest graduate schools on campus. Despite Lagemann's and a few other faculty members' efforts, only the relatively small UTEP, mid-career master's, and the one-year Teacher Education Program (TEP) master's degree existed.

As the second decade of the new millennium approached, however, the overwhelming interest in education by Harvard's undergrad population could not be ignored. As more and more graduating seniors headed off to teach in public schools across the country after their five-week TFA trainings, the Harvard education faculty split about what its proper response should be. While some advocated for increased attention to teacher preparation, others still held that it was not central to HGSE's mission.

Eventually, the champions of teacher preparation won out. In 2013, James Ryan assumed the dean position with a desire to strengthen the undergraduate-to-teacher certification pipeline, hoping that at least 10–15% of students would participate. A year into office, Ryan and his colleagues announced a groundbreaking new initiative to make good on that goal: the Harvard Teaching Fellows program (HTF). Ryan and pro-teacher education faculty members, such as Katherine Merseth, made no qualms about HTF responding to undergraduate demand largely fueled by Teach for America. In an interview, Merseth criticized TFA's model and called the new program an alternative, explaining, "We intend this to be a great way to get into teaching, but to do it right."[81] The new program intended to keep the prestige factor alive and well, making the program a competitive, fully funded fellowship for a select group of forty seniors in its first year. "I also think that up until now," Ryan said in an interview with the *Harvard Crimson*, "[teaching has] not been a career that people with a lot of choices . . . that involve higher-paying jobs, that a lot of them consider. So part of this is to try and change that."[82]

Students accepted into HTF (all Harvard undergraduates) participate in a year and a half of intensive, field-based preparation. They begin taking teaching coursework in the spring semester of their senior year and combine more coursework with student teaching experiences the summer after graduation in nearby Boston area schools. Fellows then undertake one year of a part-time teaching residency in cities across the nation while they continue to receive support from HGSE faculty and complete online coursework, then return for an additional summer of coursework in Cambridge and observed teaching. At the conclusion of this training they receive Massachusetts state licensure, which is reciprocal in many states. The program is funded by a $10 million gift from two Harvard graduates, a few other alumni donors, and funds from Harvard President Drew Faust, meaning fellows not only do not pay a dime but also receive a living stipend during their residency year. If they chose to go on to complete a master's degree at HGSE, they receive reduced tuition.[83]

HGSE's faculty are also capitalizing on increasing student critiques of TFA and other fast-track teaching programs, as well as continually growing demand for education-related resources on campus. In fall of 2014, two months before the launch of HTF, a student group called on the university to sever ties with TFA in a widely publicized protest. This sentiment reflects a growing body of criticism toward TFA's model. "We're calling on Harvard to support and provide the resources for people who want to have lifelong careers in public education, not people who want to teach for a couple of years and then go to law school or business school," said Blake A. McGhghy, one of the student leaders of the anti-TFA protest.[84]

Katherine Merseth's undergraduate course "Dilemmas of Equity and Excellence in American K–12 Education" likewise demonstrates undergraduate interest in the topic. Around 300 students have registered for the 75-person class each year since it began in 2011, necessitating a lottery. Given this zeal for all things education, Merseth is considering implementing a new Education Studies secondary field for undergrads and founding an Institute of Education modelled after the existing Institute of Politics.[85]

Meanwhile, the TEP master's program (open to non-Harvard undergrads) continues to gain credibility, both in the education world and on campus, with a cohort of twenty to twenty-five teacher candidates per year training to be teacher leaders in urban settings. The eleven-month program aims to balance theory and practice while providing a fieldwork residency component to complement coursework, similar to HTF. Students concentrate on pedagogy and teaching methods, but also address urban-specific issues of race, class, gender, and power dimensions.[86] Yet despite nearly identical curriculum, faculty, and coursework, because most of the master's candidates do not currently come from Harvard, the program is considered less prestigious on campus than the Harvard Teaching Fellows.

The lessons from Harvard's winding and troubled relationship with teacher preparation are telling. Prestige matters, at least for the fate of university-based teacher education. Harvard's experiment with a new teaching fellows program represents an attempt to capitalize on the interest and status fostered by TFA, but with a research-backed professional curriculum and a clinical training component. The next few years will offer insight on whether such efforts can finally render university-based teacher education a sought-after career path for high-achieving students, which may have a profound impact on the educational landscape. Yet most teacher preparation does not occur in hallowed halls of the Ivy League, nor does it need to. Most teacher preparation occurs in regional and state colleges and universities, where high-quality, rigorous, and well-respected professional preparation can take place, as the next case study demonstrates.

"The Harvard of Teacher Education": Montclair State University

"It's hard for a school like Montclair to get to the cutting edge," Montclair State University Provost Richard Lynde noted in a 1999 interview. "But that's exactly where we are on teacher education. . . . I would have no qualms about putting our program against any in the country."[87] While it may be difficult for public regional universities such as Montclair State to compete with schools like the University of Chicago, Stanford, or Harvard in overall rankings, many nonetheless excel in the field they were originally created for—teaching. Deemed the "Harvard of teacher education," Montclair State University is one of many former normal schools that have stayed current on the latest innovations in teacher education. Montclair State took the Holmes and Carnegie reports of the 1980s to heart and has offered one of the best programs in the country for decades. Lacking the resources and prestige of the Ivies or flagship state universities, and therefore some of the challenges inherent to the teacher education enterprise in such spaces, Montclair has produced great teachers for the state's schools for over a century.

Stories such as Montclair's therefore challenge the arguments that innovation in teacher education only happens outside the institutional framework of the university setting or that innovation within universities only results from market pressures from alternative route programs. Though Montclair became enmeshed in the heated battles over alternative certification in New Jersey in the early and mid-1980s, along with all the state's teacher-preparing institutions of higher learning, sources reveal that innovation started before the major "competitive threat" of the state's alternative route program or organizations like TFA took hold.[88]

Montclair mirrors the institutional development of many normal schools across the country over the past 100 years. First founded in 1908 as the New Jersey State Normal School at Montclair, it began, like most normal schools, as a two-year institution dedicated to preparing school teachers for service in the regional community. Such institutions became popular during the rise of the common school movement in the mid and late nineteenth century, when demand for credentialed school teachers rose dramatically in tandem with the expansion of the school system. Though the school only graduated forty-five students in its inaugural class, by 1918, 1,464 students earned diplomas, with 1,200 marching off to teach in New Jersey the following year. As the progressive era brought demands for greater professionalization of the teaching force in the early twentieth century, the school transitioned from a two-year normal school to a four-year teachers college in 1924, renamed itself the Montclair State Teachers College, and granted its first master's degree in 1932. At the end of World War II, the GI Bill led recently returned soldiers to flood the nation's halls of higher learning. So many GIs enrolled at Montclair in 1947 that classes had to be held in wooden war-surplus buildings, and enrollment only increased in the following decade. During this era, long-time Harvard president James B. Conant, who would lambast the teacher preparation field in his 1963 book *The Education of American Teachers*, had positive reviews for Montclair, granting it the title "the Harvard of teacher education."[89]

After a merger with the Panzer School of Physical Education, Montclair again changed its name to Montclair State College in 1958, and, mirroring national trends, became a comprehensive four-year college in 1966, offering liberal arts degrees. However, those first two decades of transitioning to a liberal arts college were the "dark ages of teacher preparation," according to former College of Education Dean Nicholas Michelli.[90] This happened at many other former normal schools as well. In the effort to serve a ballooning post-secondary student population, and to distance themselves from their own past, many former normal schools gave up their commitments to teacher preparation, particularly as they tried to attract larger numbers of students and earn greater levels of prestige that came with liberal arts education. Then, in 1994, the college became a regional state university, offering graduate degrees and a few doctoral programs.

Instead of abandoning its roots even further, Montclair returned to them in the latter half of the twentieth century. "By the late 1970s," Michelli noted, "the education school reasserted its bloodlines, moving in new directions that would carry the rest of the institution along as well. The education faculty began groundbreaking work in the area of critical thinking. The education school also came to recognize the need for partnerships with urban schools. On the one hand, it saw a need to help create the schools for which it was training new teachers. On the other, it wanted to enlist experienced teachers in more formal arrangements and deeper involvement in teacher training."[91]

Starting in the late 1970s, the education school faculty developed a robust curriculum centered on critical thinking, built strong relationships with its arts and sciences faculty (unlike the elite research institutions), forged meaningful district partnerships with New Jersey schools, and secured sufficient funding through engagement with national and local governments and philanthropies. In 1979, reform got under way through the emphasis on critical thinking and a new partnership with the Newark public schools. Spearheaded by Professor Wendy Oxman, Project THISTLE: Thinking Skills in Teaching and Learning launched a program to bring critical thought into K–12 classrooms by offering graduate-level professional development and master's courses to public school teachers. By 1987, the college established the Institute of Critical Thinking with a grant from the New Jersey Department of Higher Education through the Governor's Challenge grant program. Ten years later, the program had worked with around 300 Newark public school teachers.

As we noted earlier, Harry Judge reflected on the Holmes and Carnegie reports, saying that schools of education "will change only when they really wish to, and not enough yet do."[92] Montclair State did, in fact, wish to change. It very much saw itself responding to the recommendations of the reform reports, which built on initiatives already underway. As Michelli, Oxman, and their colleague Robert Pines noted in 1999, "Like teacher educators and other faculty at institutions across the country, the faculty at Montclair State College have been studying the reports that have been characterized as defining 'the second wave of educational reform' for the past several years. While most of the first set of reports, including *A Nation at Risk*, had as their primary focus the practices of the K–12 schools, the second wave extended that focus to include teachers and teacher education."

For example, they noted that the 1986 Carnegie Forum's *A Nation Prepared* was "quite explicit in urging collaboration between colleges and 'clinical schools.'"[93] Whereas others reacted defensively to the reports, Montclair took concerted effort to strengthen its district partnerships and improve its school-based pre-service and in-service training in a "clinical" setting—and to make itself better and more relevant in the process.

In the summer of 1987, a steering committee composed of Michelli, the dean of the School of Professional Studies, the director of teacher education, and the director of the Institute for Critical Thinking began meeting to put these reforms in motion. The group grew during the academic year, adding representatives from each of the college's five schools, students in the education program, and representatives from the public schools. That year Robert Pines, director of teacher education, sent letters to the superintendents of all fifteen school districts in a thirty-mile radius, outlining the program to create clinical districts and choose specific teaching schools within them. After in-person meetings and review of written stipulations and commitments, twelve superintendents followed through. One superintendent wrote, "We believe that this project will be an exciting challenge for our district and mesh beautifully with our district's own initiative to integrate a thinking skills program in our existing curriculum. Therefore, we accept your invitation to become a 'clinical district' and to work with you to make this project a reality."[94]

Montclair's experience thus complicates the story that played out in many other settings, where superintendents revolted against the schools of education that provided their teachers and decided to start their own programs. In northern New Jersey, superintendents became active and welcome partners with Montclair education faculty. District- and school-level leaders believed that they knew which colleges turned out high-quality graduates and which did not. So, while many of these district leaders welcomed alternative certification programs and publicly criticized the quality of schools of education, they also recognized quality departments when they saw them. They just did not see enough of them like Montclair.

By 1988, Montclair began selecting schools and teachers for its innovative clinical teacher training model as part of what became the New Jersey Network for Educational Renewal (NJNER), directed by Professor Ada Beth Cutler. Teachers applied based on a selective set of criteria, with sixty accepted as the school's first "clinical faculty." These mentor-teachers received an honorarium as well as targeted support and training on how to guide their apprentices and incorporate critical thinking into their daily lessons. In this way Montclair could ensure that its trainees were learning from master teachers, in line with the School of Education's pedagogical philosophy, which it set to paper in the late 1980s after much stakeholder discussion and a two-day retreat for campus- and district-based faculty. By the end of the 1990s, Montclair could boast of having over 500 school-based clinical adjunct faculty members.

Unlike other universities where the arts and sciences faculty and education faculty became estranged cousins, Montclair urged its various departments and schools to work together. Inspired by the work of Ernest Boyer and the Carnegie Foundation (the same Ernest Boyer of New Jersey's Boyer Panel; see chapter 1), Montclair started the Faculty School Incentive Program to encourage professors in the disciplines and in the School of Education to focus on work in local K–12 schools. The arrangement allowed professors in English or biology with ties to the School of Education, for example, to shift the weight of their teaching loads so that some of their hours could occur in local public schools. A professor of curriculum and teaching with an appointment in the English department could spend some hours in a local high school, supervising students, working with faculty, and developing teacher professional development seminars. By 1999, 440 faculty at Montclair had participated.[95]

Quite clearly, when Montclair became a university in the early 1990s, it did not give up on teacher education as it had when transitioning to a liberal arts college. This happened in part due to a commitment by faculty and administrators, and in part due to engagement with national networks. In the same year of the transition, 1994, the National Education Association (NEA) chose Montclair to participate in its teacher education reform plan. This ensured that innovation continued throughout the 1990s and into the next millennium as part of a broader effort to support clinical training across the country in what were termed professional development schools (PDSs). Stemming from the reform reports, the PDS model aimed to create schools that were exemplars of practice to train novices, improve veteran teachers' skills, and build and share knowledge on teacher education.[96] A 1999 article in the Bergen County *Record* detailed this type of training at Dumont High School, where a close PDS partnership linked Montclair State students and professors with the teachers union and Dumont faculty and administrators in the learning process. "In effect, they are using Dumont High School as a laboratory for portfolio assignments they have been given," Pines said. "It's like making the rounds as a doctor," he continued, foreshadowing the language that would become prevalent in the field of urban teacher residencies a decade later.[97]

After four years of planning, and based on the work of John Goodlad and the much earlier work of John Dewey at the University of Chicago, Montclair also became the first university to open a Center of Pedagogy—just as the University of Chicago was shuttering its own Department of Education. In 1998, the center offered the nation's first doctorate in pedagogy and took institutional control of all teacher education pathways. The new doctorate program aimed to provide expert training for current teachers or teacher educators wishing to grow in their practice, gain a firm grasp of pedagogical theory, develop leadership skills, and occupy a more prominent realm in education reform. The center also continued to encourage cross-campus relationships, offering a summer program for faculty in the arts and sciences to discuss issues of public education and social justice through an Institute of Education Inquiry. Over 100 arts and sciences professors participated in the summer of 2008, attending seminars in which they discussed the role of public education in a democracy and the role of the university within that mission. Today, the Center of Pedagogy still serves as the institutional hub for teacher preparation at Montclair State.

Much like Stanford, Montclair benefitted from supportive administrators, particularly from the 1980s to the present. As one 2009 case study on Montclair noted, "MSU's commitment to teacher preparation is grounded in its history as a normal school and the university's administration continues to demonstrate a dedication to educating teachers. Teacher education officials declare themselves 'very fortunate' to have had two consecutive university presidents who have been very supportive of teacher preparation. An 'ongoing legacy' of support from the Dean of the College of Education and Human Services has also allowed the teacher preparation program to pursue continual growth and renewal."[98]

What made Montclair distinctive during this era, according to Dean Michelli, was that "we have a point of view. We prepare teachers in a way that is thoroughly grounded in a set of beliefs that has evolved over the last twenty years."[99] And Montclair continued to take bold steps to improve its teacher education program at the turn of the millennium. A new teacher-as-leader program began in 2000 under the direction of JoAnne Looney, which resulted in a Master of Arts in Teaching (MAT) degree. A new initiative intended to recruit teachers of color started in the same year.[100] In 2004, Montclair launched an even deeper partnership with the Newark schools called PIE-Q, and in 2005 Montclair was chosen as one of a few universities nation-wide to receive a Teachers for a New Era (TNE) grant from the Carnegie Corporation to both strengthen their own teacher education program and serve as an incubator for best practices. In 2007, Edutopia named Montclair one of only ten schools that would "change the way we teach," reflecting Montclair's reputation as an innovator on the vanguard of teacher preparation. Two years later, in 2009, the Newark-Montclair Urban Teacher Residency kicked off with a $6.3 million grant from the U.S. Department of Education; it received another $6.2 million in 2014 to carry on the work as part of a twenty-five-university grant program on teacher education quality. In 2011, Montclair was chosen to serve as one of three TNE grantee schools, along with Arizona State University and Indiana State University, to host cross-site visits for the TNE network of twenty-five university and district partners. Montclair's Ada Beth Cutler served a valuable leadership role in that effort.[101]

After the turn of the new millennium, the school received numerous awards recognizing its quality for these myriad initiatives. In 2005 and again in 2009, the program received the Richard W. Clark Award for Exemplary Partner School Work through the National Network for Educational Renewal (NNER). In 2007, the George Lucas Educational Foundation named Montclair State one of the ten leading teacher education programs in the nation. The Newark Trust for Education named the program a "Top 11 to Watch in 2011," and the Urban Teacher Residency graduate program was recognized by the New Jersey Secretary of Education for Excellence in Teacher Education in 2012. In 2013 the Woodrow Wilson National Fellowship Foundation named Montclair one of the university partners for its Woodrow Wilson Teaching Fellowship program. Although College of Education Dean Cutler criticized the National Council on Teacher Quality (NCTQ) ranking system for being unreliable, the college's secondary program ranked fourth out of 343 in the most recent rankings, an impressive showing.[102] Efforts toward self-evaluation through the tracking of retention and student performance metrics also placed Montclair in league with other leading programs that proactively sought to evaluate their performance before any NCTQ or federal or state accountability measures were imposed. These are just a fraction of the many awards related to teacher education that Montclair has received over the years.[103]

Though this list of reforms and awards is somewhat dizzying, it demonstrates a decade of intense effort by Montclair faculty, with consistent support from long-serving president Susan Cole to maintain cutting edge programs, a rich curriculum, and strong district partnerships, as well as to participate in a number of national grant programs and professional networks. While the program is not without its challenges—no program is perfect—it is fair to say that Montclair State faculty did not sit idly by in the face of critiques of education schools in the post-war period and at the turn of the new millennium. Instead, they built on early reform work that began in the late 1970s, responded to the Holmes and Carnegie reports of the 1980s, continued to incorporate new training methods in line with educational research, and actively collaborated with school-based personnel, national and local philanthropies, and governments to evolve and grow over the years.

Rather than being reactionary, Montclair was on the cutting edge, particularly around the turn of the twenty-first century, when critics of traditional routes dismissed such university-based programs. As one commentator from the American Federation of Teachers reflected, "A look at Montclair's evolution—from a normal school founded in 1908, to a college in 1928, to expansion as a comprehensive college in the mid-60s, to its designation as a university in 1994—shows a history of innovation, mostly led by those in teacher training here."[104] While Teach for America prides itself on its core value of "continuously improving effectiveness," this quality was not the unique terrain of alternative certification programs drawing on the insights of business and the private sector. Other, less elite regional universities exemplified this quality, as Montclair and the next case study from Indiana demonstrate.

Excellence and Innovation in the Hoosier State: University of Indianapolis

Indiana has a problem. At the beginning of 2017, the state faced a potentially dire teacher shortage; it ranked as one of the lowest states for teacher recruitment and retention, with enrollment in education programs down a startling 35% state-wide, and teachers leaving the classroom at alarmingly high rates. In 2014 the state adopted a program that allowed anyone with a bachelor's degree and at least three years of appropriate work experience to become a secondary teacher in math, science, or music if they passed an appropriate content test, in an attempt to confront the pipeline challenges.[105] Still schools faced shortages. Yet unlike the early 1980s, when New Jersey and many other states faced similar trends, the conversation around how to solve this challenge sounds markedly different in the Hoosier state. "First and foremost, we must treat teachers as professionals and as role models, as they were for me, then equip them with the resources they need to succeed," Governor Eric Holcomb said in a campaign statement in 2016. "We also need to ensure teachers are a part of the conversation and have a seat at the table. Educators know what is best for their schools."[106]

Education schools, the former targets of education reformers' ire, are now considered valuable actors in bringing about that heightened professionalism, rather than eroding it—at least by some voices in the conversation. Programs across the state—such as the University of Indianapolis's (UIndy) teacher education program, which significantly revamped its teacher preparation model in the early 2000s—are held up as bastions of innovation by foundations and politicians, and are encouraged to continue their work to prepare professionals for life-long careers in education, while crash-course alternative programs meet increased skepticism. "We'd maintain we've been reformers all along," Kathy Moran, of UIndy's School of Education, told the *Indiana Star* in 2012.[107] Universities such as UIndy, along with places like Montclair State, challenge the perception that schools of education sat idly by in the face of alternative route competition at the turn of the millennium. While some schools of education complained, others took audacious new steps. Instead of bemoaning the challenges, UIndy—led by an effective provost, Deborah Balogh, who was deeply committed to teacher preparation—took action. It represents the many non-elite universities that serve as hubs of excellence and innovation in the field of teacher education—a point John Goodlad made in his national study of teacher education in 1990.

The University of Indianapolis cannot claim the long and hallowed history of institutions such as Harvard, Stanford, or the University of Chicago, nor does it have their resources. Thus, it is a far more representative case study of the thousands of institutions of higher learning that currently prepare teachers across the nation. The school's history also reflects the many changes that similarly sized regional universities underwent throughout the twentieth century.

Founded in 1902 through a partnership between real estate developer Willian L. Elder and the Church of the United Brethren in Christ, Indiana Central University was meant to attract settlers and resources to a new neighborhood in Indianapolis: University Heights. The school and its surroundings therefore "grew in infancy together" when the college officially opened in 1905. In those early years, the university contained eight schools: a college of liberal arts, a teachers college, a music conservatory, a school of oratory, the school of commerce, a Bible institute, a school of arts, and the Academy, in which students completed preparatory work and earned high school diplomas. Indiana Central received accreditation from the North Central Association of Schools and Colleges in 1947 and became a Methodist institution after the United Brethren and Methodist churches merged in 1968. Known as Indiana Central College from 1921 to 1975, it started to use the term "university" again in the mid-1970s. In 1986 it changed its name officially to the University of Indianapolis. Today, UIndy is home to a number of programs at the associates, bachelor's, master's, and doctoral levels, and the College of Education is one of seven professional colleges that educates mainly in-state students for work in Indiana and across the Midwest. As a private liberal arts college, UIndy enrolls around 5,000 students across levels per year.[108]

Through a combination of initiative on the part of key university and School of Education faculty and partnerships with national foundations, the teacher education program at UIndy is now a national model of excellence, ranked by some just as highly as places like Stanford and the University of Michigan. UIndy demonstrates that while teacher education programs at elite institutions have struggled to earn respect from their academic peers and to receive ample administrative support, education programs at smaller universities have the potential to develop strong ties with other academic departments, their administrations, nearby communities, and national foundations to provide rigorous professional preparation through a variety of degree-granting pathways.

The story of UIndy is important therefore in the larger tale of the demise of university-based teacher preparation's monopoly, namely because it refutes common assumptions. While many education schools were facing intense scrutiny and even the chopping block in the 1990s and early 2000s, UIndy's School of Education faculty stayed busy. In 2001, the School of Education partnered with the College of Arts and Sciences to create the Center of Excellence in Leadership for Learning (CELL), a research initiative focused on increasing post-secondary outcomes for Indiana students through curricular work with Indiana secondary schools. By 2002, the Association of Independent Liberal Arts Colleges of Teacher Education recognized UIndy as a program of distinction for those very efforts, which reflected a commitment to both disciplinary learning and K–12 needs.[109] As was apparent in the other university-based case studies, strong ties between schools of education and departments in the liberal arts and sciences have often been a challenge, but UIndy was able to build relationships and forge the necessary institution-wide structural changes to promote collaboration—including revising what types of activities are recognized in work load and tenure decisions, so that work with teacher education is valued and rewarded by academic departments outside the School of Education.

UIndy faculty also took the general critiques of education schools—low-quality candidates, lack of rigor, poor school-based training, and weak disciplinary training—to heart. They ensured that their professional degree was both practice-oriented *and* academically rigorous.[110] When the School of Education revised its teacher training curriculum, it decided to manage a teacher candidate's path to licensure through what they call three "gateway points." At the end of each gateway point, the candidate must pass a designated assessment, ensuring competency along the way—not unlike some of the module-based alternative programs.

Gateway I, for example, is formal acceptance into a candidate's chosen teacher education major at the end of their sophomore year. Although prospective teacher education candidates enroll in entry-level education classes during their freshman and sophomore years, a prospective teacher candidate is only officially admitted to the program once they have acquired junior standing and proven successful in their early coursework. Successful undergraduate applicants must maintain a cumulative GPA of 2.75 or higher, as well as a passing grade in four English and communications courses and two introductory education courses. To pass the first stage, applicants must also demonstrate competency in basic skills through specified standardized test scores and the successful completion of a written case analysis and an in-person interview with professional educators.[111] In short, not everyone gets in.

The School of Education aims to educate teachers within the context of a liberal arts education, requiring candidates to fulfill at least 120 credit hours within a general education curriculum.[112] Secondary education majors are also required to fulfill specific requirements in their chosen content area, such as math or history. Irrespective of grade level or subject, all candidates must complete three components: methods (pedagogy) courses, field experiences and school visits to a variety of schools, and two semesters of student teaching. Methods courses begin in a teacher education candidate's sophomore year and take place on site at local elementary and secondary schools. Courses on classroom diversity, management, special needs, and technology in the classroom are taken by all undergraduate teacher education majors.

The School of Education faculty also decided that teacher candidates needed exposure to a range of classroom environments in the early years of the major, followed by admission to a "professional semester" of two ten-week student teaching placements in the candidate's senior year (Gateway II). Giving its teacher candidates classroom experience from the start is a source of pride and again serves as a model of innovation.[113] For all teacher candidates familiarity with classrooms begins in the freshman year, even before being officially accepted into the major, through visits to urban and suburban schools as part of their preliminary requirements. Sophomores also formally observe classrooms, and juniors engage in a series of off-campus "field experiences" in which they directly interact with student populations in surrounding townships in the role of math and literacy tutors. The School of Education considers field experiences an integral part of the teacher education program; this importance is borne out in the separate course numbers under which these experiences are listed.[114] Within these field experiences, teacher candidates begin to develop a portfolio composed of lesson plans, reflections on pedagogy, analysis of student work, and videos of their teaching practice. The school requires an average of twenty supervised hours of field experiences before teacher education majors begin at their student teaching placement.[115]

A teacher education candidate begins Gateway III after completing both student teaching placements. Ultimately, the candidate submits a teaching portfolio to demonstrate his or her ability to integrate pedagogical theory with effective teaching practice.[116] Only after the candidate has achieved a satisfactory grade on the portfolio and maintained a cumulative grade point average of 2.75 or higher will the school recommend a candidate for Indiana state licensure. The undergraduate education major now offers eighteen specializations that lead to state licensure, ranging from elementary education to Spanish and German at the secondary level. Additional licenses are also available, including special education, through a Mild Intervention certificate, and a Technology certificate, leading to licensure in the growing field of educational technology.

In addition to an undergraduate program, the UIndy's School of Education offers a thirty-six-credit Master of Arts in Teaching (MAT), geared toward those already holding undergraduate training in a content area. Cohorts of twelve to sixteen are selected in the spring through a similarly rigorous admissions process as the undergraduate program. Completion of the MAT is then spread over three semesters, spanning fifteen months in total. The structure of the program draws from innovations in alternative certification programs, in that students begin and travel as a cohort throughout their training, and the structure of the program allows for students to continue full-time employment while they attend evening and weekend classes. Unlike the undergraduate program, graduate teacher education candidates also engage in a single semester of full-time student teaching. Satisfactory completion of a student teaching experience and teaching portfolio leads to recommendation for Indiana state licensure.

Arguably the most significant reform work began in 2008, when UIndy partnered with the Woodrow Wilson National Fellowship Program to devise a new clinical residency model for STEM teachers. Based in Princeton, New Jersey, the Woodrow Wilson National Fellowship Foundation is a non-profit organization committed to funding the education of future leaders. In 2006, under the leadership of former Teachers College president Arthur Levine, the foundation launched a new program of teaching fellowships designed to fill a growing national need for top-flight teachers. The teaching fellowships establish new clinical-based teacher residency programs to prepare highly effective science, math, and technology teachers in high-needs urban schools. As the foundation set out to find partner institutions, it recognized existing innovation as well as potential for further development in UIndy and eventually selected it as the only private college partner in the foundation's state-wide initiative to develop new clinical residency teaching fellowships in Indiana.[117]

In the summer of 2008, stakeholders from UIndy's School of Education gathered around the table with representatives from three surrounding urban school districts, the College of Arts and Sciences, and foundation representatives to design the new program and its curriculum. Drawing on innovations from both within and outside of schools of education, they turned to places like the Chicago and Boston teacher residencies and Linda Darling-Hammond's work at Stanford for inspiration, exemplifying an open attitude toward innovation, not rejecting solid ideas just because they began outside of the traditional university setting.

The resulting program is similar to the MAT but with a few additional components that make it a unique residency and mentor-supported experience. The process begins when a cooperating mentor teacher agrees to host a fellow in his or her classroom for the entire year. The mentor teacher then receives training prior to each semester to ensure that the candidate's experience is meaningful and aligned to the program's curricular and pedagogical philosophy. The mentor teachers also remain highly involved in the planning process, furthering their stake in the program. The fellows themselves start their journeys in the summer, after being accepted through a highly selective application process. They undergo intensive training on working with diverse learners, content standards, and core concepts in their disciplines, all part of an "educators as decision makers" curriculum.

In the fall, fellows begin observing in their mentor teachers' classrooms from day one of the school year and slowly segue into assisting with various teaching activities. Eventually the fellows teach full lessons under the guidance of their mentors. This all takes place during half-days for three of the five days of the work week, when the fellows are school-based. The other half of these days are used to visit a variety of school settings to observe classrooms in both traditional public and charter schools in the three partner districts. The other two days of the week are spent on campus-based coursework, which reflects a rich and varied professional approach and includes everything from child psychology to methods to equity and diversity courses. Fellows begin teaching a full-course load by March, with the continued support of their mentor teacher. They also meet weekly with a Woodrow Wilson Foundation director and clinical supervisor for in-time, personalized support. Students are encouraged to participate in state, regional, or national professional organization conferences for their appropriate content area.

By June, when the school year ends, fellows will have completed a substantial capstone project. After the official fellowship year, once fellows are hired in a high-needs urban district, they are assigned a content-specific mentor teacher who continues to provide targeted support and feedback, guided by Charlotte Danielson's *Enhancing Professional Practice: A Framework for Teaching* as the underlying mentoring framework.[118] Fellows also continue to attend occasional weekend workshops, and they develop, present, and execute personalized professional development plans in their first three years.[119]

The program has largely been hailed as a success. It boasts a 100% placement record, and many graduates have gone on to win awards of excellence in their districts. In January 2016, the Indiana Commission for Higher Education awarded the Woodrow Wilson Foundation another $1.3 million to train STEM teachers, a part of which will go toward UIndy's fellows program. Furthermore, in 2011 the Carnegie Corporation chose UIndy as one of only five recipients nation-wide for its 100Kin10 initiative, which aims to train 100,000 high-quality STEM teachers in the next ten years.[120] As part of this initiative, the National Science Foundation's Robert Noyce Teacher Scholarship program also granted UIndy $1.2 million to fund twenty-six Noyce Grant Scholars, who receive financial assistance to complete a rigorous one-year clinical master's degree in an innovative $(STEM)^3$ program, intended to meet the increasing demand for STEM teaching jobs state-wide, particularly in high-needs districts.[121] Dow AgroSciences likewise pledged money through the 100Kin10 initiative to further fund the Woodrow Wilson STEM scholars.[122]

Teacher educators active in UIndy's STEM Fellows program note a few key components to the program's success, characteristics they encourage other university-based programs to adopt. For one, their relationship to the faculty in the arts and sciences is strong. The Association of Independent Liberal Arts Colleges of Teacher Education recognized UIndy's College of Education as a program of distinction for its collaboration with the College of Arts and Sciences, particularly in relation to the CELL. Both the College of Arts and Sciences and the School of Education collaborated in 2008 to develop the new Woodrow Wilson Teaching Fellowship Program, arts and sciences faculty have consistently been at the table during teacher education curriculum decisions, and arts and sciences faculty tenure decisions recognize work done in collaboration with the School of Education.[123]

The teacher educators do cite several challenges for university-based clinical residency programs, including balancing the faculty's right to design their own courses with the need to provide a holistic, collaboratively developed, and uniform curriculum; balancing time between coursework and clinical practice; responding to students' real-time needs while maintaining a core curriculum; and integrating families and communities into the training process. Yet they also note that through strong relationships, by bringing all stakeholders to the program design and revision process, and by altering academic structural hurdles that prevent meaningful collaboration across campus and with districts and communities, they have been able to manage these challenges. For example, they have succeeded in revising tenure requirements and in altering the residency calendar to reflect the local schools' calendars and not that of the university.

Another key component of all UIndy STEM teacher education programs is the commitment to project-based learning (PBL), which aligns with many state-wide initiatives in K–12 schools. This approach attempts to increase retention of material through in-depth projects. UIndy teacher education faculty mirror this form of pedagogy themselves as much as possible, so that teacher candidates are familiar with teaching and learning in this format.

UIndy also cites their foundation partners as crucial to program operation, noting that they could not afford to run the program without the partnership of the Woodrow Wilson Foundation and funding from places like Carnegie, DOW, the Noyce Foundation, and the state Department of Education (although faculty also note that this reliance on outside funding continues to pose a challenge). UIndy's experience demonstrates the need for policymakers to fund teacher education adequately, for foundations to concentrate on such programs to achieve high-leverage impact, and for universities to stop treating these programs as "cash cows" and instead value them as key links between universities and the communities in which they reside. Countries with the highest quality teacher education, like Finland and Singapore, make professional teacher education free or highly affordable, ensuring that quality candidates are attracted to the profession and do not graduate with high levels of debt into a low-paying field. In an era of ballooning university tuition, this is all the more necessary.[124]

School of Education faculty members also note that being proactive about new state and federal policies that affect teacher education remains crucial to their success. When the Obama administration announced new policies encouraging states to rank teacher preparation programs, and Indiana passed their law in 2010 to do so, UIndy faculty joined a consortium with other teacher educators to ensure that they had concrete ideas to bring to the table regarding how programs should be evaluated—a far cry from the hostile relationship between education reform governors and the superintendents who revolted in the 1980s and 1990s against their local schools of education.

UIndy's university-based innovation also reflects a larger state-wide trend. While education-school bashing continues in some quarters, and teaching programs still fight an uphill battle in terms of public perception in the face of growing alternative route programs, many schools of education across the state have made important reforms in the last decade in an attempt to improve the Hoosier state's teaching pool. Teaching fellows programs at Butler University, the University of Indiana, Purdue University, Ball State University, Valparaiso University, and IUPUI (the joint Indiana University/Purdue University at Indianapolis campus), to name a few, have all taken steps to reform and meet the changing demands put forward by new state and federal legislation that calls for greater accountability. Butler University's College of Education Dean Ena Shelley, for example, told the *Indiana Star* that in relation to the new teacher evaluations, she wants to see portfolios, peer reviews, and parent surveys, among other metrics, included in the final ratings of education schools.[125] Most importantly, however, she wants the state Department of Education to include her and her fellow teacher educators in the process: "It would be a real travesty if they don't, because we have so much to offer to one another. This isn't about power and control."[126]

In an era when education schools faced intense external scrutiny and often internal administrative pressure, not all succumbed under the weight of the challenge. Many, like the University of Indianapolis, took action in the belief that quality teacher preparation is possible through careful program design that draws on the best innovations developed in and outside of the university under the guidance of professional teacher educators.

Go Online, Young Man: Western Governors University

Western Governors University (WGU), which now enrolls a total of 16,000 teacher candidates in its undergraduate and graduate programs, did not originally plan to prepare teachers. Instead, it began as an online university in the midst of the 1990s tech boom, bent on shaking up the broader world of higher education by revolutionizing its institutional structure. Gone were the days of the Carnegie Unit, WGU boosters proclaimed, the outdated system that determined credits by hours of "seat time" instead of learning outcomes. And gone were the days of large brick-and-mortar colleges and universities, making way for an era of online distance learning where students could earn a degree from anywhere, at any time, and at their own pace—as long as they had access to a high-speed Internet connection.

Western Governors University takes its name from its founders, a group of nineteen governors from western states who announced the idea for a new online, non-profit, regional university at a conference in 1995. Led by governors Roy Romer of Colorado and Mike Leavitt of Utah, the group placed its new idea at the intersection of three colliding developments: rising college enrollments across the West, shrinking state budgets unable to fund more campuses for two- and four-year colleges, and a dot-com bubble that exuded energy and faith in "disruptive technologies" like online education.[127] For Romer, the chief concern was workforce development and a move to competency-based education from what he viewed as anachronistic measures of seat time. Leavitt's priority was to take advantage of the Internet, especially to serve potential college students in remote western settings who could not travel to a college campus.

Thus came the first ever "high-tech regional university." The announcement immediately garnered attention from the media, politicians, tech enthusiasts, business leaders, and voices in higher education. Many inside the education establishment raised skeptical eyebrows, but political opposition proved slight. "I haven't sensed any state at all saying this is dumb and we shouldn't be doing this," Jeff Livingston, Utah's WGU coordinator, noted in 1996. "No one has said they won't join."[128] Other enthusiastic supporters voiced their approval as well. "This will put education in the hands of people who can't take advantage of a traditional college because they're working or live too far away or can't leave home," WGU representatives explained. "It won't replace the present university system but expand it to new markets."[129] The idea was perfect for the unique landscape of the West, spokespeople further argued, with its vast stretches of land and rural populations. "Imagine: A Bonners Ferry worker could learn electronics at his kitchen-table computer, taking classes via Internet after his shift at the sawmill. A mother in Omak, Washington, could, through two-way video hookup, realize her dream of getting a teaching degree," a reporter from the *Spokane Review* mused in a November 1996 article.[130] "The genie is out of the bottle," announced Governor Phil Batt of Idaho that same year.[131] A new era in higher education had begun.

Nevertheless, expansion was slower than some of the school's initial proponents hoped. Online learning was new. Potential students as well as education theorists were skeptical of such a vastly different enterprise from what they knew from their own educational pasts. And places like the University of Phoenix, whose online programs were also on the rise and gaining a bad reputation in many circles as diploma mills, were not helping the cause. The revolution therefore did not happen quickly, and those involved in WGU's creation have admitted that the project faced difficulties in its infant years. Leaders busied themselves with extensive public relations campaigns that gained them flashy headlines, often at the expense of hammering out the gritty details of operations and development.[132] The university's mission also seemed unclear in the beginning, as the WGU administration struggled to decide which degree programs it should offer and eventually opened with just two associate's degrees, one in arts and one in applied science in electronic manufacturing technology. When the university opened its virtual doors in 1998, it struggled to attract enrollment and fell far short of budget projections. Meanwhile, the dot-com bubble began to burst, causing a crisis of faith in the transformative power of online anything. In its early years, the long-term success of WGU was far from inevitable.

At the turn of the millennium the "Virtual U" received a boost, though. In 2001, then-president George W. Bush proposed the No Child Left Behind (NCLB) Act, which passed through Congress with strong bipartisan support. Among other new rules and regulations, the act mandated a "highly qualified teacher" in every classroom. Suddenly, a high demand existed for programs that could grant the "highly-qualified" status. Since WGU was the brainchild of the state governors themselves, few state-level legal barriers prevented WGU from playing a hand in the teacher preparation game.

In late 2001, WGU's then-president Robert Mendenhall and Governor Leavitt met with Bush's Secretary of Education Rod Paige to discuss the possibility of an online teacher preparation program. After sitting quietly through much of the conversation, Paige eventually announced, "I like it."[133] In 2002, WGU received a $10 million federal grant to begin planning its teacher preparation curriculum, and other federal funds followed. In designing the curriculum, WGU's leaders called on a variety of stakeholders, but most of all they involved school superintendents, whom they asked to describe what they saw as the skills and attributes needed for teachers in their districts. From the planning stages onward, WGU's teacher preparation curriculum was more superintendent-driven than university education school–driven. Not surprisingly, superintendents liked it that way. Like other WGU programs, the question of "industry" needs came first. Capitalizing on these trends, the university opened its Teachers College in 2003.[134]

By the early 2000s the national debate about teacher education had been in full swing for two decades, with traditional colleges of education no longer credited as the only valid preparers of K–12 teachers. More and more people looked to alternatives like competency-based curricula and online tools as the future. President George W. Bush, as a previous western governor who expressed support for the program, also gave the model backing from the White House. Thus, not only did WGU receive federal funding in the form of grants at a crucial moment in its institutional development, but the Higher Education Act listed WGU explicitly by name so that students could use federally subsidized loans for tuition there. Sure enough, online teacher preparation proved to be a winning strategy. Enrollment climbed, particularly after WGU gained NCATE accreditation in 2008, and expanded exponentially thereafter. WGU is now available as a pathway to teacher certification in all fifty states, a vision that went beyond even the original dreams and confident talk of the western governors.

Currently, the university offers both bachelor's and master's degrees in information technology, nursing, and business, in addition to its largest field—teaching, which makes up about two-thirds of total enrollment, according to 2006 numbers.[135] WGU's Teachers College offers seventeen degrees, including bachelor's and master's degrees, as well as post-baccalaureate licensure programs, in various K–12 fields, and a master's in educational leadership. By 2017, WGU had not only far exceeded the competition in terms of sheer number of enrolled students, but also surprised many when it was ranked first out of over 800 programs in preparing middle and high school teachers in NCTQ's 2014 rankings. Nevertheless, the question remains whether online teacher preparation is the exciting new frontier of teacher education, or if we should be wary of the great unknown. Are not-for-profit online programs "diploma mills" akin to the University of Phoenix or a bold new platform to democratize quality teacher training? WGU perhaps suggests a bit of both: that new models need to be managed with great care, but that they also hold great potential.

In order to answer these questions, it is important to know what teacher preparation looks like at an online university. The WGU model is somewhat different from its original incarnation. Students still complete degrees based on competencies and not credits, but the experience has improved in a number of ways since the university's opening. Each teacher candidate, for example, is assigned a personal mentor who helps students design an individualized study plan. Students then take classes at their own pace via the WGU online learning platform, with average time to completion for a bachelor's degree ranging from two to two-and-one-half years for those with some college credits in hand, and four to five years for those who start fresh. Students can speed the process along by demonstrating early success with competencies they already possess; for example, if an engineer decides to switch careers and gain licensure in high school physics, they could theoretically pass through the math and science requirements quickly. Students also work on their own schedules, whether late at night or during the daytime, a perk intended to benefit those with jobs or childcare duties, though the program recommends devoting around twenty hours per week of study. Perhaps most important, particularly in the field of teacher preparation, the online nature of WGU's programs means that someone living in an isolated rural area can prepare to be a teacher in their own town without leaving home or family. In response to the oft-voiced complaint that a young person from a small town who attends the campus of a state university seldom wants to return home, WGU allows a not-so-young person with family responsibilities to stay where they are, prepare to be a teacher, and teach close to home, an especially important concern in the kinds of isolated places where teacher shortages are the most acute.

Teacher candidates must pass a wide range of competencies, complete a curriculum meant to impart the same type of learning as a liberal arts education for bachelor's degree candidates, and advanced learning at the master's level. A candidate securing a bachelor's degree in secondary mathematics education, for example, must take several college-level mathematics courses as well as liberal arts requirements such as English composition and a U.S. history survey, in addition to courses on content-related pedagogy, educational psychology, classroom management, engagement and motivation, and "fundamentals of diversity, inclusion, and exceptional learners." The curriculum is overseen by an Education Program Council, a seven-member group consisting of professors of education with PhDs in the field, as well as current and former school superintendents, and Sharon Robinson, former president and CEO of the American Association of Colleges for Teacher Education (AACTE).[136] A move away from superintendent output and a focus on state-level and CAEP compliance has tended to make the curriculum shaped more by accreditation agency requirements than by faculty input in recent years, however.

Courses are all online, often consisting of both print and online textbook lessons, web-based tutorials, and online simulations (see Figure 3 for an example of what a module looks like). If students desire, they can also have access to online learning communities of peers, though there are few to no real-time interactive learning experiences during coursework, since students are encouraged to complete lessons at their own pace and on their own schedule. Emphasis also tends to be on completion and progress, rather than on learning and inquisitiveness.

Although modules are pre-designed, if students have questions they

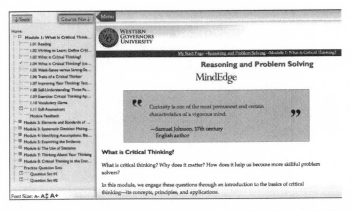

FIGURE 3. Example of a module in an online course offered through Western Governors University. Students complete modules at their own pace through an online platform. *Source*: Western Governors University, https://www.wgu.edu/sites/wgu .edu/files/custom_uploads/SampleLearningResourceMindEdge.png

can reach out to mentors and course faculty for clarification on subject matter. They are also provided with additional learning resources, such as e-textbooks, online modules, study guides, simulations, and virtual labs. Students can communicate with other students through a mix of blogs, chat rooms, and discussion portals if they so desire. Yet many students, concerned with proving competency quickly, go it alone. Course faculty and student mentors are required to hold a master's degree in their subject, and each course is overseen by a PhD-holding content expert who helps design the curriculum. The responsibilities of different faculty sometimes cause confusion, but as WGU's President Scott Pulsipher explained to National Public Radio:

- **Program faculty** include outside experts from academia and business, who decide what should be taught at a high level. Program faculty also design curricula, working backward from necessary skills, called competencies, to create content and design assessments.
- **Course faculty** have specific expertise in a given topic. They may give feedback on student work, run discussion groups, or work directly with students who are falling behind.
- Finally, each student has a single assigned **program mentor** for his or her entire time at WGU. Mentors have advanced degrees in the student's discipline: health sciences, IT, business, or education. They help students

understand the content, and connect what they are learning in different courses; they also assist with project planning and assessment scheduling. Emotional support is part of the job description. Pulsipher says program mentors reach out to their students by email, phone, and text at least once a week, much more if students are struggling.[137]

Various assessments, such as multiple-choice tests, portfolio assignments, research projects, and essays, prove competency on a pass/fail basis. These assessments are evaluated by WGU subject-area mentors and are overseen by an Assessment Program Council to ensure quality and rigor. Students have the option of taking their multiple-choice exams remotely, with webcam monitoring by WGU proctors.

Once students master WGU's competency modules, teacher candidates embark on a clinical teaching component. WGU breaks with its general commitment to online learning when it comes to student teaching; it partners with schools to hire mentor teachers to provide in-person, on-site clinical training. Candidates first undergo a pre-clinical experience, observing lessons from experienced teachers and writing sample lesson plans. Then candidates complete a twelve- to twenty-week "demonstration" or student teaching experience in a local district where they are evaluated on performance by an on-site WGU supervisor. At their schools, candidates receive feedback and are evaluated by their mentor teachers as well as WGU specialists, who conduct in-person visits at least six times—twice as many visits as in some traditional university programs. To graduate, proficiency in the classroom must be demonstrated, a fact WGU likes to tout.[138] Kate Walsh of NCTQ stated, "The instrument Western Governors uses to determine whether teachers are ready for the classroom is one of the best in the country."[139] Candidates also produce a teaching portfolio at the end of their degrees, which includes a philosophy of teaching statement, as well as a resume and proof of in-classroom success in the clinical component. WGU then mentors candidates through state-specific licensure requirements.

WGU prides itself on its low cost, an issue of increasing importance as tuition rises in more traditional public and private universities, and as teaching salaries remain stagnant. Students pay a flat rate of under $6,000 per semester, meaning they are incentivized to complete modules as quickly as possible. If a candidate finishes the bachelor's program in the standard four years (the usual time it takes to complete an undergraduate degree at most institutions), the program will cost around $48,000 total—a significant investment, but around half the cost of most other preparation programs, including online and traditional campus competitors like the University of

Phoenix and Grand Canyon University.[140] Most WGU candidates finish in much less time, generally four to six semesters. While WGU seeks grants and state funds for new program development and special projects, the core instructional budget is completely tuition funded. It aims to avoid a situation where it must close a program because of a shortage of grant funding. The fact that WGU owns and maintains no real estate beyond administrative office space in Salt Lake City and pays its mentors—as faculty, all of whom work from home, are called—solely for their mentoring work and not for time devoted to research makes the low tuition possible.

WGU's Teachers College can claim, with some convincing metrics, that it *is* a high-quality program, despite being fully online and its faculty producing no research of its own. Although WGU initially struggled to gain accreditation, it became the first online teacher preparation program to do so when it received NCATE recognition in 2008.[141] The much-discussed 2014 NCTQ rankings, which placed WGU first in middle and secondary preparation programs, gave the school new, if controversial, status.[142] Although WGU's elementary program was ranked lower by NCTQ, it still placed at the top of the list for some western states. WGU representatives and enthusiasts also highlight the fact that WGU succeeds where traditional programs fail: in attracting diverse and previously unreached populations. Flexible online programs, they argue, allow parents to simultaneously fulfill childcare duties and study for a teaching degree, or the late-in-life career changer to keep earning income while training for entry into the classroom. Statistics confirm some of these claims. The average age of WGU students is thirty-six, 19% of students are people of color, 33% live in rural areas, and 41% have parents who never went to college—all demographics that policymakers would like to draw into the teaching force in larger numbers. WGU has also conducted surveys that reported very high satisfaction rates by principals and superintendents, an expected response given their primary input into the curricular design from the beginning.[143] In one survey, 99% of employers agreed that WGU graduates met or exceeded expectations.[144]

The quality of a WGU education, however, was greatly called into question in September 2017, following an audit by the U.S. Department of Education's (USDOE) Office of the Inspector General. After a much-anticipated report, the USDOE concluded that 62% of students were enrolled in courses not meeting the standards of Title IV of the Higher Education Act, guidelines outlined by the USDOE to guard against risks in involved in distance learning. The report called on WGU to return at least $713 million in federal financial aid. Specifically, the relationship between faculty mentors and students was determined to be lacking the necessary substance required by distance-learning courses as outlined by the 1992 federal law and clarified by a 2006 revision. WGU's program instead fell under the model of a "correspondence course." The report noted that interaction was not substantive or required in many programs, and often occurred only at the initiative of the student. Although the report did not specify which courses failed to meet the requirements, and therefore the compliance rate within the Teachers College is unknown, the report nonetheless dealt a harsh blow to WGU and its reputation, and provided fodder to those critical of online competency education. "The audit's findings should be taken very seriously, as the regular and substantive interaction requirement draws a clear distinction between self-learning and education and protects the integrity of federal student aid programs," associate professor of education at George Mason University and former Obama administration deputy assistant secretary for higher education Spiros Protopsaltis said.[145]

The school's representatives and other voices championing competency education challenged the Inspector General's findings. Moreover, they critiqued Title IV, claiming that it was premised on an outdated definition of faculty and distance learning incompatible with changing educational structures as represented by new competency models. Senior vice president for government and public affairs at the American Council on Education Terry Hartle, for example, told *Inside Higher Ed* that that the Inspector General had applied an obsolete, twentieth-century definition to a twenty-first-century institution: "At the end of the day, we need a clear federal policy toward definition of 'online education.' Until we have that, we are dealing with round pegs and square holes."[146] WGU also critiqued the law, while contending that it did comply with all legal regulations. WGU president Scott Pulsipher stated, "We vehemently disagree with the inspector general's opinion. We've been compliant with the law and regulations since our founding."[147] Others point out that the school had and continues to enjoy strong bipartisan support. The Obama administration often praised WGU, and the Trump administration is not likely to follow through on the Inspector General's recommendations. The recent controversy, however, brings to light the need for more legal clarity on the ever-expanding frontier of online education, as well as the need to define what, exactly, defines teaching at the university-level and who should responsibly be called a university teacher, including a teacher educator.[148]

Critics point to other drawbacks of the model and caution potential teacher candidates and policymakers against becoming overly excited about the promise of online programs such as WGU. After all, the verdict is still out on the efficacy of online education in general and for teacher preparation in particular. There is no conclusive evidence that affirms the quality of such programs, and many criticize the metrics that the NCTQ report used to rank WGU so highly.[149] Of course there are no widely accepted metrics for affirming the quality of more traditional programs either, and those measures that do exist—like value-added measures—are subject to intense debate. Nevertheless, critics worry that the field of online teacher preparation is expanding too rapidly without the benefit of time-tested results and recommend more small-scale pilot programs before many new teachers enter the classroom through this pathway. Moreover, while WGU boasts that it successfully reaches previously underserved populations, others point out that online education keeps already isolated populations isolated, as students have less incentive to travel to college campuses to meet people of other backgrounds, leading to more race and class stratification. Some critics point to what seems to be low graduation rates at WGU—only 40% of enrolled students actually finish to completion, which skeptics say speaks to the allure of online education but its ultimate weakness. On the other hand, traditional campuses apart from elite universities have similar problems. In WGU's home states, Utah State has a four-year graduation rate of 28.6% and a five-year rate of 44%, while the University of Wyoming maintains a four-year rate of only 26% and a five-year rate of 50%.

Others have pilloried WGU as a "university without intellectuals," that is, a program that will provide the needed licensure and certification but not an actual professional education. Competency-based programs, some argue, reflect a vision of education that boils all knowledge down to measurable skills and facts, to the detriment of more nebulous but highly valuable aspects such as critical thinking, intellectual curiosity, learning how to interact with a diverse group of peers, and the ability to choose one's own teaching philosophy after being presented with the full range of thinking on that topic. In so doing, critics claim, these types of programs bow to the whims of business and district interests who want compliant yet skilled workers and not a more autonomous and critical teaching body. As education scholar Johann Neem writes, "The problem is that the very thing that makes WGU valuable for certification—its competency-based approach—prevents it from providing the kinds of learning experiences that define liberal arts college education." Such programs therefore help "students pass the licensing exams, but [they do] not help them become drivers."[150]

Debates, of course, remain whether teacher preparation *should* mirror a traditional liberal arts education, and whether face-to-face time with professors and other students is actually valuable or if the same type of rigorous learning can happen through an online, or at least a blended, interface.

No studies conclusively prove that online education is better or worse than traditional campuses. In fact, WGU argues that it does, in fact, provide the rich, professional curriculum that combines theory, practice, and content that can be found at other universities—it just happens on a computer. This makes WGU different than something like the Relay Graduate School of Education, which also embraces the competency approach but focuses on skills far more than on learning theory and content knowledge. Another camp of opponents, however, cites online programs and their federal support as excuses by state and federal governments to continue defunding traditional public institutions of higher education and education schools in particular.

In these early years of online education, credibility is perhaps the biggest hurdle. Online learning is radically different from what happens in a traditional college, and it is hard for many to adjust. Many still question the validity of online programs, seeing them more as diploma mills than as reputable institutions of learning or professional training, even when they are not for profit. In the world of higher education, where brand matters, WGU still lacks cultural capital, even when those making these judgments do not know much about the program. Massive degree-granting online programs, some argue, hurt the status of teachers; if anyone can earn a teaching degree online, it cannot be that serious of a profession. This view is beginning to change as online education expands and universities that *do* have brand-name credibility enter the fray. The University of Southern California (USC) has thoroughly embraced online teacher preparation and now offers fully online master's programs that promise to democratize high-quality, holistic teacher preparation. Others, including our own home at New York University (NYU), are also launching fully online master's programs. Neither USC nor NYU are at the low end of the status spectrum, so they may in time lift the status of online teacher preparation across the board.[151] Faith in Silicon Valley–style "disruptive innovations" and "social entrepreneurship" likewise continues to grow, lending more integrity to new tech-based solutions that draw on startup lingo to promise "high-leverage practices," "twenty-first-century tools," and "innovative technology platforms" to revolutionize the way that education schools "do business." Yet with that growth and visibility comes increased and justifiable criticism.

As technology continues to take over more aspects of daily life in the twenty-first century, it is unclear whether the burden now falls on the defenders of traditional programs to make the case for themselves, or the other way around. Similar to establishment-based opponents of alternative certification in the 1980s, something more than self-interest needs to convince policymakers and teacher candidates that what happens in-person and in traditional classroom settings matters. And something more than affordable tuition needs to convince those same candidates, hiring principals, and the public that what happens online is legitimate. The fate of the new frontier is yet unknown.

Conclusion

The preceding case studies focus on institutions that have responded to the challenges of the last thirty years—whether that response was the closing of old programs and the reopening of new ones, a recommitment to programmatic excellence, or a fundamental rethinking of the institutional direction in teacher education. The examples given are but a few of the many that could be offered. From California to Maine, institutions public and private, large and small, elite and non-elite have developed significantly new approaches to teacher education on their campuses. But is it also important to note that although there are many institutions of higher education that belong in this category, there are others that have not done so.

As we have said, we take seriously Harry Judge's observation that efforts to restructure teacher education "stalled (which is not to say terminated) when the colleges and schools of education had to think seriously about reforming themselves. They will change only when they really wish to, and not enough yet do."[152] This judgment remains true in the second decade of the twenty-first century. There are university-based programs in every part of the United States that have done very little to seriously reform themselves. As state governments or accrediting agencies have added requirements, they have complied. As public pressure has demanded some reforms, they have made them. But the changes have been minimal and too often grudging. It is far easier to explain why calls for change are misguided—from blaming neoliberal market forces to continuing to critique efforts to evaluate programs—than it is to make change. Faculty politics in departments and schools make maintaining the status quo far easier than undergoing deep-seated change. Different faculty factions can quickly checkmate each other. Faculty reward systems encourage individual scholarly productivity, often at the expense of the investment of time that curricular reform demands.

Arthur Levine's 2006 work in the Education Schools Project found that there were 1,206 schools, colleges, and departments of education in the United States, located at 78% of all four-year colleges and universities. Levine notes, "They award one out of every 12 bachelor's diplomas; a quarter of all master's degrees; and 15 percent of all doctorates, more than any other branch of the Academy."[153] Other studies have used slightly different but similar numbers. While battles rage between proponents of university-based programs and those devoted to alternative routes, and while many on all sides use international comparisons to critique their opponents, the very diversity among schools of education in the United States and the very size of the enterprise makes most generalizations about their work meaningless.[154]

When Linda Darling-Hammond calls for increased professionalization of teacher preparation through improved certification programs on college campuses, she also notes, "Education schools have been variously criticized as ineffective in preparing teachers for their work, unresponsive to new demands, remote from practice, and barriers to the recruitment of bright college students into teaching."[155] The reality is that both sides of the coin are true. There are university programs that have done amazing work in professionalizing their efforts, raising standards, and, as Darling-Hammond asks, moving to "prepare teachers for more adaptive, knowledge-based practice, while simultaneously tackling the redesign of schools and teaching."[156] But there have been others that have been every bit as ineffective, unresponsive, and remote as the critics charge. To try to paint all programs with the same brush is to misunderstand the very nature of campus politics and twenty-first-century teacher preparation.

CHAPTER THREE

The New Hybrids

I N THE SPRING OF 2016, the *Hechinger Report* and *The Atlantic* published a three-part series on the current state of teacher education. They profiled three teachers, one from a traditional university-based education school, one from the quick-prep TNTP (formerly The New Teacher Project) Teaching Fellows program, and one from the Urban Teachers Residency in Washington, DC. While each installment revealed the challenges first-year teachers face in America's public schools, from quieting chattering students to providing sufficient levels of rigor, the last part of the series implied that a hybrid residency approach, which includes a full year of classroom apprenticeship coupled with coursework, provided the best preparation before assuming one's own classroom.[1] As the series asks, can residencies and other hybrid models lead to better-prepared, life-long educators?

Many education experts and commentators seem to think so, hailing residencies and other hybrid models that combine elements of traditional and alternative programs as the future of teacher preparation. In the first two decades of the new millennium, a groundswell of new institutional models for teacher education arose, attempting to draw the best of traditional university-level education together with the benefits of alternative routes. This effort often translates into some form of school-based, year-long clinical training paired with coursework embedded in the clinical experience rather than prior to it, all before a teacher candidate assumes the position of lead classroom instructor. Reminiscent of Ernest Boyer's suggestion after he chaired the Panel on the Preparation of Beginning Teachers in New Jersey in 1984 (see chapter 1), perhaps the ideal professional training for a K–12 educator happens in some sort of institutional hybrid that brings in various stakeholders from institutions of higher learning and public schools.

University-based teacher educator Kenneth Zeichner notes, "There has also been a growth in hybrid programs (e.g., urban teacher residencies) that are centered in a rigorous clinically-based education for teaching under the supervision of an experienced teacher which offer the potential to utilize the strengths of both university and school-based teacher educators. Carefully structured and well-supervised clinical experiences like those that exist in the education of other professionals [are] absolutely essential for the education of teachers no matter what pathway into teaching is taken."[2] Seth Andrew, founder of Democracy Prep Public Charter Schools, agrees; in a statement before the U.S. House Subcommittee on Early Childhood Education, Elementary and Secondary Education in 2012 he noted, "We have a problem of quality. And we need to find more quality people coming into the profession. And we need to be agnostic about how they got there."[3]

Such hybrid programs could include district-based residencies, like the ones in Boston, Denver, and Chicago; new stand-alone graduate schools of education like Relay Graduate School of Education (Relay GSE); teaching "academies," such as the new Woodrow Wilson Academy of Teaching and Learning; or even charter-chain preparation pipelines that train teachers for specific school environments, such as High Tech High in California or the more controversial Success Academy in New York City. The most recent large-scale philanthropic effort to reform teacher education, the 2015 $34.7 million Gates Foundation program to create innovative "transformation centers" for teacher preparation supports this catholic attitude toward preparation route, funding alternative providers, district-based hybrids through the National Center for Teacher Residencies and the Massachusetts Department of Education, and traditional programs at the University of Michigan and Texas State University—very much reflecting the changing tenor of the teacher preparation debate that transcends the university versus alternative divide.[4] This chapter will explore these new hybrid models and attempt to evaluate their potential for the future of American teacher preparation.

Residency Models

District-based residency programs are of relatively recent vintage, but in their roughly decade-long existence they have managed to garner accolades from both alternative certification advocates and the staunchest supporters of teacher professionalization. Former President Barack Obama, former Secretary of Education Arne Duncan, and philanthropist Melinda Gates, all alternative route supporters, have expressed enthusiastic public support for district-based residencies and made site visits to the first such program in Boston.[5] In a 2008 *Phi Delta Kappan* article, teacher professionalization crusader Linda Darling-Hammond also sang the model's praises, noting, "The teaching residency model holds particular promise for addressing the problems of teacher preparation, recruitment, and retention for high-need districts—and may constitute one of the most important reforms of teacher education generally."[6] The 2008 bipartisan reauthorization of the Higher Education Opportunity Act also allocated $300 million toward strengthening district and university teacher preparation partnerships, with a large portion of that money supporting clinical residency programs.[7]

The model was first created by people with the same disenchantment about the university-based teacher education system that fueled the New Jersey alternative route, Teach for America, and programs like Relay GSE. Yet it also drew from some early recommendations in the Holmes and Carnegie reports, which encouraged clinical training and district partnerships through professional development schools. Tim Knowles, formerly the director of the Urban Teacher Education Program (UTEP) and Urban Labs research institute at the University of Chicago, has no qualms about the fact that residencies act as a "competitive threat" to traditional university-based programs. Self-identifying as falling outside the alternative certification movement, however, residencies act more like apprenticeships with ties to a university than earlier fast-track alternative programs like Teach for America (TFA). These programs do not ask whether preparation is necessary or theory is valuable, Boston Teacher Residency's founding director Jesse Solomon explains, but seek to find better ways to prepare teachers, give them both theory and practice, and keep them in the classroom.[8]

Residencies can also operate within the more traditional university setting. Programs such as Stanford's Teacher Education Program (STEP) and the University of Michigan's well-respected teacher education program have adopted many of the aspects of the clinical residency approach, while residencies are proliferating across university campuses from Columbia's Teachers College, to the University of New Hampshire's Rural Teacher Residency, to Virginia Commonwealth University and Texas State.[9] As a model with origins and advocates on both sides of the debate, residencies make sense as bridge-builders and can operate at a variety of institutions, large and small, elite or not.[10]

The residencies themselves can also take credit for spreading the model. In 2007, the three leading residency programs—Boston, Chicago, and Denver—joined together to form the Urban Teacher Residency United (UTRU), now called the National Center for Teacher Residencies (NCTR), which promotes the national expansion of the residency model and allows programs to share innovations and best practices. So far, twenty-eight programs across the country have joined, in such varied locations as Los Angeles, California; Vermillion, South Dakota; Richmond, Virginia; and Minneapolis, Minnesota.[11]

In addition to gaining the blessing of many university-based teacher educators and alternative certification advocates, residencies also solve the "revolt of the superintendents" problem, even if they leave some critics of today's schools dissatisfied. Under residencies, superintendents maintain real power in the running of the program and, in many ways, maintain more control over their teacher workforce than through any other model. According to surveys, principals also seem happy. One principal noted,

> Seeing [residents] in the fall as I begin my observations, I know that they have some skills that I don't necessarily need to worry about as I do a teacher that I hire from a traditional program where that student taught for 10 weeks. I know that a teacher from a traditional program, I need to get in there immediately to set up the rituals, routines and the management, and I have approximately three weeks to do that. Otherwise I lose. I don't need to do that with a resident—and I have 15 on staff—I have not needed to do that with a resident. I have not yet hired a teacher from a traditional program that I haven't needed to do that. As far as the time and the support, it's different. While I'm supporting in the fall a new teacher from a traditional program, I'm supporting around management. When I'm supporting a first-year resident, I'm supporting on instruction, and that's a significant difference.[12]

With this model on the rise, district residencies are simultaneously challenging and affirming many aspects of university-based and alternative models, raising the question of whether some sort of hybrid is the way of the future. Yet high price tags, unconfirmed impact, and delayed gratification are leaving others to wonder whether these programs are worth the cost, as just the latest reform du jour. Moreover, changes in federal policy following the election of Donald Trump jeopardizes some of the federal funding that was previously flowing to academies and residencies through Teacher Quality Partnership grants, which only lasted for five years and began under President Barack Obama. It is too early, however, to analyze the impact of such a political shift at the writing of this book.[13]

Charter and School-Specific Teacher Education

Another type of hybrid model also brings the training close to schools—charter schools, that is. These programs, such as High Tech High in California, Great Oaks on the East Coast, Aspire in California and Tennessee, and KIPP in cities across the United States, offer in-house training that prepares teachers in specific pedagogical philosophies to work in specific charter school environments.[14] In many ways, these programs operate just like residencies, beginning with summer coursework before a year of clinical training coupled with more coursework, but with training that addresses the perceived needs of specific schools and charter networks. This "homegrown" approach allows networks to maintain full control over their teacher training, manage their pipeline, and ensure that teachers are only exposed to that network's methods and teacher mentors. This approach avoids a phenomenon that university educators complain about—after a year or more of coursework, a student enters student teaching with a cooperating teacher who tells them to "forget all that theory stuff you learned in university." A downside to this model, however, is that participants arguably fail to receive a robust professional education and gain exposure to a variety of schooling environments, thus limiting their ability to fully critique their own practice or the school's underlying philosophies.

Teaching Academies

Beyond the district and charter residency models, other hybrids are cropping up across the country, including the new hot-button issue in teacher preparation following the passage of the Every Student Succeeds Act (ESSA) in 2015: teaching academies. The act allows states to grant up to 2% of their Title II funds to new teacher and principal training academies, which are defined as not-for-profit entities operating either within or in partnership with an institution of higher education (schools like Relay GSE count) and are intended to train teachers and administrators for high-needs schools through some form of clinical preparation. Although these academies will be evaluated based on their ability to raise student achievement—meaning, controversially, they will be using value-added measures to assess their graduates—they are not beholden to the same state and federal legislation as other certification programs, such as faculty having to hold advanced degrees or conduct research, students having to complete credit hours, or accreditation from recognized accrediting bodies.[15]

The idea derived from leaders at the New Schools Venture Fund, an influential education reform organization; allies at Relay GSE; and former Chicago UTEP director Timothy Knowles. Things got off the ground in 2009, when New Schools partnered with the Carnegie Foundation for the Advancement of Teaching to host a "community of practice" summit, which brought together leaders from both sides of the teacher preparation divide in order to devise solutions for how to scale-up quality preparation through a variety of certification pathways, embracing the idea that quality teachers can be built—in an education school or outside of one. In what must have felt like an interfaith ecumenical council, teacher educators from Stanford, the University of Michigan, the University of Southern California, and the University of Washington broke bread with the leaders of Relay, Match and its new Sposato Graduate School of Education, the Urban Teacher Center, and Boston Teacher Residency, among others, and discussed how best practices could be shared and programs reformed to improve teacher preparation across the country.[16] While not everyone within this umbrella organization of roughly forty organizations agrees on all issues, program leaders from various preparation pathways visited each other's trainings for observations, shared materials, and engaged in spirited dialogue. Enthusiasm for academies grew in part from this experience.[17]

In 2011, New Schools and Relay teamed up to help draft legislation to implement the academy idea, resulting in the Growing Excellent Achievement Training Academies (GREAT) Act. A bipartisan coalition of senators including Michael Bennet (D-CO), Lamar Alexander (R-TN), and Barbara Mikulski (D-MD) sponsored the bill and brought it to a vote during the term of Undersecretary of Education Ted Mitchell, former CEO of New Schools Venture Fund. The act called for federal funding, administered through states, of new academies to train principals and teachers. The academies would include three key characteristics: rigorous admissions processes, an emphasis on clinical instruction, and graduation tied to student achievement as measured through test scores. Harkening back to the logic behind charter schools, advocates claimed, "In return for accountability, academies will be free from burdensome, input-based regulations that are unrelated to student achievement."[18] Although the act failed to pass as standalone legislation, the idea was folded into the Every Student Succeeds Act that replaced No Child Left Behind in 2015 as the over-riding federal education law of the land.

While proponents claim that academies overcome the divisive nature of teacher education debates, providing a middle ground between university and alternative route preparation, others see new battle lines drawn. In October 2016, when the Obama administration released new teacher education regulations, Ken Zeichner and Lauren Anderson forcefully critiqued academies, particularly programs like Relay GSE that are rapidly expanding without proving their efficacy. They also highlighted the equity issue at stake, considering these academies are largely directed at high-poverty communities and their teacher graduates are not expected to serve middle- and high-income students—the "other people's children" problem. "There *is* wide variation in quality among all types of teacher education programs and ongoing improvement of *all* programs is needed," Zeichner and Anderson noted, "That said, the new federal regulations will not bring us where we need to go. We *can* promote innovation *and* reasonable, high standards for all programs; it's possible if we allow states and accrediting bodies, with *real* involvement of educators, to engage in a process that has professional integrity, rather than one hijacked by educational entrepreneurs who know little of the work."[19] Anderson, Zeichner, and many others see support for these academies as one more victory for the corporate reform movement.

Whether new residency models, academies, or reforms in traditional university-based and alternative route programs, a thousand flowers still seem to be blooming in the field of teacher preparation, nearly forty years after New Jersey's first alternative route program. What that means for the quality of the American teacher force is yet to be determined.

Finding the Middle Ground in Bean Town: The Boston Teacher Residency

Drawing on the much-used medical analogy in the *New York Review of Books*, education historian Jonathan Zimmerman noted in relation to teacher education, "Imagine if an Ivy League student started Nurses for America, giving highly qualified recruits a quick five-to-seven-week training (which is all that TFAers receive) and then sending them into hospitals to draw blood, administer vaccinations, and monitor life-support machines. Newspapers and patients' rights groups would immediately mount a strong political protest, and personal injury lawyers would see fertile new ground for lawsuits."[20] Yet rather than just casting doubt on the quick-prep TFA model in and of itself, this analogy also critiqued schools of education. Zimmerman continued, "Everyone understands that you can't be a nurse without attending a nursing school with carefully developed standards that must be met if candidates are to be systematically inducted into the profession. Most of our schools of education lack such high standards. If they did, TFA and other 'alternative routes' into teaching wouldn't exist." In a similar vein, John Jacobson, dean of the Teachers College at Ball State University, responded to a 2014 Indiana law allowing schools to hire anyone with a bachelor's degree and three years of relevant work to teach certain secondary subjects by noting, "If traditional programs knocked it out of the park, there would be less need for alternative programs."[21]

In that spirit, the Boston Teacher Residency (BTR) and residencies like it set out to create a new teacher preparation route that responsibly prepared teachers and elevated the status of the profession while transcending perceived problems with traditional schools of education *and* with five-week crash-course alternative routes. "[BTR] was a competitive threat—and that was intentional," Timothy Knowles, a BTR co-founder who later led the Urban Education Institute at the University of Chicago, said in reference to schools of education, which he and his Boston colleagues saw as not adequately graduating prepared professionals.[22] He and his colleagues also believed BTR was just as much a competitive threat to programs like TFA, which were also causing harm by not providing enough preparation and producing high turnover in classrooms that needed career teachers the most. In an interview with the Public Broadcasting Service (PBS) in 2015, Jesse Solomon, one of the founders of BTR, also drew on the medical analogy to explain, "Our country right now invests in the preparation of doctors to the tune of about half a million dollars per doctor. . . . I'm not arguing we should spend half a million dollars per teacher. But if education is really as important as everybody says it is, and if teachers are really as important as everyone says they are, then we should be thinking about how we as a country invest in the recruitment, preparation and support of teachers."[23]

As a best of both worlds–style compromise, BTR relies on a selective application process to choose its residents, who then embark on a thirteen-month training program that includes a year-long classroom apprenticeship coupled with coursework and a post-graduation mentoring experience intended to increase retention. In the first year, residents spend the summer taking theory and methods coursework. During the school year, they apprentice in a classroom four days a week, from the first day of school year to the last, while attending master's-level courses on Fridays and one night per week. Over the course of the year, they gradually assume teaching responsibilities in their school placement. The residents also participate in "clinical rounds," observing other master teachers at their host schools, and participate in mentorship experiences with other BTR colleagues. After the school year finishes, residents complete one additional month of coursework before graduating with a Massachusetts Initial Teacher Licensure and a master's degree from the University of Massachusetts, Boston. That fall, they take up a position in the Boston Public Schools (BPS), with a commitment of at least three years. BTR reasons that this training cycle allows students to observe crucial tone-setting moments on the first days of class, to benefit from the mentorship of a master teacher and an entire school community, and to experience a full school year with a group of students before taking the lead themselves. This way they are "safe to practice," just like any medical professional.

The program also prepares teachers for the challenges and frantic pace of first-year teaching. The intensive schedule, requiring students to take courses, work in a school, and produce papers and research projects simultaneously, is intentionally challenging, again mirroring the well-known rigor of a medical residency. "We try to overload people," Solomon told *Scholastic Administrator* magazine in a profile on the program. "You have to be able to balance lots of competing demands and do that across cultures, across race, across age. If you are overwhelmed by our residency, you will be overwhelmed by your first year of teaching. You've got to be able to hang in and have this bottom-line attention to student achievement."[24]

In addition to the apprenticeship model, BTR also has other unique aspects. For one, it was a program built in mind solely for and in collaboration with the Boston Public Schools (BPS). In 2003 Thomas Payzant, superintendent of BPS, and Timothy Knowles, then-deputy superintendent of teaching and learning, were approached by the foundation Strategic Grant Partners and asked what initiative they would fund if resources were limitless. Their response: a teacher preparation program that would provide a steady stream of high-quality, well-prepared teachers to meet the district's needs. Thus began a brainstorming session about the best model to make good on that dream. Both Payzant and Knowles agreed they did not want the program fully housed in BPS central offices due to cumbersome bureaucracy and internal politics. They turned to Ellen Guiney at the Boston Plan for Excellence (BPE), a local education foundation, to create a "one foot in, one foot out" model that would allow them more autonomy. Knowles then recruited Jesse Solomon, a ten-year teacher leader in the district, to take on a founding and directing role in the new program. A graduate of the Massachusetts Institute of Technology with ample experience teaching in Boston schools, Solomon founded a school-based teacher preparation program at the City on a Hill charter school after becoming disillusioned with the high turnover rate and overly harrowing first years of his colleagues. Solomon, like Knowles and Payzant, believed that the teacher education programs at nearby universities were just not getting the job done and that there must be a better way.[25]

What eventually became the Boston Teacher Residency program, Solomon explained, was not based on one particular model or charismatic figure, but drew on a variety of people and practices. The founding team looked to the professional development school movement that had emerged from the Holmes Group in the 1980s, the school-based teacher preparation programs at the private Shady Hill School in Cambridge, Massachusetts (which partnered with Lesley University but essentially ran its own internship program), and the teacher induction program that Solomon had launched during his time at the City on a Hill charter school. The team also drew from the rounds model developed at Clark University in Worcester, Massachusetts; the descriptive review process developed at the Prospect Center in Vermont; and critical friends group work pioneered by the Annenberg Institute, as well as ideas and practices from teacher educators such as KIPP's teacher muse, Houston math educator Harriett Ball; Bob Moses and his civil rights-oriented Algebra Project; and Michigan State University education professor Deborah Lowenberg Ball's work on core teaching competencies. BTR's founders also studied other clinical traditions in the professions, such as law and medicine, and borrowed ideas where appropriate. The BTR curriculum therefore reflects a concerted effort to blend theory with practice, provide residents with contextual information about the neighborhoods they will be working in, and includes coursework on such issues as child development and content methods so that residents gain not just knowledge of their subjects or a set of mechanical skills learned through an apprenticeship, but what teacher educator Lee Shulman calls "pedagogical content knowledge"—knowing how to teach a subject *and* run a classroom.[26]

In offering courses that stressed pedagogical content knowledge and foundational issues like child and adolescent psychology, BTR's founders avoided the critique that they sent teachers into the classroom with skills but no professional understanding of their work. By having these classes taught by district affiliates rather than university faculty, they avoided the concern of many superintendents like Payzant that the graduates might develop ideas inconsistent with those held by the district leadership.

BTR was also careful in selecting its host schools and mentor teachers to make the clinical experience meaningful. Schools applied to serve as host sites and agreed to receive at least six BTR residents in a cluster each year. BTR staff screened the schools and observed their teaching methods before placing residents to ensure the residents would have access to quality mentoring and multiple examples of master teaching. Mentor teachers at the selected host schools applied for their positions and were likewise observed, screened, and trained. They received $3,000 compensation for their work—significantly more than most universities offer their cooperating teachers.

Starting in 2012, the Boston Plan for Excellence also embarked on a new teaching academy initiative, which would create new schools more explicitly modeled after teaching hospitals to train new residents. The first academy opened as the Dudley Street Neighborhood Charter School in September 2012, and the second as the Dearborn STEM Academy in September 2015.[27]

With their needs-based and Boston-specific approach, BTR focused on recruiting teachers for the areas where the district faced shortages—mainly in science, math, special education, and English language learner (ELL) classes. Although many qualified applicants submit applications each year, BTR often turns down qualified candidates if they do not match the content areas in which the district needs teachers. All BTR candidates also have the option of adding a certificate in special education or ELL to their content specialties, ensuring that residents are prepared to meet the needs of Boston's diverse student population.

The program is surprisingly affordable—at least for residents. Wanting to provide a reasonably priced option for mid-career professionals looking to enter teaching, or highly-qualified recent graduates, Solomon and his team crafted a model in which residents take out an interest-free loan for $10,000 at the beginning of their training, then one-third of that amount is forgiven upon completion of each year spent working in Boston Public Schools. At the end of the three-year contract, students are paid back the entire cost of the program. Residents also receive a $12,100 living stipend during their residency year and receive an AmeriCorps education award worth $5,775. While the district absorbs much of this cost, BTR and other similarly structured residency programs still rely on outside funding to make the model financially feasible, as it can get quite expensive.[28] Boston Plan for Excellence, for example, helps raise a percentage of program costs. Proponents argue that due to the high retention rate of graduates—80% remain in BPS for at least five years—the upfront cost is a wise investment for the district and promotes stability within school communities.

Lastly, BTR's founders feel strongly that the residents ought to reflect the demographics of the school system itself. According to program statistics and an outside assessment, cohorts are in fact impressively diverse, better reflecting the racial and ethnic make-up of BPS than the teaching population more generally does. Overall, BPS teachers are 68% white, while roughly 84% of students are not. By contrast, in the 2014 BTR, nearly half of the residents were people of color.

What began as a small initiative with fifteen residents in its first year has now grown into a leading supplier of new teachers for the district, training 100 residents per year. It also serves as a national model of district-based teacher education. Yet despite these positive attributes and much public acclaim, the data on the program's effectiveness are still mixed. BTR waited anxiously for a Harvard team to release evaluation measures based on student achievement data, hoping that the numbers would prove what they believed all along—that a first-year residency really does make a difference. Yet BTR graduates were actually shown to struggle *more* in their first three years than other incoming BPS teachers with similar experience, especially in math. In their fourth year and beyond, however, BTR graduates displayed higher student gains than veteran teachers, showing a capacity to improve rapidly.[29] To fully accept these conclusions, one must put faith in the ability of value-added measures to reflect actual teacher impact, which remains a controversial topic. Moreover, despite these studies, BTR and proponents still believe that the residency prevents terrible first years for teachers and that better teachers are staying in classrooms longer, which is the ultimate goal. Ninety percent of BTR grads remain in the field of education in some capacity, 87% are still teaching, and 80% are still teaching in-district after five years. Among principals, 97% reported that they would recommend hiring a BTR graduate to a colleague. Furthermore, a study by the Institute of Education Sciences and the U.S. Department of Education reported that most of the thirty residency programs being funded by the federal government under the Higher Education Opportunity grants program, including BTR, successfully aligned classroom practice with theory-based coursework, provided strong mentorship experiences for candidates, and expanded the labor force beyond traditional teacher candidates. National Council on Teacher Quality rankings also looked favorably on BTR, granting it an A grade.

Despite these accolades, the program is not without its skeptics. Some wonder just how much the program benefits from its University of Massachusetts partnership—whether BTR really is "university affiliated" or simply has a "paper stamping" arrangement to achieve a degree and state licensure under the aegis of the university. Although graduates receive a master's degree upon successful completion of their thirteen-month training, the courses are designed and taught by BTR employees, not by university faculty, rendering the partnership more in name than in practice. BTR claims it seeks teacher educators who demonstrate a blending of theory and practice in their professional work, such as a literacy coach with a doctorate in language acquisition or a professor at a local university with urban teaching experience. Other critics raise skeptical eyebrows about the ability of teachers to critique district leadership or policies if they are trained by the district itself. They question BTR's effect on teacher workforce autonomy and whether residents receive the preparation for professional leadership that ought to be a hallmark of the best teacher preparation programs.

Despite these criticisms, BTR is lauded as a darling in the education reform world, reflected in such honors as the Harvard Kennedy School's Innovation in American Government nomination and the recognition given to BTR by organizations as diverse as the Organization for Economic Cooperation and Development (OECD), the National Council on Teacher Quality, and the University of Pennsylvania's Center for High Impact Philanthropy. BTR also serves as a potential olive branch to bring together teacher professionalization crusaders and alternative route boosters, both of whom want to see high-quality candidates coupled with high-quality preparation and manageable student costs. As BTR shines as the city on the hill, other residencies around the country are also looking to the Boston beacon and experiencing success.

Navigating Complex Partnerships in the Emerald City: The Seattle Teacher Residency

In 2013 Seattle experienced something all too rare in the education world: consensus. Touted as a "local miracle" on the front page of the *Seattle Times*, the newly created Seattle Teacher Residency (STR) program brought together four major, sometimes combative, partners—the Seattle Public Schools (SPS); the Alliance for Education, Seattle's local education fundraising nonprofit; the University of Washington (UW) College of Education; and the district's teachers union, a newcomer to teacher residency partnerships.[30] "The teachers union and the Alliance don't see eye-to-eye about much," wrote John Higgins in the *Times*, "but they both agree that the residency is a good thing for students and teachers."[31]

Similar to the Boston residency program, STR prepares residents in and for the classrooms of Seattle's Title I public schools. During a fourteen-month program, residents are trained through a combination of rigorous university-based coursework and a full school year clinical experience. After completing the program, they are supported through continued coursework and mentoring experiences. A new cohort of carefully selected candidates (typically twenty to thirty) begins the program each year, with direct curricular instruction in coordination with the University of Washington and hands-on observation and practicum with SPS mentor teachers. Residents are trained as either elementary teachers with an ELL or SPED endorsement, or as special education teachers with general education training.[32] Upon completion of their training, STR graduates make a five-year commitment to teach in Seattle public schools in high-need environments. Graduates receive targeted and sustained support from the district's STAR Mentor Program to ensure retention, success, and continued growth as new teachers.

To date, the program has proven quite successful. Like Boston, STR teachers are known to stay in classrooms longer than their peers and reflect the diversity of their students far more so than the teaching body at large. Furthermore, achievement data were shown to improve at a higher rate in schools with greater numbers of STR teachers.[33]

Despite these successes, for a brief moment the future of STR came into question, reflecting the challenges that sometimes arise in programs that rely on so many competing interests and perspectives. For this reason, STR offers an important case study as a unique model for quality teacher preparation, an unusually diverse multistakeholder partnership, and as a lesson in how programs can overcome challenges, adapt, and thrive.

DISTRICT–ALLIANCE PARTNERSHIP

As senior leadership changed in all four partner organizations over the first few years of the STR program, tensions emerged between the school district and the Alliance for Education. At the fall 2015 school board meeting, the Seattle school board went so far as to vote to cut ties with the foundation, the major funder of STR. Citing disagreements with Alliance leadership, but also reservations about the "long-term sustainability and cost" and "low system-wide impact" of the teacher training program, the superintendent and the school board reprioritized district funding and took a less enthusiastic stance in their support for the residency program.[34] The challenges in the SPS–Alliance relationship were complex and not specifically related to the functionality and impact of STR—the district faced serious budget challenges—but the vote proved dramatic and troubling for supporters, nonetheless.

The problem stemmed more from competing ideas about the actual function of the Alliance for Education and its proper relationship vis-à-vis the district than the residency model itself. Like the Boston Plan for Excellence and education foundations in many other districts around the country, Seattle's non-profit Alliance functions as a stand-alone, independent organization in order to raise funds from private donors, businesses, and philanthropies outside the usual political fray. The Alliance sprung from the desire of diverse leaders in the Seattle area, including the superintendent, mayor, and corporate leaders, to direct private sector resources to the local school district. The organization formed in 1995 as a merger of three smaller, pre-existing education foundations and became the leading means of channeling private dollars into the public schools, mainly from the city's major companies such as Microsoft and Boeing.[35] In most cities where these local education foundations operate, they have been praised for raising funds and adding new resources and flexibility to otherwise tight, and tightly designated, school budgets. They have also been criticized for representing unwelcome business involvement in the management of the public schools since their additional dollars, even if a tiny percentage of school budgets, represent an important resource that often comes with strings attached.

"When the organization started, there was great sensitivity to needing to take cues from the school district, rather than coming up with an agenda and then imposing that agenda on the school district," the Alliance's first executive director told a local radio news service in a 2013 interview.[36] Yet over the years, and with a change in leadership, the Alliance began developing stronger, and more independent opinions about the best reform policies and the way to spend its dollars, opinions that didn't always align with district superintendents' agendas. Former Alliance President and CEO Sara Morris, for example, characterized the relationship differently; "Really our work is to be the 'critical friend' of the district," she said in the same 2013 radio interview, through finding the "right balance between support and pressure."[37] As a private sector–funded organization, and with Morris coming to the work from a career at Amazon, the Alliance began favoring some policies popular in corporate reform circles, especially teacher evaluations tied to student testing data and accepting TFA teachers—opinions not always readily embraced by the union and other Seattle education stakeholders.

In the early 2000s, the Alliance became intrigued with what Boston was doing with its district-based teacher residency program. The residency model of teacher preparation reform was on the rise, money was flowing readily to them, and more research began supporting district-based clinical training as the way of the future for teacher education. Unlike some of the other reforms on the Alliance's wish list, this one also received backing from the then-district superintendent, Susan Enfield, and prominent teacher educators at the University of Washington's College of Education, especially then-dean Tom Stritikus. Soon after the idea was launched, the Alliance invited the union to join the effort, particularly under the urging of UW professor and teacher educator Ken Zeichner. The union did join—a major departure from other residency programs around the country. With the teachers, teacher educators, the district, the nearby university, and the business community on board, it went very smoothly in the beginning, Morris remembered. Two STR teachers even provided testimony to the U.S. Congress regarding the value of residency models with the support of the local teachers union.

Yet after only two STR cohorts, the partnership began to face serious problems, finding itself at real risk as a result of conflict between the Alliance and district leadership. The health of the partnership was further affected by high leadership turnover in the district in the years surrounding the creation of the residency, with five different superintendents rotating in and out in the last decade. Larry Nyland, who assumed the position in 2014, was particularly frustrated that the Alliance seemed to be directing its resources toward its own agenda, as opposed to simply providing funds to meets the district's needs and desires, though the district's three previous leaders expressed similar frustrations. The teachers union also butted heads with the Alliance in 2013 during new contract negotiations. The Alliance wanted student testing data to be taken into account in teacher evaluations, while the union did not. The conflict reached its peak in the fall of 2015.[38]

On October 7, the school board sent the Alliance a letter saying that it would be officially dissolving its relationship with them. The letter detailed concerns and frustrations with Alliance leadership and the direction of the organization from the past four years. In the school board's proposed action report, which it shared at a public meeting on October 9, 2015, the board stated: "While SPS is thankful for the funds granted, the funding priorities of the Alliance and the funding priorities of SPS Superintendent and SPS Board of Directors ("Board") are not aligned." The report concluded with the news that the board would in fact be cutting the district's share of the funding for STR, from $200,000 to $50,000.[39]

"This has been a very intense and public unraveling of what we had hoped would be a strong partnership," said Anissa Listak, founder and CEO of the National Center for Teacher Residencies, in an interview with the *Huffington Post*.[40] "Whatever this political in-fighting is all about, it's become an adult issue and is not at all about kids and education." The *Seattle Times* editorial board shared a similar sentiment in an open letter, expressing hope that the two entities could repair their relationship.[41] Both the school board and the Alliance wrote op-eds expressing regret (though not changed minds) over the development, as did Zeichner.[42] "These relationship woes are not entirely uncommon among residencies," Listak added, "although they occur more frequently between a university and a school district."[43]

In time, however, political winds changed course, and the partnership was revived. Dramatically. With new leadership at the Alliance and in the school district, and bolstered by positive evaluations of the program, there has been a renewed and expanded commitment to the residency program. Early in her tenure, new Alliance CEO Lisa Chick prioritized rebuilding relationships with STR partners, particularly with senior leadership. Chick instituted a listening tour, for example, to connect with multiple constituents, which included meetings with district leadership to understand where things went wrong and what was needed in order to move forward. While the Alliance and SPS continue to rebuild their relationship, both parties have consistently agreed that STR was valuable to the district, and district leadership has continued to work closely with STR to ensure program success. As a result of meaningful discussions regarding the specific program attributes of STR, by the summer of 2017 commitments were made to demonstrate clear alignment between the program and district initiatives. The end result was the successful repair of a once faltering relationship.

In a press release jointly vetted by the Alliance, the Seattle Education Association, SPS, and UW in April 2017, Clover Codd, assistant superintendent of human resources at Seattle Public Schools, declared, "The Residency directly addresses many of the goals Seattle Public Schools has for recruiting a strong teacher pool. Its focus on providing high-quality teacher training to a diverse pool of candidates, along with ongoing support for its graduates in Seattle Public Schools, creates a pipeline of exceptionally well-qualified teachers committed to serving students in our highest-need schools." As this statement shows, stakeholder support for the program was restored.

UNIVERSITY PARTNERSHIP

Partnership with UW's College of Education is another critical asset of the residency's successful functioning. University faculty who participated in the design of the program and who now teach in it are committed to innovation and integration with district programming. When political tensions arose, UW faculty were right there to defend the program. In fact, STR serves as a kind of laboratory for those who work in the university-based teacher education program, reflecting a relationship between "traditional" and "alternative" that is far more complementary than combative. In an April 2017 press release, Mia Tuan, dean of the UW College of Education, highlighted the college's support of STR: "At the College of Education we believe, as do our partners, that ensuring children in our Title I schools have highly effective teachers, who stay and continue to grow in their practice must be a top priority. The Seattle Teacher Residency is a key strategy for diversifying the teaching force, improving retention, and providing children in Title I schools with excellent teachers."

The university-based partnership ensures that critical theoretical and pedagogical training is not given short shrift in STR's curriculum, as it is in some alternative programs where skepticism of the ideas of university-based educators abounds. The partnership also allows instruction to be strongly aligned to classroom practice. UW faculty helped create the curriculum and the "learning cycles of practice" that help teachers develop a set of STR- and UW-defined core practices of effective and equitable teaching in the classroom. Residents, for example, learn many aspects of their curriculum content, aligned with special education and English language learner methods, within the context of their mentor teachers' classrooms as opposed to in university classrooms, but their learning is still under the supervision of UW instructors. In this way, the university partnership is much stronger than some other residencies. Real-time coaching, immediate debriefs, and video analysis allow targeted strategic feedback of both teaching and student learning. Residents therefore learn content methods in the classroom, receive feedback in the moment, and analyze and reflect on their teaching practice as they go. Resident instruction is also specifically designed to prepare graduates to teach in the SPS system. STR's team of leaders and UW faculty create alignment between the STR curriculum and the SPS vision to best prepare the residents to teach within the context of Seattle's schools—making teachers, teacher educators, and district leaders happy.

In addition, the program is aligned with the college's commitment to equity and to the diversification of the teaching corps. Under the guidance of STR and UW, residents engage in deep exploration of their own identities and of how power and privilege affect the biases and assumptions that individuals make about others. This exploration is informed by the insights of educational sociology, history, anthropology, and economics, among other academic disciplines. The residents also integrate this "classroom learning" with real-world environments, specifically exploring and experiencing what that type of knowledge means in the classroom and community. As an example, they regularly visit the Monroe Correctional Complex to engage in conversations with the Black Prisoners' Caucus and reflect on the school-to-prison pipeline with men and women who have experienced it in order to better understand how to interrupt that pipeline in their own classrooms. Residents are also charged with challenging their own assumptions and are supported to leave STR with the belief that not only can all children learn and be held to high expectations, but also that Seattle students, their families, and their communities are partners in education, bringing rich resources and assets to the classroom. They also leave with a university-approved professional education to ensure that they can continue to serve as intellectual and political leaders in their communities.

UNION PARTNERSHIP
STR's partnership with the Seattle Education Association (SEA) may well be the most unique aspect of the Seattle residency. With the organized voice of teachers in support of and participating in the design and implementation of the program, district-wide support was reinforced, even given the

fact that the program only serves the district's Title I schools. The partnership also mitigates the tensions that sometimes arise between "professional" educators and alternatively certified new teachers, the latter sometimes seen as undermining the authority of the former. Rather, STR serves as a valuable political partner to the union and was able to secure support on many agenda items, including substitute certificates, mentor selection and responsibilities, and fundraising. The union in turn helped STR secure funding from the National Education Association and continues to submit grant proposals on the program's behalf. In addition, union leadership includes STR in negotiation strategies to seek out budget allocation opportunities. In the fall of 2014, in collaboration with the National Board for Professional Teaching Standards, SEA sent a mentor and resident graduate to Washington, DC, to testify to congressional staff on the contribution of the residency model. This was a significant step toward both labor support and national recognition of the residency model.

NATIONAL IMPACT, LOCAL SUCCESS

Despite some rocky moments, STR is thriving. In a 2015 report, "Clinically Oriented Teacher Preparation," the National Center for Teacher Residencies (NCTR) cited Seattle for its comprehensive, performance outcomes –driven assessment process; effective restructuring of clinical roles for faculty, staff, and mentor teachers; and instructional innovations. In spite of the aforementioned tensions, the report also cites leadership engagement and commitment as a critical component of STR and its success.[44] STR teachers are staying in-district and continue to reflect the diversity of their students. "Forty-one percent of them are teachers of color—double the 20 percent diversity rate for all teachers who work in Seattle Public Schools, and four times the state rate of 10 percent. And nearly all the residency graduates who start teaching in a high-needs school returned there for a second and third year. That's much higher than the 71 percent retention rate for other Seattle teachers hired in the same year," the *Seattle Times* reported in 2017.[45] Though student testing data is a notoriously difficult mode of evaluation, they also noted that student test scores are rising in schools with STR-trained teachers. The program's commitment to offering on-going support, training and guidance to graduates of the residency program, including a collaborative community across cohorts and targeted curricular offerings designed to increase teacher success and longevity, aids in this retention and performance.

There is no denying that the conflict between the Alliance for Education and Seattle Public Schools was real and significant, and posed a true threat to the sustainability of the Alliance for Education itself, as well as the Residency program. However, the Seattle Teacher Residency managed to endure despite that conflict, and in some instances, even served as a bridge to rebuild the district/Alliance relationship, as both entities saw the value of their shared work. The Seattle case also serves as a model for other districts experiencing tensions among stakeholders, as an example of the value of working through disagreements amongst sometimes antagonistic groups.

As mentioned earlier, by 2017 the *Seattle Times* described STR not as the center of a citywide political fight, but touted it as an innovative program that "seems to be fulfilling its mission to help develop a more diverse teacher workforce in the city's public schools."[46] While the model's need for significant funding was acknowledged, attention to the conflict between the school district and the Alliance in 2015 clearly took a backseat to identifying the value of the residency program at a time when teacher shortages are predicted and opportunity gaps continue to exist. Though obstacles arose on the winding road to the Emerald City, the residency program did not fall on its way.

Despite the still inconclusive data, worries over expenses, and recent political complications in Seattle, the residency model is still thriving in many parts of the United States. From the 2008 Teacher Quality Partnership grants to the present, state and city officials, as well as foundation officers, are giving increased attention and support to the residency model. Indeed, some officials have expressed recent interest in eventually having all of their new teachers enter through the Urban Teachers residency pathway, reflecting the growing hold of residency programs across the country.[47]

Teacher Education for the Twenty-first Century: The Woodrow Wilson Academy of Teaching and Learning

When Arthur Levine speaks at education events, he often shares the same message: America's education system is sorely out of date. "The United States is making a transition from a national, analog, industrial economy to a global, digital, information economy. All of our social institutions—education, finance, government, media, and healthcare—were created for the former. Each works less well than it did in the past; they seem to be broken today. They need to be refitted for a new era," he stated.[48] A new stand-alone education school run by the Woodrow Wilson National Fellowship Foundation and partnered with the Massachusetts Institute of Technology (MIT) intends to do just that. Led by Levine, the school will shift the educational program from an input-oriented process centered on the Carnegie

Unit, or seat-time credit hour—a direct relic from the industrial age—to a knowledge- and skill-based, time-variable competency curriculum in a blended online and offline setting—a product of our tech age. Unlike other voices in the debate who demand revolutionary changes in teacher preparation, however, Levine does not advocate the end of education schools. More research and expertise, not less, are necessary for increasing the quality and rigor of teacher education, he and his Woodrow Wilson colleagues believe.

Levine has long served as a critical voice in the world of teacher preparation. As former president of Teachers College at Columbia University, he ruffled feathers with a highly critical 2006 report on the state of teacher education in the United States. "Educating School Teachers" lambasted the field, concluding that most programs at education schools were engaged in a "pursuit of irrelevance," with shoddy and disorganized curriculum, and faculty that remained disconnected from real-world classrooms.[49] In an oft-cited passage, he wrote, "Teacher education is the Dodge City of the education world. Like the fabled Wild West town, it is unruly and chaotic. There is no standard approach to where and how teachers should be prepared, and the ongoing debate over whether teaching is a profession or a craft has too often blurred the mission of education schools that are uncertain whether to become professional schools or continue to be grounded in the more academic world of arts and sciences."[50] The report also revealed that 61% of teacher education alumni believed that their programs did not prepare them adequately. Principals largely concurred, with only 30% reporting that the education school graduates were ready to face the challenges of their classrooms.

Rather than remaining a critic, however, Levine acted. As president of the Woodrow Wilson National Fellowship Foundation, he reoriented the organization's work from a focus on fellowships for future higher education faculty to elite teaching fellowships in the style of a Rhodes scholarship that would bring top-flight candidates to graduate programs in schools of education while at the same time demanding fundamental rethinking of the teacher preparation programs at the universities that received Woodrow Wilson fellows. In doing so, Levine launched what he and his colleagues saw as the new frontier in teacher education. In the summer of 2015, after several years of research on the lessons learned from the fellowship program and consideration of the viability a new enterprise, the Woodrow Wilson Foundation announced the launch of the new Woodrow Wilson Academy of Teaching and Learning, a stand-alone education school that will partner with MIT and Boston-area school districts to provide a new type of preparation and serve as a research laboratory meant to conduct and disseminate important findings to other education schools and policymakers at the state and national level. Levine sees the teaching academy as the Google or Bell Labs of the teacher training world, bringing elite teacher candidates together with cutting-edge research scholars in an innovative laboratory approach.[51]

The school will receive its first cohort of aspiring teachers in the fall of 2018, after a year working with a smaller cohort of "design fellows." The 2017–2018 design fellows are expected to help develop and test the program. Like other new hybrid approaches, the curriculum will be based on a research-backed assortment of skill and knowledge competencies, completed at each student's own pace through a blend of online modules and in-person learning experiences rooted in the latest learning science and in the context of real-life classrooms. Students spend around twenty hours a week in schools at the start of their clinical placements, beginning with the first day of school, and take on an increasing amount of instruction time as the year progresses.

Over a roughly year-long course of study, students must also pass twenty "challenges" that combine four to five competencies each, a curricular model that mirrors the project-based learning method. One example of a challenge, for instance, asks a fellow to respond to a prompt about a first-year teacher learning that their entire class failed a unit test that the teacher created and administered. The candidate must then figure out what to do and produce a "challenge solution" consisting of a series of artifacts and performance assessments. This challenge would be rooted in the competencies of content knowledge, assessment, learning sciences, and instructional design, while assessing the candidate's skills and knowledge in working with students and families in a simulated meeting with irate parents. To pass such a challenge and proceed to the next competency, students must demonstrate mastery through their artifacts and performance assessment, judged by teaching academy faculty, most of whom come from a background in teaching themselves. In this way, the curriculum can cover a variety of scenarios that might not appear in student teaching experiences, but which teachers will undoubtedly encounter in their careers. As with WGU and residency models, the Woodrow Wilson Academy developed the curriculum through conversations with a number of stakeholders, including university-based teacher educators, current and former teachers, superintendents, and other school-based personnel. The first cohort of design fellows will provide feedback on what works and what needs improvement or revision.

The academy is also pioneering a new approach to the clinical component of teacher education. Rather than focusing on time as the sole indicator of utility, the program is based on a combination of in-school training along the lines of a traditional student teaching experience, simulations, and out-of-school time (OST). During the in-school period, teacher candidates observe master teachers and practice teaching lessons while receiving feedback, similar to the best-designed student teaching and residency experiences. Simulations occur out of the classroom and are meant to expose students to an even wider array of events and challenges that teachers may face in the classroom. For example, a certain type of behavioral challenge may never come up in real time, but students will nevertheless be trained in how to approach that situation. The academy is working in close collaboration with MIT to develop a number of "practice spaces" that leverage the power of emerging technologies to create these scenarios, particularly learning games and virtual simulations.

As a final part of the clinical component, students visit innovative learning sites so that they are trained not only to succeed in the classrooms of today, but also the classrooms of tomorrow as Woodrow Wilson founders would like to see them: personalized, innovative, and drawing on the best of technology and learning science. Fellows spend time in such innovative spaces as the Computer Clubhouse, an afterschool and weekend program at Boston's Museum of Science and founded in collaboration with MIT's Media Lab. According to the Woodrow Wilson Foundation, the academy prioritizes environments that offer examples of personalization, maker spaces, gaming, new instructional designs, and student-driven and adaptive learning through advanced technology. Teacher candidates can then practice teaching in these learning environments of "tomorrow," which rarely surface in traditional school environments.

The design fellows are a small initial cohort of ten students receiving free tuition for their role in testing the new curriculum in middle- and secondary-level STEM subjects of biology, chemistry, and mathematics, but there are plans to expand to 200 students and to more subject areas in the future, with enrollees paying around $25,000 for their master's degree. What separates the Woodrow Wilson Academy from WGU, Relay GSE, residency programs, or many other new experiments, however, is its emphasis on research, and the fact that everything—the research and the academy's curriculum—will remain open-source and will be free to other education schools and available for a fee to districts to use in professional development trainings. The idea is that the academy will eventually serve as a "library" or resource center dedicated to teacher education—a "pool of research on effective teacher training methods" for all to use. In this way, the academy dismisses the idea that competition breeds the best results.

The Woodrow Wilson Academy also hopes to move beyond the "traditional" versus "alternative" divide by drawing in ideas from both traditional university-based programs and alternative and hybrid programs. The program has already received buy-in from both teacher preparation camps: the defenders of the traditional route and their critics. Sharon Robinson, former head of the American Association of Colleges for Teacher Education, told a reporter that although she is usually wary of sweeping proposals like that of the academy, she finds this one promising since Levine, despite being a critic, comes from the education school world and recognizes the value of university-based programs.[52] The American Federation of Teachers has also expressed tempered support, and the program has received impressive backing from reform-minded philanthropies such as the Bill and Melinda Gates Foundation, the Carnegie Corporation of New York, and the Amgen Foundation, as well as a number of other foundations and individual donors, which together have provided $20 million to launch the initiative.[53]

Another unique aspect of the new program stems from its relationship to MIT, one of the most elite and renowned research universities in the world. Although MIT can boast a long history of providing support to elementary and secondary educators, from writing math and science textbooks in the 1960s to the more recent pioneering work of teaching coding to kids, these initiatives always remained ad hoc and disorganized. One representative from MIT noted that, as late as 2015, over 125 initiatives and research projects related to K–12 learning existed at MIT, but none of them were coordinated. Interest in creating an MIT School of Education has even surfaced over the years, noted Professor Sanjay Sarma, MIT's vice president for open learning, but enthusiasts always hit road blocks from a less-than-interested administration and a faculty that seemed unenthusiastic about risking their prestige by opening an education school.[54]

Things began to change in 2014, however, with the release of a forcefully written and highly publicized institution-wide task force report. In it, MIT expressed the desire to become a world leader in open-source education, both in terms of actual courses offered through new platforms such as Massive Online Open Courses (MOOCs) and in terms of innovative pedagogy, particularly related to new technologies, game-based learning, and blended learning in a global, diverse context. The Woodrow Wilson Academy curriculum attempts to respond directly to these recommendations. One recommendation for "Extending MIT's Education Impact" explicitly called for a more comprehensive K–12 strategy and a consolidation of efforts under currently disparate programs, such as the existing MIT Edgerton Center and the Scheller Teacher Education Program, both of which provide targeted professional development trainings to current teachers related to technology and science teaching.[55] While elite universities without schools of education like MIT may be reluctant to open an education school, and universities like Duke, Yale, and Princeton that closed their education schools or departments in the 1970s and 1980s share that reluctance, some may be willing to partner with new experiments in teacher training to bring the benefits of elite higher education into the teacher and principal preparation world.

While it is still too soon to evaluate the impact or efficacy of the Woodrow Wilson Academy, it is certainly a program to watch. It reflects a general trend in hybrid models, an interest by elite universities to enter the teacher preparation enterprise, and an embrace of new technologies without dismissing the importance of educational theory and research.

Job-Embedded Training: High Tech High

If the twentieth century was the Century of the Atlantic, the twenty-first has been billed as the Century of the Pacific, with Asia ascendant and California's Silicon Valley shifting the center of power in the new technology-filled millennium. Teacher education, even if symbolically, reflects this shift. Our examination of alternative certification began in New Jersey, reflecting the 1980s and 1990s faith in Wall Street–style markets and competition to solve social problems, and ends in California, with a new model of teacher education that embraces the new twenty-first century gospel of Silicone Valley entrepreneurship. High Tech High (HTH) has led the way in what are perhaps the two newest waves in hybrid teacher preparation: charter network certification programs and an embrace of tech-based education solutions.

High Tech High was founded—or "launched" to use the language of start-up culture—in 2000, ushering in the new millennium with a novel model of schooling. Echoing Arthur Levine's description of the needed educational changes for a new era, Gary Jacobs, a San Diego–area businessman and current chair of the HTH school board, argued that the structure of most American public schools was based on an outdated industrial economy. "On all fronts, the teaching and learning experience here is keenly attuned to the demands of today's world, not the industrial world that existed a hundred years ago when the American school model came into being," he explained to *Edutopia* in 2008.[56] Progressive-era education reformers drew on the latest innovations in factory management to churn out workers for a newly industrialized world at the dawn of the twentieth century, creating graded and tracked classrooms and echoing the division of labor through the division of disciplines. Education leaders in the twenty-first century likewise needed a new model, he and his supporters claimed, one that reflected the increasingly technology- and information-based global economy for which American workers would need to be prepared. Drawing insight not from industrial shop floors but tech startups, this new model would do away with the tracking, subject-area divisions, and textbooks of the last century, and embrace interdisciplinary project-based learning and technology.

Resembling a combination of John Dewey and Mark Zuckerburg more than Wendy Kopp, Rob Riordan, HTH co-founder and president emeritus of the HTH Graduate School of Education, and Larry Rosenstock, current CEO of the HTH network, explain their pedagogical philosophy as such:

> For more than a century the whole point of schooling has been to restrict the curriculum, specify the required content, and limit the entry points to it—often by means of a watered-down, already obsolete text, mediated by a classroom manager whose task is to transmit the subject matter to 30 or more individuals of diverse backgrounds, experiences, interests and resources. This is particularly true of the "big four" core subjects the Carnegie Commission decided, nearly a century ago, are the subjects that matter. English, math, science (biology, chemistry, physics) and social studies count for much, and the fine and practical arts for much less. Why not study anthropology, or zoology, or environmental science? Why not integrate art with calculus, or chemistry with history? . . . It has long been axiomatic in the United States to separate students according to perceived academic ability. . . . Instead, our aim in this century should be to integrate students by eliminating tracking, to integrate the subjects via problem-focused experiences, and to integrate school with the world beyond through fieldwork, service learning, and internships.[57]

What this looks like in practice is something that more closely mirrors Google and Facebook headquarters than a public school: students and teachers work in glass-pod classrooms, solving real-world problems, often with the aid of cutting-edge technology and laboratories. As shown through a documentary produced on HTH, instead of learning about DNA in a textbook, biology students might develop ways to test meat samples to detect the presence of poached animals in African marketplaces and then travel to Tanzania to work with community groups to implement a new solution to the problem of poaching. A combined art and biology class might produce digitized 3-D artistic representations of the body, while a history and literature class allows students to spend a semester writing a play about the experience of LGBTQ+ individuals during World War II. Visiting a HTH campus in San Diego, one sees individual students and clusters of students hard at work on their various projects, some in consultation with instructors and some on their own. The intensity of the student focus and the lack of students acting out their dissatisfaction with the school day is striking to even the most casual visitor.[58]

The first of HTH's four design principles is equity, although as its leaders explain, equity is always a goal and never a finished accomplishment. The organization attempts to focus on both innovation and equity, "working to fulfil the unrealized promises of *Brown v. Board of Education*" while simultaneously employing new technology-driven solutions and an innovative curriculum to do so. The other three design principles are personalization, which emphasizes a learner-centered, inclusive approach; authentic work, in which students engage in work that matters to them; and collaborative design, in which all teachers, students, and external partners participate in designing individual projects, the school's culture, and assessment.[59]

HTH began as a single school serving 200 students with some start-up money from Gary and Jerri-Ann Jacobs. This funding enabled the acquisition of the initial site on a decommissioned Navy Training Center in the Point Loma section of San Diego. Supporting an initiative of Irwin Jacobs, CEO of the multinational telecommunications company Qualcomm, a coalition of San Diego–area business leaders responded to public demand and procured additional funding from the Jacobs family, Qualcomm, the Gates Foundation, and other local and national philanthropies. HTH grew dramatically in the following decade. Now with thirteen K–12 schools in southern California and a total of 4,500 students, HTH relies on a zip code–based lottery to create student bodies that attempt to match the diversity of California's neighborhoods and to provide opportunities to low-income students from under-represented and working-class backgrounds. All students are in the same classes. All students are expected to produce the same quality of work. Around 90% of HTH students go on to college.

While many applaud these innovations, others worry about the unintended consequences. For one, High Tech High's requirement to submit an application for the lottery already implies that only the most-motivated students and families will likely enter—the same critique levelled at many charter schools. Recent media publicity has made HTH somewhat of an education gem in California, meaning that many middle- and upper-income students apply as well as those from working-class backgrounds. Nevertheless, HTH has been able to maintain a high level of diversity, with 46% of students qualifying for free or reduced lunch, compared to 40% of students at nearby San Diego High School.[60] By insisting that all of San Diego's zip codes are included, HTH has achieved some level of socio-economic and racial integration in an era when charter schools are being blamed for further segregating students along lines of race and class. HTH boasts a demographic makeup that is around 44% Hispanic, 33% White, 9% Black, and 13% Asian, with almost 10% English language learners and 13.5% special education students, challenging the idea that choice and diversity are mutually exclusive.[61]

In addition to its curricular innovations, High Tech High is also in innovator in teacher preparation, as the first charter network to train its own teachers and prepare them for state certification—a growing trend in the teacher preparation landscape. Although HTH has a good working relationship with nearby schools of education, its leaders felt the need for more teachers who would fully buy into HTH's unique approach. In response, they started their own non-degree teacher credentialing program in 2004, as well as the degree-granting Graduate School of Education (HTH GSE) in 2007. Today HTH prepares teachers for careers in the HTH network and outside of it, provides professional development, and produces research on student and adult learning. Under California's Alternative Certification Internship law, which allows teachers to earn certification during their first year on the job after 120 hours of pre-service training, HTH GSE was able to run its own pre-service training and provide the follow-up coursework.

The HTH teacher credentialing program offers two tracks—both based on the assumption that all teacher candidates are already teaching, though not necessarily at HTH. The two-year teacher preparation program is embedded in a K–12 school and includes attention to project-based pedagogy as well as to the theory and skills needed to effectively teach English language learners and diverse student populations. Courses and programs are delivered in a standard sequence and lead to a California teaching credential. The induction program serves already credentialed beginning teachers through a two-year program and advanced study aligned with the California Standards for the Teaching Profession expectations.[62]

Aspiring teacher candidates can therefore receive their teacher education entirely through the network in a two-year, non-degree granting program. Once offered employment in a HTH school (or another school, upon approval by HTH), teacher candidates complete their 120 hours of pre-service with HTH GSE faculty, most of whom have some combination of teaching experience and a background in education studies, though a PhD is not required and few faculty hold one. (A number of HTH board members, however, come from the university-based education world.) Summer training consists of two courses: Foundations in English Language Development and the New Teacher Odyssey, a course intended to provide the basics in topics like lesson design and classroom management. First-year teachers then take five courses while teaching full-time. The courses include everything from teaching methods to integrated educational technology. They take four courses in their second year, on such topics as methods of English language development and philosophy of education.[63] Unlike Relay GSE and some other charter-inspired or in-network residencies, HTH does not endorse a Doug Lemov–style, technocratic, skill-based teaching style. It instead offers a curriculum that promotes teacher autonomy, professionalism, equity, collaboration, and deep learning. Graduates of the HTH program, far from wanting to institute classroom drills, are prepared to foster student engagement in their own learning, especially through the project-based HTH approach.

The desire of High Tech High and other charter networks to enter the certification field grew from the same concerns voiced by Norm Atkins of Relay GSE and Tom Payzant of the Boston Public Schools: not enough teachers were ready to teach on day one in the right subjects and with the right expectations, particularly for networks expanding at exponential rates. For example, Uncommon Schools, which runs charter schools in six cities on the East Coast, had to hire 1,000 teachers between 2005 and 2015 to keep pace with its rapid expansion.[64] Charter chains, at least the ones with very specific and well-defined pedagogical philosophies, such as HTH and Uncommon Schools, also thought that they could do a successful job themselves in attracting high-quality personnel and in growing their own crop of mission-aligned educators and school leaders who would be inclined to stay in-network longer than a two-year stint and who would buy into the networks' philosophy wholesale. As Larry Rosenstock has also noted in regard to certification, "If the aim is to attract significant talent to teaching, including individuals with advanced degrees and industry/business experience, then the best approach is to offer alternative paths to teacher certification (e.g., via internships and apprenticeship) in the context of professional, growth-enhancing conditions of work: reasonable teacher load, opportunities for professional collaboration, influence on decision-making, and autonomy in curriculum development."[65] He also noted that "an infusion of younger teachers who are digital natives will do more than professional development for existing staff." Indeed, the average age of teachers at HTH is 31.

While High Tech High was the first charter chain to offer a program leading to teacher certification, now a number do, such as the Aspire network in California, Great Oaks Charter Schools on the East Coast, and the controversial New York City-based Success Academy. While some partner with universities, such as Great Oaks and New York University, others conduct everything in-house. Networks *and* teaching candidates, boosters argue, see it as a win, win. For the Great Hearts Academies charter network, which partners with the University of Dallas to award their residents master's degrees, "Teachers receive a heavily subsidized master's degree without having to step away from teaching, and once it's completed, they will receive the customary pay increase on Great Hearts' salary scale. The network develops its most promising teachers and secures a five-year commitment from them (the two years of the program plus an additional three years)."[66] Such models are appealing pathways for late-in-life career-changers or recent graduates with mountains of debt from their undergraduate degrees who want a faster pathway into the classroom, a guaranteed paid position either quickly or immediately, and more preparation and support than older alternative route programs provide.

Unlike the alternative certification advocates of the 1980s and at the turn of the millennium, charter school leaders and their aspiring teachers also began to believe that at least some serious coursework and clinical training was preferable to the crash-course–prepared teacher, who often struggles with management their first year or two and leaves the profession quickly thereafter. A U.S. Department of Education survey in California confirmed that the youngest and least-prepared teachers, often prepared through alternative routes, generally cluster in the highest-needs schools. This became a recognized problem on both sides of the certification debate by 2010.[67]

Philanthropies and state governments have responded enthusiastically to charter school teacher preparation programs. Each state maintains a different law regarding whether teachers in charter schools require the same level of certification as traditional district public schools. As of 2012, only twenty-three states mandated that charter school teachers be licensed. The 2016 changes in federal education policy embedded in the Every Student Succeed Act's "Teaching Preparation Academy" stipulation make it even easier for charter chains to manage their own teacher preparation in order to meet state law, though each state must approve such proposals.[68] In this conducive policy setting, education reformers and pro-charter lobbyists are ramping up their efforts to enlarge the number of charters that are certifying teachers. The Gates Foundation recently allocated $60 million to promote in-network charter school teacher training programs.[69]

Critics raise alarm bells, however. Many worry about the consequences of allowing charter chains to prepare their own teachers.[70] For one, teachers are only educated in that network's educational philosophy, which sometimes can be very narrow and even ideological. New York's Success Academy, for example, is extremely polarizing, not only for its controversial leader Eva Moskowitz, but also for its no-excuses, test-prep heavy curriculum, harsh discipline, and anti-district school stance. Teachers trained in Success Academy's residency program only receive instruction on how to teach according to its model, not how to become an autonomous professional educated in a full range of pedagogical philosophies. To be fair, some say the same of traditional schools of education, where education professors often cling tightly to their own pedagogical philosophies—whether they are based on John Dewey, Paulo Freire, or something else—and only expose students to that way of thinking.

High Tech High has received similar criticism. Though HTH is less divisive than Relay, TFA, or Success Academy, some question the unintended consequences of HTH's innovations. For example, some see the project-based approach as lacking in rigor and breadth of learning. While students may spend multiple weeks delving deeply into a topic of interest and community concern, this may come at the expense of a wider curriculum. The student spending an entire semester writing a play on the Lavender Scare might walk away knowing a lot about playwriting and that one topic, but little to nothing about other aspects of mid-century U.S. and global history. Others fear that such rapid innovations in K–12 schooling leaves students unprepared for college, where lecture hall–style learning and traditional assignments can become overwhelming. What happens when university-level pedagogical innovation does not keep pace with K–12 reforms? In a 2015 interview with the *Hechinger Report*, one HTH graduate at the University of California, Santa Cruz, discussed her struggles: "I didn't really learn study habits at High Tech High. . . . We definitely did testing, but it wasn't emphasized as important as it is here. Learning how much time I should be studying or even how to study was difficult in my first quarter."[71] Another HTH alum attending Cornell also struggled in her first year of college. She concluded that the benefits outweighed the temporary struggles, however. "High Tech High very much teaches you about life," she said. "It might not teach you as well for being prepared for college, but in the long run, I think life is more important."[72]

The research wing of High Tech High's Graduate School of Education also draws praise and criticism. As the first fully charter-embedded graduate school of education, it draws on the aforementioned medical analogy to liken itself to a research and teaching hospital, "where graduate students and faculty participate in courses and conduct research in a clinical setting while engaging daily in the real world of effective, innovative schools."[73]

HTH GSE publishes a peer-reviewed journal on K–12 and adult education, including teacher education, and attempts to serve as a site where researchers and practitioners from other institutions, university and non-university alike, can come together to share findings. In addition to training teachers working toward certification and conducting research, HTH GSE offers a master's degree in educational leadership, through which aspiring school leaders take classes, conduct research, and combine theory and practice in HTH's network schools and online, all in the same pedagogical style as HTH K–12 students. The graduate school also offers professional development residencies for teachers at other schools on topics such as project-based learning and assessment, and it has hosted thousands of visitors from around the world. For HTH leaders, the idea is to embed adult and student learning together, tearing down the barriers that traditionally separate them. Critics worry that in an era of data-driven reforms, such charter-chain research sites are only producing studies to support their own pro-charter agendas. Proponents of independent graduate schools of education disagree. They in turn point out that university-based researchers often also use research to support their own agendas. In the case of HTH, GSE president emeritus Riordan wants to ask larger questions, such as "How can we make group work more equitable? How can we ensure that all students have a meaningful internship experience? How can we increase students' sense of agency and authority in math so they learn to trust their own thinking and value the thinking of their peers? How can we cultivate a sense of belonging and strengthen peer networks among boys of color so they experience academic success in our schools and beyond?"[74] Yet as with other programs, the challenge of evaluation—even agreeing on the basic standards for evaluation—remains, for teacher candidates and for the research that supports their learning.

At the beginning of the twentieth century, when progressive-era school reformers set out to reform public schools in the image of business and industry, there were certainly gains and losses. While schools arguably became more efficient, professional, and open to a larger student population, they nonetheless tracked students by race and class, solidifying social divisions and inequality, and in many ways distanced themselves from the communities they served, sacrificing democratic practices in the process. Similar unintended consequences occurred in the 1980s and 1990s when the world of education took its cues from Wall Street. At the beginning of the twenty-first century, education leaders are likewise looking to the current industry du jour—the Silicon Valley–fueled tech industry—with equal potential for gains and losses. Moreover, teacher educators, policymakers and citizens must evaluate whether they want the structure of education to constantly serve business and industry needs, as opposed to the needs of a democratic and equitable society. Often those needs stand in conflict. In making these evaluations, those involved in teacher education should heed the lessons of the past, weighing the costs and benefits of googling the classroom.

As diverse as the case studies presented here are, they have one overarching theme in common. After the early 1980s, the seemingly stable and settled world of teacher preparation in the United States came unglued. The reform agenda of the 1980s, which began as a critique of both teachers and schools, became a critical call for a fundamental reform of teacher preparation. After the reports of the Holmes and Carnegie commissions in 1988 and the establishment of the National Board for Professional Teaching Standards, business as usual within education schools no longer seemed to be a viable option. At the same time, beginning in New Jersey and continuing across the country to California, alternative approaches to the preparation of teachers emerged, some linked to universities and others—proudly—with no link. While some within universities reacted only in condemnation of the commissions and the alternatives, many others, even if skeptical, sought to fundamentally rethink their work, resulting in major changes within as well as outside of university programs for teachers. Most recently, an array of new hybrid models has appeared on the scene, from district residencies, to charter-schools that award academic degrees, to competency-based and online programs. Late in the second decade of the twenty-first century, there is no sign that the teacher education wars are abating. The range of options is only increasing, and, we argue, the quality of many different offerings is improving.

Lessons Learned

WE STARTED WORK on this book with a question: "Why has teacher preparation changed so dramatically in the past three decades?" When we began our work, we did not have an answer to our question, but as we pursued our case studies—and many other case studies would have worked just as well—we came to a complex and partial answer, or rather to several partial answers. After a period of relative stability, from 1960 to the mid-1980s, teacher preparation in the United States changed dramatically for several closely connected reasons.

First, the sense that schools of education were bastions of mediocrity was widespread and a matter of growing concern in the 1980s, and the concern has never faded. The evidence seemed to be piling up. Within schools of education, the actual work of teacher preparation was too often left to the least prestigious and respected members of the faculty. Observers argued that faculty seemed to design programs to ensure that they could teach their favorite courses rather than focusing on what future teachers needed. Student teaching experiences were too short to create the kind of practical wisdom that new teachers needed and were often directed by cooperating teachers who had little knowledge of or respect for what was taught in education school methods courses. Theory and practice were divorced from each other, and many critics said that teacher preparation included "too much theory, too little practice." As we have recounted in this book, the 1986 reports of the Holmes Group and the Carnegie Commission called for radical reform of teacher preparation programs—a call that presumed the programs were sorely in need of such reform. Calls for reform have continued to appear virtually every year since that time.[1] In this volume, however, we have documented some of the schools where radical reform did indeed take place, in response to either the Holmes and Carnegie proposals, later reports, or other internal or external calls for change. If we look at curriculum reform at Stanford University in California or Montclair State University in New Jersey in the 1980s and 1990s, we see faculty and administrators demanding radical change and a refocus on teacher education. Portraying all teacher preparation programs as caught in a pre-1986 time warp and still in need of such change is simply inaccurate.

Nevertheless, at the conclusion of our work, we have a sense that we have documented the exceptions rather than the norm in twenty-first-century teacher education. While pursuing the case studies we report here, we have continued to hear other faculty and education school staff insist that the reforms from the 1980s to the 2000s are a mistake, that students need every one of the methods courses currently offered, that pedagogical content knowledge means a primary focus on pedagogy and not so much on content (an argument that drives Lee Shulman, who coined the term, to distraction), and that calls for teacher candidates to have an arts and sciences major is an attack on the work of schools of education. The circle-the-wagons mentality is alive and well even as we write. We remember Harry Judge's 1998 lament that the effort to reform university teacher education in the 1980s stalled "when the colleges and schools of education had to think seriously about reforming themselves" and that change will come "only when they really wish to, and not enough yet do." He hoped that change was still just around the corner on a majority of campuses.[2] Twenty years later, we continue to have that hope—but we also are concerned that for many education schools, reform is not yet happening.

A second reason for the major changes in teacher education came about in response to the complaints about university-based programs and especially the fact that many universities seemed glacially slow to change. The push for alternative programs outside of universities accelerated in the late 1980s and has never slowed down. While some reformers continued to work for change within universities, others simply said, "we give up," and moved to create alternative programs outside of any university connection. While TFA may be the best-known alternative certification program, the New Jersey alternative route program actually pre-dated the founding of TFA. The New Jersey effort, TFA, and many other early alternative routes echoed much of the same rhetoric: university teacher preparation programs involved far too many courses, many if not most of which seemed irrelevant to teaching. Thus, teacher education took too long, cost too much money, and was sometimes plainly boring. If the universities could not or would not change, why bother with them.

The argument had resonance, especially starting in the 1980s when many were losing faith in public institutions, such as the public universities that house the vast majority of teacher education programs. It is also important to recognize that just under the surface was a second argument for alternative routes to teaching. The Reagan Revolution of the 1980s was a time of unlimited faith in markets and private enterprise—at least among those who were fans of the revolution. For true believers in the 1980s agenda, which came to be known as the "neoliberal" agenda, privatizing public institutions, turning away from government and other large institutions, and "letting a thousand flowers bloom" provided the answer to many diverse questions. TFA certainly, and others to varying degrees, bought into and was strongly supported by neoliberal advocates of letting the market solve all problems.

We found a third reason for the dramatic changes of the last few decades. We have called it "the revolt of the superintendents." Boston school superintendent Thomas Payzant spoke for many of his fellow superintendents of large urban districts when in his famous—in some circles—talk to AACTE in 2004 (see Introduction), he voiced his deep dissatisfaction with how schools of education were preparing teacher candidates who were entering the teaching force at Boston Public Schools. A result of that speech was the creation of the Boston Teacher Residency program, which has led to a nation-wide movement for school district–based teacher preparation programs—sometimes with a tangential link to a university, and sometimes with none. These programs have become one of the fastest growing routes to teaching in the twenty-first century.

These residency programs can be viewed in many different ways. On the one hand, residencies can be seen as a practitioner-led effort to embed teacher preparation in professional practice in a thoughtful and sustained way, in contrast to the much-criticized fast track of TFA-type programs. Most residency programs require a year-long supervised internship as well as focused study in the disciplines of education—understanding human development, addressing the needs of special education and English language learners, and knowing the fundamental theories that underpin professional expertise. Residencies also prepare aspiring teachers for the specific context in which they will teach. Graduates of the Boston residency teach in Boston, the Denver residency in Denver, and the Seattle residency in Seattle. In January 2018, AACTE, an organization often highly critical of alternative routes to teaching, seemed to bless teacher residency programs as excellent examples of just the sort of university–school district partnerships the association wanted to see expanded.[3]

On the other hand, these same programs can be seen as an effort by school superintendents to control the ideology of teacher preparation. While university programs are often criticized as overemphasizing theory, part of that theory is a commitment to social justice that may lead young teachers to challenge authorities and rules in their district. No leader likes such challenges, and school superintendents seem to be especially sensitive to challenges to their authority. Controlling their own entry programs, having oversight of the curriculum from the beginning, and conducting the clinical supervision and induction of new teachers is a way to ensure a work force that is more skilled but perhaps also more docile.

Finally, the changes that began in the 1980s and 1990s created a sense of momentum in their own right. While those who follow teacher education have often focused on the intensity of the debate among advocates of different camps in the teacher education wars, the reality is that the different camps have learned a great deal from each other. And at least some have taken the criticisms of their own programs to heart. Two examples stand out. First is the story of the Harvard Graduate School of Education, which in 2000 was seriously considering getting out of the teacher preparation business to focus on professional development and research. Instead, Harvard decided to respond to the challenge posed by Teach for America. If so many Harvard students were applying to and participating in TFA, members of the Harvard faculty reasoned, couldn't they do it better? Could they build a teacher preparation program at Harvard that would borrow the best of the alternative routes and the best of Harvard's expertise? They did. At the same time, TFA, which started with a clear sense that teachers did not need much preparation and that methods courses were a waste of time, has over the years significantly strengthened both its pre-professional summer institute and its in-service mentoring and course offerings for TFA corps members who are struggling through the first difficult years of teaching. In part because of state regulations but also on its own initiative, TFA is strongly encouraging corps members to pursue an on-the-job master's degree. In fact, most TFA corps members who stay in the teaching profession beyond the required two years have met their state's requirements for teacher licensure, as if they followed a more traditional university path. Perhaps most importantly, TFA has responded to criticisms of its early elitism by attending seriously to issues of diversity so that today half of new corps members are people of color. From Harvard to TFA, and from the

Seattle residency to Montclair State, teacher education programs are better for listening to their harshest critics, even if their public rhetoric seldom reflects this reality.

At the conclusion of our case studies, we find that we respectfully disagree with many other studies of teacher education. To say that education schools and their teacher preparation programs are hopelessly out of date and "an industry of mediocrity" is simply wrong. Whether one looks at the Urban Teacher program at the University of Chicago or the revised curriculum at the University of Indianapolis or the continuing commitment to improvement at Montclair State, there are top flight programs for the preparation of teachers all across the United States. Yet, to claim that these outstanding programs and others like them are the norm in university-based teacher preparation is simply not true. The examples of mediocrity are legion. Of course, almost the exact same conclusion is true of alternative routes. Some are good and have gotten much better. TFA has recruited some extraordinarily able candidates to teaching, is doing a better job than most universities to recruit a racially and ethnically diverse corps of future teachers, and is taking the mentoring and continuing advising of teachers seriously. However, we have seen alternative routes that allow virtually anyone not only to enter the program but also to graduate and be certified through what is truly a "quick and dirty" preparation—short on pedagogy, short on content, short on the ability to do what a teacher needs to do.

We find teacher residencies an especially promising approach to teacher preparation, blending a year-long internship under supervision that deeply immerses teaching candidates in a classroom with thoughtful seminars and opportunities to learn the theories behind the pedagogy. We have our concerns about some residency programs, though. When the partnership with a university is "university lite" and mostly consists of rubber-stamping a completely independent program, especially a program that is directly under the control of a single superintendent who may not want to hear criticism, then it lacks crucial attributes of professional preparation. We were struck by the fact that residencies seem to be willing to address these concerns. Indeed, in some—particularly the Seattle Teacher Residency—the university, the district, and (all too rarely) the teacher union are all involved.

We also note a very recent development in the field of teacher education: the growth of competencies-based programs in which a candidate for teaching must demonstrate clear mastery of a list of specific competencies rather than complete courses or seat time. Competency-based programs have the potential to allow for a fast adjustment to individual needs while appreciating the diverse strengths of different candidates, allowing a person who has recently graduated with honors but needs to hone pedagogy and a person with experience with young people but less content knowledge to focus where they need to grow. When competency-based programs are linked with an online platform such as Western Governors University, we are optimistic about the programs' ability to reach individuals who because of location or other responsibilities cannot attend a more traditional campus program. We think the criticism of these programs, such as WGU—which has sometimes been seen by traditional education schools as "the enemy"—is unwarranted and unfair.

We have high hopes and expectations for some new programs still in the design and early implementation phases, including the Woodrow Wilson Academy at MIT and the program on our own campus at New York University (which we have not included in this study out of a concern for a conflict of interest). We also have grave reservations about the online programs of for-profit universities, especially that offered by the University of Phoenix. While gathering information is difficult, we have not seen evidence that would convince us of either the rigor of the preparation or the ability of the Phoenix program to control costs. We fear that too many for-profit programs like the University Phoenix combine the worst of the "industry of mediocrity," high costs for teacher candidates, and a lack of the direct contact with children and schools that is essential to foster the wisdom of practice.

As we have seen, since the mid-1980s, the field of teacher education has been both rapidly changing and filled with contention. In 2004, Frederick Hess, Andrew Rotherham, and Kate Walsh wrote, "In recent years, the debate over teacher quality and preparation has gained new urgency. During that time, competing groups of partisans have dominated this debate, one seemingly eager to assail the nation's education schools and to suggest that there is an insufficiently defined body of professional knowledge, and the other committed to advancing professionalism by ensuring that all teachers are prepared and licensed through a prescribed and formal training program. The conflict is suffusing research, confusing policy makers, and stifling potentially promising reforms."[4] At about the same time, but coming from a different perspective, Marilyn Cochran-Smith and Kenneth M. Zeichner wrote, "Almost everyone agrees that teacher education needs to be improved, but there is a vast disagreement about how, why, and for what purposes."[5] Looking at the field a decade later, and based on the case studies considered in this volume, and dozens of others that could have been included, we conclude that the debate is certainly alive and well. The happy news, however, is that far from stifling reform, the debate has led to new and creative approaches to the preparation of teachers.

While it is certainly true that there are deeply divided and hostile camps made up of critics and defenders of schools of education, there are others who are developing important new blended ventures, taking what they consider the best from both traditional and alternative routes and creating new models of teacher preparation for the United States. Calling these new ventures a third way misses the point. It is not that they represent a compromise in the teacher education wars so much as they represent an effort at experimentation and learning from mistakes in all routes to teaching that may lead to a brighter future—for teacher preparation and for the schools and children who depend on the ways teachers are prepared. We hope the next decade will see many more such experiments coupled with a much more robust evaluation system that will help us gain new and much needed clarity on what really works in preparing the next generation of teachers.

Of course, change and contention are not new to teacher preparation. As long as there have been teachers, there have been arguments about how to prepare them—or whether any preparation was necessary. Since the end of World War II, as nearly all U.S. teacher preparation became based at universities, there have been critics—some harsh, some more judicious—of the ways universities go about their work in this field. But with the exception of the short-lived National Teacher Corps of the 1960s, only a few of those critics proposed alternatives for teacher preparation. As this volume shows, that situation changed—quickly and radically—after 1986. Today, depending on how one counts, perhaps one third of those entering the nation's teaching force come from alternative routes. That is a huge change. In previous chapters, we explored the nature of the change through a series of case studies and asked the larger—and too seldom asked—question of *why* the change took place. As we noted at the beginning of the book, we could have chosen quite different case studies for both the university programs and the alternative providers. Our conclusions, we expect, would be the same.

While some university-based programs have adopted a "this too will pass" attitude—either ignoring or dismissing the voices calling for change—many other universities—including those described in our case studies—have taken criticism and calls for change seriously. Individuals as well as whole faculty within education schools have been among the leading voices of reform. Indeed university-based professors and deans began criticizing their own programs before there were alternative providers. Among our case studies, Stanford and Montclair State come to mind as advocates for change from within the Ivory Tower, but one would also certainly have to include many others, especially Michigan State University under the leadership of Judith Lanier and the work of John Goodlad and his many colleagues the University of Washington and their successors at both institutions. In the best universities, teacher preparation is dramatically better than it was thirty years ago, and university faculty have helped make it that way. Candidates for teaching spend much more time in schools, engaged in actual teaching, with careful supervision and time for reflection. Candidates for teaching are also expected to know more than was the case before; more states are calling for a bachelor's degree or the equivalent in a specific content area in order to be licensed to teach in that area. The much—and rightly—criticized education major is passing away, replaced in more and more places with a program that blends top-flight academic content knowledge in the traditional disciplines with practice-based clinical experience. While courses in teaching methods remain—appropriately—a part of the teacher preparation curriculum, they no longer dominate teacher education.[6]

In these same thirty years, alternative routes to teaching—virtually unknown in the United States in 1985—have grown rapidly and changed significantly in response to criticism. Many alternative routes—including the often referenced Teach for America—began with an assumption that virtually any smart person (often defined as any graduate of an elite liberal arts college) could teach after a few short weeks of preparation in core issues of pedagogy and classroom management. While some programs still embrace that philosophy and some states seem to be moving in that direction, many of those in the field, especially those like TFA who have been engaged for some time, have moved in the direction of significantly more professional preparation—even though they remain skeptical of university schools of education, with their emphasis on courses, credits, and seat time.

Then there are the programs we have called hybrids—district-based residency programs that have a university partner or competency-based programs, both within and independent from education schools—are blending university and non-university alternative route thinking. We certainly see examples of programs drawing from multiple perspectives in the Seattle Residency or the Woodrow Wilson Academy, described in chapter 3.

Lessons That History Can Teach

We believe that this research has satisfied our contention that taking an historical view of the changes in teacher education has benefits as compared to other approaches. In the Introduction, we wrote that we believed that viewing the very contentious history of teacher education through the prism of the discipline of history allows one to embrace the complexity and contingency of historical developments, move beyond simplistic good-versus-bad value judgments, and begin to understand the historical context that shaped reforms, reactions, and unforeseen outcomes. Having completed this work, we believe in this position even more strongly. Far too much of what has been written about recent developments in teacher preparation betrays too fully the biases of those doing the writing. Those defending education schools seek to prove the superiority of a university-based preparation program while "exposing" the dangers lurking behind the alternatives. Those defending alternative routes tend to see themselves as the virtuous reformers challenging an impervious and irresponsible status quo. History allows us to step back, to ask larger questions of national and international context, and to see in the push and pull of contending forces the working out of long-standing differences as well as the emergence of new priorities.

Our look at the last thirty years through an historical lens has also convinced us that it is foolish to assume that support for universities is by definition progressive and support for alternative programs is conservative. We need to keep the focus where it must be—on young people who are taught by graduates of these programs. It is important to know and think about the history of teacher preparation programs. Indeed, there were progressive origins on both sides of the certification debate, supporting our argument that quality, equity-based preparation can happen through a variety of pathways.

In many places, support for state-approved, accredited, university-based schools of education is seen as a liberal position. Support for alternative routes to teacher preparation is most widespread among conservatives and usually a badge of one's involvement in the conservative cause. This is an odd development. As Harvey Kantor and Robert Lowe have argued, "During the 1960s and early 1970s, criticism of the bureaucracy of public schools came chiefly from intellectuals, writers, and activists on the political left." Kantor and Lowe, however, noted that this changed with the growing conservative critique of American schooling and its concomitant call for charter schools, vouchers, and alternative routes to a teaching career. According to Kantor and Lowe, much of the left responded to the conservation criticisms by defending the very public schools that their predecessors had labeled seriously flawed if not bankrupt. Kantor and Lowe concluded, "Discourse about public education has been circumscribed by the left's abandonment of its earlier critique of the way schools are controlled and organized. . . .

[T]his abandonment has, ironically, allowed the right to define the main agenda for substantive change in cities."[7] We agree. Moreover, this shift has allowed conservatives to define much of the agenda for change in teacher education, while liberals have been oddly defensive. This is especially ironic because, looking at the issue of teacher preparation historically, it was progressives who first argued for alternative methods of teacher preparation. The National Teacher Corps of the late 1960s was a liberal response to the perceived racism and lack of contact with communities of color in education schools. Along with calls for equity and integration in K–12 schools, civil rights leaders argued for new forms of teacher preparation, outside of universities if need be. The lesson we take from this history is that we need to put aside automatic defenses or critiques of any particular institutional construct and ask about the outcomes—what is working to prepare competent teachers and what is working to ensure a better education for the nation's children.[8]

What Comes Next?

The question remains: What comes next? Having reviewed three decades of rapid and sometimes dramatic change, where do we—at least we, the authors, as two historians who have been looking at this story—believe the country and the teacher education enterprise need to go next? We have come to several conclusions.

First, after all the debates, we still do not know nearly enough about what constitutes good teacher preparation or how to evaluate preparation programs. We need significantly more research. Specifically, we need more research that will let us evaluate how well individual teacher preparation programs prepare effective teachers. Some of us had high hopes for so-called value-added research on this topic, but the hopes have not been justified. When we say one program is good and another not so good, how do we know? When we point to the University of Chicago or Stanford or the Seattle Teacher Residency as models of teacher preparation, others rightly ask, how do you know? When we complain about methods of evaluation, it is incumbent on those of us working in teacher education to find better models.

Second, whether teacher preparation remains in universities or moves into alternative institutions, teacher educators also need to disconnect from the university status game and assert their own independent professional norms. The quest for university acceptance and status, we believe, is a significant barrier to what matters most—the preparation of top-flight teachers for the nation's schools.

Members of education school faculty in most institutions, including the teacher education faculty, spend far too much time looking over their shoulders at other parts of the university—at the arts and sciences faculty or at elite professional schools like medicine—and far too little time on professional practice. This is not to say that keeping an eye on their peers across the university is a foolish preoccupation. Important issues of professional status, salary, and tenure are usually based on standards designed for other parts of the university. The most research productive professors are the most honored (and highest paid) faculty members. Those who actually spend significant time in classrooms, supervising and working with aspiring teachers, are nearly always the lowest status (and lowest paid). The result is that schools of education are producing significant research about education— some useful and good, some not—and far too little research and far too few new initiatives in the realm of teacher preparation and practice.

But professors of education are not the only problem. Schools of education complain about being "cash cows" for other parts of the university that have higher status. One of us had quite direct experiences with the way a change in provosts led to a change in focus for a school of education, from radical and thoughtful experimentation to develop new community-based models of teacher education into an education school staffed by clinical faculty and meant primarily to provide funds for the expansion of the more-traditional, discipline-focused efforts of the university.

Far too few professors in the core disciplines seem to care a wit about how those disciplines are taught at the K–12 level or about the preparation of the teachers who teach those subjects at the "lower" levels. Some fifty years ago, in the midst of a biting critique of schools of education, former Harvard president James Bryant Conant turned his frustration on the arts and sciences faculty, noting that "the faculties of arts and sciences had shown little interest in school problems. . . . With few exceptions, college professors turned their backs on the problems of mass secondary education." He continued, "Many academic professors believe that the courses given by professors of education are worthless, and that the degrees granted students who have devoted much of their time to these courses are of little value . . . [even though] it is generally the case that the academic professors who advance these arguments know far too little about education courses."[9] Far too little has changed in this arena.

Third, we believe that it is time—or well past time—to stop the hostility between traditional and alternative routes to teaching. There are programs that fall into each category that are excellent. There are programs that fall into each category that are mediocre, if not downright terrible. And there are blended programs that draw on the best from each and that may well be the leaders in teacher preparation in the twenty-first century. The dividing line must not be whether a program has university affiliation but whether it demonstrates programmatic excellence in the service of student learning and equity. In the process of seeking that kind of excellence, teacher educators, wherever they are based, need to listen to a wider range of voices. Those seeking to become teachers often know a great deal about what they need next. A twenty-one-year-old who has just graduated from college at the top of her or his class but has not set foot in a K–12 school since high school graduation, a thirty-five-year-old paraprofessional who has spent a decade with young children but needs more subject-matter expertise in order to teach, and a sixty-year-old researcher taking early retirement from a lab to pursue teaching as a second career in teaching need radically different forms of preparation. None of them are probably ready to enter a classroom without some preparation. But none of them should be seen as only having deficits; rather, each has a combination of expertise to draw on and needs that must be met. Until we know a great deal more than we do now about how to prepare effective teachers, we need to try many different approaches while maintaining appropriate safeguards and robust systems of evaluation. Parents and community leaders also know things about what their children, or the children of their community, need that professional educators and educators of educators may not. The goal here is not to privilege a new set of voices but to encourage a dialogue in which multiple voices help with the difficult task of building a new consensus.

Finally, we believe that the kind of preparation that today's and tomorrow's prospective teachers need simply cannot be done within the shell of the old-style teaching profession. We need to develop a different professional model—one that takes induction into the profession seriously.

Research

Teacher education is a seriously under-researched field. In a 2013 National Academy of Education study, *Evaluation of Teacher Preparation Programs*, Michael Feuer and his colleagues began with a modest understatement, noting that "many aspects of the relationship between teacher preparation and instructional quality are not fully understood, and existing approaches to TPP [teacher preparation programs] evaluation are complex, varied, and fragmented." They elaborated on this comment: "Social science is still far from reaching a conclusive judgment about how to measure pedagogical skills, content knowledge, temperament, interpersonal styles, empathy, and understanding of the learning needs of children, and how those attributed, however they might be measured, combine to make the most difference in teacher's effectiveness. . . . But by and large the knowledge base about essential qualities of teaching is still at a rudimentary stage, a reality that necessarily places limits on the design of valid measures for assessing TPPs." While Feuer outlines a robust program to remedy this situation, the funding and commitment to the work by skilled researchers are far from realized.[10]

This complaint about the lack of meaningful research may seem odd given the plethora of research studies, monographs, and arguments that have poured forth from so many sources in the last thirty years. But the problem remains. We still do not know far too much basic information that would be helpful in designing quality teacher preparation.

In 1970 Lee Shulman, then still a young researcher, wrote, "If the goal of educational research is significant improvement in the daily functioning of educational programs, I know of little evidence that researchers have made discernible strides in that direction. . . . researchers must step back, regain perspective, and then identify clearly the most fruitful routes toward development of an empirically based discipline of education."[11] Thanks to Shulman's tireless efforts over the following forty-plus years, educational research as a whole is in a much different place now than it was in 1970. But when we turn to the field of teacher education, when we ask, "how do we know which programs and types of programs produce the most effective classroom teachers?" the answer is that we do not know, not with any degree of confidence or agreement across the field.

Starting in the 1990s and continuing well into the 2000s, Linda Darling-Hammond did more than almost anyone else to lead efforts to define a research base for teacher preparation. In a 2005 study sponsored by the National Academy of Education's Committee on Teacher Education, Darling-Hammond and Joan Baratz-Snowden summarized research that they hoped would help teacher preparation programs deliver what prospective teachers needed for success. Darling-Hammond and Baratz-Snowden outlined a framework for understanding teaching and learning that included expertise in three essential areas: knowledge of learners, knowledge of subject matter, and knowledge and skill in teaching. The last area—knowledge and skill in teaching—included the former skills but also assessment and classroom management, or what many call pedagogical skills. Having identified these skills, Darling-Hammond and Baratz-Snowden also outlined the elements that they deemed essential to quality teacher preparation programs, including a core curriculum, case studies, and extended clinical practices. Finally, they advocated strongly for the accreditation system of the then dominant National Council for the Accreditation of Teacher Education.[12]

While Darling-Hammond's contribution was significant, her animus toward alternative routes to teaching, and especially Teach for America, led others to distrust some of her conclusions. Led by economists, a number of scholars—some more conservative, some not—concluded that the evidence in favor of university-based programs and against alternative providers of teacher preparation was at least flawed. By 2003 a report of the Education Commission of the States concluded that there was little or no conclusive evidence about the value of most elements that some insisted were essential to teacher preparation.[13] Two years later an American Educational Research Association panel on research in teacher education came to a similar conclusion: "Studies comparing the effectiveness of various kinds of traditional and alternative teacher education programs and 4-year versus 5-year programs in relation to a variety of outcomes generally provide conflicting findings about the efficacy of different forms of teacher preparation and do not enable us to identify the specific program features that are related to the achievement of particular outcomes."[14] Few developments in the last decade would lead to a different conclusion.

We know enough now to be fairly sure that good teachers do make a huge difference. At least since the 1990s, William Sanders, among other leaders, has argued that effective teachers make a significant difference in the lives of students. As Sanders and colleagues wrote in 1997, "The effectiveness of the teacher is the major determinant of student academic progress. Teacher effects on student achievement have been found to be both additive and cumulative."[15] Indeed, proponents of the value added by teachers insist that contrary to earlier research, their findings prove that teacher effectiveness is more significant than race, socio-economic level, class size, and classroom heterogeneity in student academic achievement. Value-added research has been questioned and has become highly controversial, especially when used (inappropriately, we would argue) to evaluate individual teachers for merit and salary. But even if one accepts the core conclusion—that effective teachers make a huge difference for their pupils, and ineffective teachers make an equally important negative impact—there remains a core problem with the research as it affects teacher preparation. We may know that excellent teachers make a much bigger difference in the academic achievement of their students than average or poor teachers, but we know far less about what the good teachers know and are able to do. And we know even less about how to ensure that any particular preparation program will provide the education they need. Without knowing what highly effective teachers do day to day in their classrooms, we end up with a circular definition of good teachers. Good teachers are teachers who make a difference. But what their characteristics are, what sets them apart from average or poor teachers, and what kind of preparation programs will produce more like them is far less clear. Least clear of all is the question of what we mean by good teaching.

The fact that this problem remains true today is ironic. In the last two decades we have learned much more about how people learn and comprehend. Research in the biological sciences has taught us a great deal about how the brain works, how individuals engage with knowledge, and how they come to an ability to read, do mathematics, and gain understanding of the world around them.[16] If teacher educators study the latest research—sometimes a big *if*—they have available to them a wealth of data about learning that previous generations did not. What they do not have is meaningful data about how to educate teachers, what brain research means for the act of teaching, and especially what sorts of preparation will enable a new teacher to help a student exercise their minds in the ways we now know minds can be exercised.

We simply do not have a meaningful research foundation for saying "this type of teacher preparation is better or more effective than that kind of teacher preparation." We have passionate arguments. We have research, but most of the research has equally well-researched counter-research. We have hints. We know that real-time involvement in teaching—not just learning about teaching—seems to make a difference. We know that content knowledge matters. But we know far too little. Moreover, for all the millions of dollars poured into experiments in teacher preparation, there is still far too little funding for research and experimentation. Until state and federal governments, private foundations, and universities find significant new ways to support high-quality research focused on the question of "what works" in teacher preparation—specifically, how to mentor large numbers of individuals to be the kinds of highly effective teachers who put what we know about learning into the practice of teaching—all of our progress will be marginal, and even the best experiments will have limited value since no one will really be able to say if this or that change makes a difference for large numbers of aspiring teachers.

Robust Experimentation

In May 1932, while seeking the party nomination that would make him president, Franklin D. Roosevelt gave a speech in which, looking at the crisis of the Great Depression, he said, "The country needs and, unless I mistake its temper, the country demands bold, persistent experimentation. It is common sense to take a method and try it: If it fails, admit it frankly and try another. But above all, try something."[17] That approach to federal policy characterized the New Deal and defined federal policy for the rest of the 1930s.

Nearly ninety years later, the nation needs a similar approach to teacher preparation. We may not have the research we need to be absolutely sure of the next step, but there are models of teacher preparation that seem promising and that need to be developed and tested in as many different contexts as possible. We have emerged from our study of a number of programs more convinced than ever that bold experimentation is what is needed and that regulations that stand in the way of such experimentation need to be abolished.

In light of the failure of research to give us sufficiently clear answers—to date—about what good teachers actually do or how to prepare such excellent teachers, we find ourselves arguing that the best course of action may well be to give both university programs and alternative providers much more freedom to pursue their hunches and develop programs as they see fit —and at the same time develop a culture of using evidence to show the world the value of their approach. It is important to allow different programs to appeal to students who will be best served by their models, whether they are a recent college graduate, a retired engineer, or a paraprofessional wishing to transition to lead teaching, each of whom may need a different type of program. Until we know a lot more about what constitutes good teacher education, we should lighten up on regulation and do everything we can to foster experimentation. At the same time, we need to develop research tools to track what seems to make a difference and what does not, so that in the not-too-distant future we will be able to point to certain models of teacher preparation and say "this works" based on clear and specific evidence.[18]

A word of caution is due here. As in any important field, "first, do no harm" is a good working limit on experimentation. We do not want to prepare architects whose buildings routinely fall down or doctors whose patients die. We also do not want to prepare teachers whose students fail to learn or are not treated with equity and respect. State regulations and accreditation standards can help ensure that bad things do not happen, which is important—indeed, essential, but regulation alone will never produce excellence. And we need excellence.

Superintendents and principals are not going to hire teachers whom they think are ill-prepared. There is far too much accountability pressure on school leaders today for them to hire less-able teachers when they have the opportunity to hire those they consider more able. School leaders may not be the perfect judges of who is best prepared to teach, but they are probably in a better position to evaluate fitness than any other authority.

At the same time, one good limitation on any program is to ask, "would the developers allow their own children (or in the case of some of us grand-children) to be taught by the graduates of the program?" Unless the answer is a resounding "yes," the program should not proceed. We do not need programs that prepare teachers for "other people's children." When the founders of High Tech High send their children to that school to be taught by graduates of its internal teacher preparation program, we have reason to trust what the school is doing. The same should be true in all cases.

The important issue is not whether a prospective teacher took a particu-lar course or where the course was offered—in an accredited school of edu-cation or a non-traditional program. The issue is the capability of the teacher and the quality of their future practice. Do new teachers know what to teach and how to teach? Are their students engaged in learning in ways that will result in their long-term academic achievement (which is much more than the skill of passing one standardized test)? Are students, including special education and English language learners, treated with respect, and do they feel safe in the classroom? Are we sufficiently nimble in our programs to attract and support seasoned adults who have much to offer but may not need every course in our program?[19]

We understand that our argument flies in the face of work that many of our colleagues are doing to strengthen the standards of excellence in teacher preparation. Especially since the launch of the Council for the Accreditation of Educator Preparation (CAEP) in 2013, some of the best minds in teacher education, representing a wide spectrum of opinions, have come together to develop significantly improved standards for maintaining excellence in the field.

Building on the important work of the former National Council for the Accreditation of Teacher Education (NCATE, founded 1954) and the Teacher Education Accreditation Council (TEAC, founded 1997), CAEP has sought to move standards for teacher education from a focus on specific requirements to a focus on the skills and competencies needed for effective-ness in teaching. At their core, the CAEP standards seek to create a culture of evidence in which programs consistently ask what evidence do they have to demonstrate that what they say about their program is true and how can they, as program faculty, use this same evidence for continual program improvement. The fifth of the 2013 standards specifically asks whether the provider meets the following criteria: "The provider maintains a quality assurance system comprised of valid data from multiple measures, including evidence of candidates' and completers' positive impact on P–12 student learning and development. The provider supports continuous improvement that is sustained and evidence-based, and that evaluates the effectiveness of its completers. The provider uses the results of inquiry and data collection to establish priorities, enhance program elements and capacity, and test innovations to improve completers' impact on P–12 student learning and development."[20] At their best, the CAEP standards seek to create a culture in teacher education programs where every teacher preparation course and every program is consistently looking at the evidence from multiple sources—not just test scores but student work and other indicators—and is improving as a result. We certainly applaud that goal. The federal government and many states have adopted the CAEP standards as the new norm for acceptable teacher preparation programs.

We support these efforts as long as CAEP accreditation remains optional and other programs are free to experiment unhindered by accreditation. While we applaud CAEP's effort and especially the dialogue it has spawned, we believe that the pitfalls of implementation are significant. Seeking and winning accreditation takes a significant investment of time and money, which are necessarily diverted from continuing research and/or development of individual aspiring teachers. While the goal of the standards is to create a culture of evidence, the search for evidence can all too easily lead to a culture of compliance. Even more significant, accreditation standards, by definition, limit experimentation. While the University of Chicago's Urban Teacher Education Program and the online programs of Western Governors University are accredited, they may represent the outer limits of what is deemed acceptable and could be constrained in their efforts by CAEP's standards. We have also heard from deans and other teacher education leaders about the degree to which state and voluntary accreditation standards limit creativity and foster an attitude that hinders new kinds of thinking, as faculty and staff spend time searching for the required evidence to prove what a program is doing in a way that will satisfy accreditors rather than asking larger questions about direction, goals, and purpose. Certainly meeting all of the many requirements of state governments and accreditation agencies exhausts many faculty who otherwise might spend their time and creative energies working with individual students or on new program development. Indeed, more than one dean told us that leadership in the field had become creative compliance. But too often following rules and regulations wins out over more creative approaches. Why not, we argue, encourage the most diverse range of efforts, even radical ones that are beyond the limits of current standards or are not amenable to short-term evidence collection? The efforts may not all succeed, but we also are not at a point in the development of a knowledge base to say with any confidence that current educational structures represent best practices. Until we are, we believe that limitations on experimentation provide undue hindrances to the bold efforts—sometimes linked failure—that will generate a better future.

Five Questions Yet to Be Addressed

While we offer some tentative answers in explaining the history we have reviewed, we are left with questions about what comes next and what ought to define the future of teacher preparation in the United States. Among other avenues for research, we ask the following five questions.

HOW CAN WE DEVELOP AN EQUITY AGENDA FOR ALL THAT SERVES TO SIGNIFICANTLY IMPROVE TEACHING?

Talk of equity and social justice has been part of teacher education discussions at least since George Counts published *Dare the School Build a New Social Order?* in 1932.[21] In our judgment, the most important thing any teacher can do for justice, and therefore must be prepared to demonstrate in a pre-service program, is to teach all students effectively, especially poor students, students of color, students with disabilities, or English language learners. Teachers must imbue all students, privileged and unprivileged, with a sense of democratic values and the ways of democratic discourse. Of course that simple statement opens a range of complex issues, but for us an equity agenda in teacher preparation means starting with two key issues.

Teaching Diverse Learners

All teachers should be prepared to address the needs of special education students and English language learners (ELLs) and able to give thoughtful attention to a range of multicultural issues, including race, class, gender, sexual orientation, and religion. Most teacher education programs claim that they do this, and we believe that they want to. We are less convinced that many do so effectively. By 2025, when many of today's graduates will be hitting their stride as teachers, an estimated one in four public school students will be classified as an English language learner.[22] All teachers must be prepared to confront this fact by receiving at least a baseline education in how to best reach students with language needs. Teachers will also need to serve students with varying special education requirements and should be prepared to employ the most effective and research-proven strategies to provide students with disabilities with the education they need and deserve. We worry that while we have seen specialized programs for special education and ELL teachers that are excellent, too few general education teachers are getting the preparation they need to serve today's diverse student body.[23] Teach for America, to its credit, places diversity at the center of their training both during induction and in the summer institute. TFA's Diversity, Community, and Achievement curriculum requires pre-service teachers to consider issues of race and class as they relate to educating students in urban and rural low-income communities and provides methods for approaching learners across lines of difference. Others may learn from it.

Preparing a Racially and Ethnically Diverse Cohort of Teachers

Today's teaching force is too white. Preparation programs in all forms have a core responsibility to prepare a diverse generation of teachers. There is strong evidence that students, both white and non-white, prefer being taught by teachers of color. Student perceptions of their teachers are a strong predictor of academic achievement; thus, failing to prepare and supply such teachers is one of the main failings of the field of teacher education nationally. We are not saying there is not also a need for highly qualified and committed white teachers. There is. But many schools need a much more diverse faculty, and to accomplish that, teacher education programs, both university-based and alternative routes, need to take diversity among teacher candidates much more seriously.[24]

Kenneth Zeichner has recommended several strategies that teacher preparation programs can use to increase the racial diversity of their students, including more thoughtful recruitment and admission standards that focus on aptness to teach, establishing articulation agreements with two-year community and technical colleges, expanding outreach to historically black colleges and universities (HBCUs) and Latinx-serving schools, and perhaps most important strengthening faculty commitment and competence with regard to issues of diversity so that students of color feel welcome and included in the life of an education program.[25] While significant increases in financial aid for future teachers is needed across the board, it is especially important for future teachers of color, some of whom come from low-income backgrounds and some of whom are offered enticing financial aid packages in other fields.

We have seen significant developments in some of the programs that we have studied. After beginning as a program focused on elite (read: white) college students, Teach for America has taken the issue of diversity seriously, so that today almost half of its new corps members are people of color, significantly higher than the 15% national average among educator preparation programs. Among university programs, Stanford has led the way in recruiting students of color, so that today the Stanford Teacher Education Program can also boast that half of its students are people of color. Stanford's financial resources and prestige have been important to this effort, but so has a deep institutional commitment to creating a welcoming learning community.[26] The Seattle Teacher Residency likewise has taken steps to attract a teaching corps that reflects the diversity of the district's student body, and has succeeded. Whatever the route, we know that it is possible to create a more diverse teaching force, and we need more programs that aim to do so.

HOW CAN TEACHER EDUCATORS MORE EFFECTIVELY LEARN FROM CURRENT TEACHERS, PARENTS, AND THE COMMUNITY?

Teacher education programs are too isolated. Even in the best of the programs —traditional and alternative—that we studied, we found far too little interest in listening to a broader audience. We did not see sufficiently strong evidence of the voice of today's teachers in planning teacher education curricula, though we did note that some schools, like the Relay Graduate School of Education, only hire former teachers for their faculty. We likewise saw little evidence of the voice of parents and community leaders in the development of teacher preparation programs, though the residency programs, such as those in Chicago, Boston, and Seattle, seem to be doing the best in this regard.

There is a long history of teacher complaints that their pre-service programs did not prepare them for what they experienced in their first years of teaching. Indeed, education school alumni are among the fiercest critics of schools of education, and alternative route alumni are almost equally critical of their programs. Criticism of TFA by its former corps members has become a virtual cottage industry.[27] Yet across the board, we saw far too little evidence of program leaders listening to teachers. This is not to say that teachers have all the answers or that practice should suddenly be elevated above theory. Neither of those statements is true. However, those who study a field but no longer practice directly in it can also be wrong and can all too easily miss factors that seem obvious to a current practitioner. Unless theory, including theories of what constitutes good teacher preparation, are tested through meaningful engagement with practice and practitioners, something important is lost.

Kenneth Zeichner and the late Peter Murrell have been the strongest recent advocates of bringing community voices—parents and community leaders—into the dialogue about teacher preparation, in the process developing what Murrell called "the community dedicated teacher."[28] In a recent paper, Kenneth Zeichner, Katherina Payne, and Kate Brayko Gence argue that "teacher education needs to make a fundamental shift in whose knowledge and expertise counts and should count in the education of new teachers." The authors call on faculty in schools of education to "cross institutional boundaries to collaborate with communities and schools."[29] While acknowledging that such collaboration is not easy, Zeichner, Payne, and Gence insist that until not only the voices of teachers but also those of parents and community leaders are part of planning teacher education programs, the curriculum will not only be incomplete but misguided. This is not a matter of discounting the professional expertise of those who study and teach about the process of teaching and learning. It is not about privileging a new voice. It is about adding essential voices—from practicing teachers, their students, and parents and community residents, who because of their perspective have their own wisdom to add to the knowledge base needed for teacher education to effective. As Zeichner and his colleagues note, this approach will sometimes lead to misunderstanding and will try the patience of all involved as people of quite different perspectives try to understand each other and work together. Nevertheless, we believe that the diversity of voices represented in this radically revised approach to planning and implementing a teacher preparation program—one that solicits and values community input and participation along with that of scholars and researchers—is a key component of excellence.

An ideal program for aspiring teachers should ensure that candidates are well versed in the kinds of communities they will likely serve. Aspiring teachers need to learn how to live comfortably in the communities they serve, not just commute to work from a different world. They need to learn how to translate important theoretical knowledge on community and diversity into successful classroom practices, teacher–parent relationships, and school leadership. Empirical research on the efficacy of student and community engagement supports this stance, and a value-system committed to democratic and public education demands it.[30]

Such an approach to teacher preparation is not new. When the federal government launched the National Teacher Corps as part of the Great Society programs of the 1960s, a key element in the preparation of Teacher Corps members was developing a close connection to the communities where they planned to teach. Teacher Corps candidates were required to live with a local family while preparing to teach and were expected to be active in the community as well as the classroom once on the job. The notion that community residents, especially residents of often-marginalized, poor urban and rural communities, would help shape the education of teachers was a radical approach to teacher preparation, embraced by some while discounted by others.

We found too little evidence of this approach in our case studies. We were delighted when Stanford graduate and Woodrow Wilson Teaching Fellow Lydia Cuffman wrote that she lived where she could walk to school:

> My first commitment to the community where my students live is living there myself. I see my students at restaurants and at the movies. I attend their arts performances, and even occasionally make it to a sporting event. I perform with a local theater group that uses our school's stage. I march in the annual Fourth of July Parade, waving at all my students as I see them in the crowd. When my school raises a bond issue to pay for renovations, I walk to the firehouse in my neighborhood to vote on issues that affect me and my students.[31]

We would be happy to hear more such comments. As we noted, we were impressed that the Seattle Teacher Residency included the teachers union in the leadership of their program, an anomaly among residency programs. We also have been impressed by the ways in which the University of Pennsylvania prepares teachers through a deep partnership with the neighboring community of West Philadelphia, and we are intrigued by the degree to which Miami University in Oxford, Ohio, embraces Murrell's ideas. We want to know more. Such an approach is never easy and always essential.[32]

WHAT IS THE RIGHT MIX OF THEORY, PRACTICE, PEDAGOGY, AND CONTENT?

When Lee Shulman coined the felicitous term "pedagogical content knowledge," he was pointing out a simple truism: You can't teach what you do not know.[33] He was also saying something else: You have to know how to teach what you know. We have listened to debates—too many debates—between those who demand more time for aspiring teachers to be immersed in practice and in learning how to teach and those who insist that teachers simply need to know their content much more thoroughly and that anyone who knows content well can teach. Such a debate is wrong headed

As Shulman himself defines the term, "pedagogical content knowledge" certainly involves rich knowledge of the subject matter or, in the case of elementary teachers, the multiple subjects that a teacher is going to teach. Those who argue for more content in teacher preparation are not wrong; they are simply insufficient in their argument. As Shulman has noted, his definition "goes beyond knowledge of subject matter [though it certainly assumes it] per se to the dimension of subject matter knowledge for teaching." In this expanded definition, teachers need to know how to make their subject comprehensible to others and "must have at hand a veritable armamentarium of alternative forms of representation, some of which derive from research whereas others originate in the wisdom of practice." Finally, he added, "pedagogical content knowledge also includes an understanding of what makes the learning of specific topics easy or difficult: the conceptions and preconceptions that students of different ages and backgrounds bring with them to the learning of those most frequently taught topics and lessons."[34]

Real expertise in pedagogical content knowledge implies learning many things in many different places. We believe that a quality teacher preparation program must have four elements, wherever it is located. First, good teachers need to know their subject—their content—very well. In nearly all cases, this involves a full major in an academic discipline, especially for secondary teachers who will teach that discipline, but also for elementary teachers who need depth of subject matter knowledge in at least one field rather than a smattering of knowledge in many. While a solid undergraduate major is essential, it is not sufficient. In any field, someone cannot master one part of the work, then forget it and move on to another. Aspiring teachers and practicing teachers need continuing work in content. They not only need to know the latest research, but also need to love their subjects and love learning enough to want to continue learning in the field. The old conception of a MAT degree as one half graduate courses in a discipline and one half in the teaching of that discipline was not a bad idea.

Second, good teachers need much-maligned methods courses. Learning to teach is a skill, and people need to be taught that skill. Some of the wisdom of practice can only be learned through actual practice, but some also needs to be learned in a classroom devoted to teaching that skill. Whether through the Friday pedagogy sessions of the Boston Teacher Residency or the competencies of the Woodrow Wilson Academy or the discipline-specific pedagogy courses offered on school sites by the University of Indianapolis, teacher preparation programs need to include, as Shulman stated, "understanding what makes the learning of specific topics easy or difficult."

Third, foundational courses are also essential. A teacher who does not know child and adolescent development, who has not thought about Piaget's stages of development, Vygotsky's zones of proximal development, or Bruner's views of active learning, will be shortchanged in key tools of understanding student strengths and weaknesses, as well as the opportune moments of learning. Teachers also need to ask the larger questions, like "what is the purpose of schooling anyway" or "what has worked or not worked in educational innovation in the past?" A person who enters teaching and is not armed with that expertise may get by, but they will not be a professional or a leader in their field.

Finally, it is time to get rid of student teaching and move all aspiring teachers through a full school year internship prior to their assuming the responsibility of being a teacher of record. Residency programs have mastered this approach. Stanford demands it. Many other places, in our estimation, fall short. Traditional student teaching—a few weeks in one school setting, perhaps another few weeks in a second setting—is simply insufficient. Schools are different places during the excitement of September, with the energy before the winter holidays, during the long break from instruction for standardized tests in the spring, and with the exhaustion of students and teachers at the end of the school year. The teacher who has not seen all of these moments has not been prepared. When a teacher candidate is in the same classroom for a full year, they are seen by the students as a kind of co-teacher. As the year progresses, they can assume more and more responsibility, not in the absence of the supervising teacher but through co-teaching responsibilities in which the students gain from the energy and diverse knowledge base of two adults. The aspiring teacher grows through practice, constant feedback, and new-found confidence. Happily, in January 2018, the AACTE strongly endorsed just this sort of enriched and deeply engaged effort as the heart of teacher preparation.[35]

WHAT ABOUT THE COST?

In most other nations with which the United States compares itself in the field of education, teacher preparation programs are highly subsidized if not free. In Finland and Singapore, for example, both places held up as models of how schools do it right, preparing to be a teacher is fully funded by the government. As a result, teacher preparation programs are able to be highly selective. This is not even close to being true in the United States, and in fact the problem is getting worse. Universities are not prepared even to subsidize their teacher education programs. Much if not most private philanthropy has turned from funding university teacher preparation programs, including the kind of robust experimentation that is so badly needed, to pouring most of their resources into alternative programs. In addition, the federal government and state legislatures have dramatically reduced the percentage of the costs of higher education that they provide, with the result that tuitions are rising, student debt is soaring, and institutional resources are constantly strained. Cost of a master's degree with certification can be up to $70,000, or even more at a private university, and a four-year undergraduate program in education may be four times that. Public universities and some experimental programs can cost much less, though a cost of $10,000 or $15,000 is still significant when teacher starting salaries hover around $30,000 per year in some states. Put simply, the United States will not get the quality or diversity of teachers it needs until the issue of the cost of teacher education is addressed. Yet cost is surprisingly absent from the discussion of teacher education reform, and CAEP says nothing about it in its new accreditation standards.

In general, residencies and other alternative programs are far ahead of the universities in addressing the issue of cost. When a candidate is accepted as a TFA corps member or participates in one of the teacher residency programs (see chapter 3), tuition is free, or close to free, or can be "paid back" through the initial years of service as a teacher. In fact, in many residencies, those enrolled in the programs are paid a modest stipend. Through TFA and other alternate programs, the route to teaching is quicker than traditional programs, so aspiring teachers are soon earning a full teacher salary (modest as that may be). Happily, some of the university-based programs are also working hard to keep costs manageable. Stanford is close to providing scholarship funds that cover the full cost of the teacher education program and has made doing so a university priority. Competency programs, from WGU to the Woodrow Wilson Academy are holding costs low; in fact, the Woodrow Wilson Academy will be free in its first year.

Nevertheless, the bottom line is that the cost to become a teacher is too high in the United States. As foundations and other funders have turned their support primarily to alternative programs, it has been harder and harder to raise scholarship funds for university teacher education programs. Moreover, too many senior administrators of universities continue to view teacher education as a "cash cow" that can be tapped to support other programs. Few school districts have taken any interest in financially supporting the preparation of their future teachers, apart from those few enrolled in district-controlled residency programs—even though a well-prepared teacher is a valuable asset to a district. In addition, the federal government, apart from occasional loan forgiveness programs, has never taken the necessary steps to address the issue of cost. Until this situation changes, preparing to be a teacher is likely to be out of reach for many who might make excellent teachers and will continue to involve unseemly levels of debt for individuals who do become teachers.[36]

WHY CAN'T WE THINK ABOUT A DIFFERENT STRUCTURE FOR THE TEACHING PROFESSION?

The current structure of the teaching profession—that is, the job description for most teachers in their day to day work—makes no sense. It does not sufficiently allow for professional growth or advancement, and it certainly works against the meaningful induction of aspiring teachers into the profession.

The reform reports with which we began our study—*A Nation Prepared*, from the Carnegie Forum on Education and the Economy, and *Tomorrow's Teachers*, from the Holmes Group of Education Deans, were both issued in 1986.[37] Both transformed the debates about school reform and teacher education. While both reports called for significant improvements in teacher education, they also spoke to larger issues of the teaching profession. A common theme in the two reports was that the current flat structure of teaching impeded effectiveness. They called for a profession led by lead teachers or career professionals, highly prepared, expert teaching veterans who supervise and support the work of larger numbers of professional teachers, who in turn would be supported by instructors, interns, paraprofessionals, and other instructional assistants, all of whom might, in time, move up in the system with further preparation or might elect to stay in a junior role. A short time after the reports were released, Albert Shanker, then president of the American Federation of Teachers and a member of the Carnegie Forum, explained, "If all the people working in hospitals had to be doctors, we would have seven million doctors instead of 500,000—and they would all be paid like teachers. There would be too many to educate as rigorously as we do now, so the standards of medical practice would probably be much lower than they are now."[38] Shanker's point was that the teaching profession's status would improve, and the quality of American education would also improve, if the staff of schools became more like that of hospitals. It was not to be. In spite of significant support and much national discussion, virtually nothing has been done to change the basic structure of the teaching profession in the last three decades.

The failure to implement changes in the structure of the teaching profession means that the effort to reform the initial preparation of teachers is doomed to half measures. First-year medical residents, even though they hold an MD degree, do not perform brain or heart surgery unsupervised. First-year law school graduates with a JD do not try cases before the Supreme Court; indeed, in many cases they work as associates in a larger law firm until, after years of supervision, induction, and testing, they become partners and take on an elevated role. In many other professions, from architects to engineers to the clergy, new professional school graduates, degree in hand, become assistants and associates; in time, with supervision and mentoring, they move into more senior roles. Yet the average June graduate of an education school program becomes the teacher of record and solo classroom leader only a few months later. TFA insists that its corps members be teacher of record after completing the initial summer program, no matter what sorts of internship opportunities are available. This is simply foolishness. Stated bluntly, we believe that no first-year teacher should be a teacher of record. Co-teaching, deep-level university–school partnerships, and the kinds of paid internships offered through residency programs make much more sense and would contribute much more to children's learning. The fact that the University of Chicago program includes the initial years of teaching as part of the official graduate program is a significant step in the right direction. It is well known that new teachers need time to mature. Yet, they cannot go without salaries; like medical residents and associates at law firms, they must be paid, rather than expected to accept more debt. Although there are some things—the hard-won wisdom of practice—that only come with time on the job, that job ought to be much more closely supervised and mentored. At the other end of the profession, more senior teachers gain much by being mentors and taking on new responsibilities. As is well known, the job description of a twenty-year veteran teacher is the same as that of a brand-new teacher. The only way up is moving out of the classroom, which impedes the profession's growth at all stages. Teachers unions and school districts are the drivers here. They need to do much more.

Learning from Each Other in Spite of Ourselves—and Getting Better as a Result

As we began organizing this book, we planned case studies on models of excellence in both university-based programs and alternative providers. Fairly quickly, it struck us that some of the programs that we found most promising were hard to classify as one or the other. We looked at the new effort by the Woodrow Wilson National Fellowship Foundation to create a laboratory in partnership with the Massachusetts Institute for Technology for experimentation in teacher education—the Woodrow Wilson Academy of Teaching and Learning; the University of Washington's serious partnership with administrators, teachers, and funders to create a truly blended Seattle Residency Program; the University of Chicago's Urban Teacher Education Program (which is thriving in spite of the fact that the university closed its education school two decades ago), or the efforts of Western Governors University to develop a completely online teacher education program. In each case, we asked, was the program university-based or alternative? Clearly in all of these and other cases, a university was a significant player in the effort. Yet, none of these programs looked like a traditional education school program. If we had looked at the online programs of the University of Southern California or our own New York University or many other similar ventures, we would have faced the same problem of trying to classify the program. Perhaps in the second decade of the twenty-first century, some of the best efforts at teacher preparation simply cannot be classified as falling into the old dichotomy of traditional or alternative.

It is also true that in spite of the conflict and the deep hostility between traditional and alternative programs, many programs that fit clearly in one category are learning from the other (reluctant as they may be to acknowledge it). Many schools of education are moving away from the traditional "drop-by" student teaching placements to a year-long internship in a school that involves significant co-teaching, so that by the end of the year the novice teacher has had a long and meaningful experience with her or his students. As noted earlier, the association representing education schools—AACTE—has endorsed this approach. Among the alternative providers, Teach for America is not the only one to acknowledge that a few weeks of preparation through a summer boot camp were not sufficient and that more extensive support both before and during the crucial first years of teaching was absolutely essential for any level of sustained success in the profession.

Not everything we have studied gives us reason for optimism. At a meeting of the American Association of Colleges for Teacher Education or at other gatherings of teacher educators, one will hear plenty of voices still arguing that talk of reform is a conspiracy by those who want to undermine university education schools and must be stoutly resisted. At the other end of the spectrum, the efforts of some states to completely deregulate the licensing of teachers clearly opens the door for charlatans who are prepared to offer "quick and dirty" preparation programs or for harried superintendents to hire unqualified candidates to fill last-minute vacancies in August. Both of these scenarios leave new teachers completely unprepared for the rigors of the work and assign the students to months without learning until the new teacher flees the scene. Some for-profit providers have used the new openness in the rules for teacher preparation to offer unethical programs that, while convenient for aspiring teachers, are needlessly expensive and, more seriously, so removed from practice that the graduates cannot be expected to be effective teachers without significant additional training. We will continue to worry about these trends.

Nevertheless, we conclude our study of the changes in teacher preparation with a sense of optimism. Many good people are devoting their professional lives to the work of ensuring that a new generation of American teachers are better prepared than their forbearers were. Many are dreaming up, planning, and studying ways to improve professional practice, while others are engaged in always-underfunded research about what needs to come next.

Will all of the necessary steps be taken? Will the rift between traditional and alternative routes to teaching be healed? Will different models of professional education for teachers learn from each other and grow better in the process? We do not know. Historians make poor prophets. Nevertheless, in light of our study of recent history, we believe that those engaged in policymaking, philanthropy, and direct efforts in all forms of teacher preparation have much to learn from history. All involved in the teacher preparation enterprise need to remember the quip attributed to John Dewey that the most fundamental thing about being a progressive educator is ensuring that we are always making progress. There is much progress being made—and yet to be made—in the preparation of America's teachers. Whether we are based in a university or a non-traditional institution, we must not become defenders of the status quo or let ourselves believe that our latest innovation is the end of the line. We need to recognize our failures and our successes, and we need to critique where we have fallen short or fallen into self-serving moments, even as we critique others who have failed in other ways. In the end, the goal of everyone associated with the enterprise of teacher preparation must be the same: ensuring that every child in this nation has a fully qualified teacher who knows his or her subject matter, who equally knows how to teach and engage young people in learning, and who is absolutely committed to the academic and personal success of every child.

A Concluding Word

In 1993 Lee Shulman wrote an essay about teacher education entitled "Calm Seas, Auspicious Gales." In it he found himself wishing for a few more gales in the calm seas of 1990s teacher education. He wrote, "I find the world of teacher education all too comfortable and consensual in its attitudes. Whether advocating the magic of reflective practice, the routines of Madeline Hunter, or the organizational rhetoric of professional development schools, this beleaguered field has circled its wagons and developed the appearance of consensus far too readily."[39] Shulman was, in fact, writing at the beginning of decades of extraordinary gales that would rock every aspect of the field of teacher education. While there was no way for Shulman to know what was coming, he had a sense of what lay in store. After all, he had done as much as any educator in the previous decade to lay the foundation for some gales himself: calling for new, more focused research on questions of teaching; proposing new forms of assessment of teachers that mixed portfolios with direct observation; developing the idea of *pedagogical content knowledge* to address the split between those who said teachers needed to focus on the how of teaching and those who focused on the what by saying that both were essential; helping to launch the National Board for Professional Teaching Standards; and much more.

As we reach the end of this study of the history of the wars in teacher education over the last thirty years, we have seen very few calm seas. Advocates of almost every perspective on teacher preparation have been happy—too happy, we sometimes think—to point gales of criticism at alternative approaches. Defenders of traditional university-based programs happily dismiss alternative providers as driven by a neoliberal desire to undermine public schools and all public institutions, including education schools, the majority of which are located in public universities. Advocates for alternative routes routinely dismiss university-based programs as bastions of faculty privilege that preserve professors' favorite courses at the cost of creating an over-long, over-expensive, and irrelevant curriculum that fails to prepare novice teachers for what they need to know and be able to do on the first day of school. Even those who are launching blended programs, including teacher residencies, seldom acknowledge the contribution of either camp to the ideas that are creating the new models.

Nevertheless, within each camp the situation that Shulman described a quarter century ago still prevails. Within each camp, "this beleaguered field has circled its wagons and developed the appearance of consensus far too readily." Within each group, there has developed an us-versus-them mentality that promotes self-satisfaction much more than self-critique.

In our study of the history of the past thirty years of American teacher education, we have seen lessons that those in every camp, and those who seek to stand a bit outside of all of them, may want to learn; indeed, they often have been learning from each other, in spite of the heated rhetoric. Many universities have improved their teacher preparation dramatically, devoting more time to supervised practice, taking seriously the merger of pedagogy and content implied in *pedagogical content knowledge*, inventing their own fast-track programs that save time and money for those who might otherwise consider only the alternative routes, and developing online and competency-based approaches to teacher education to serve a more diverse student body in different locations and coming to teacher preparation at different starting points. Some in the alternative preparation world have taken heed of the "quick and dirty" critique of their work. TFA is far from the only program that has developed more robust preparation and more careful supervision for its fellows seeking to enter teaching. Many of the residency programs that have emerged are taking far greater advantage of the connections to theory as well as practice that a university partnership can offer. What started out as a kind of "rubber stamp" of the residency program by university partners has become—certainly in the case of newer programs like the Seattle Teacher Residency—a deep partnership between university and school district to produce teachers who can benefit from both.

The gales of the last thirty years have been auspicious, leading to better teacher education and better teachers. It may also be time for some calm seas to reflect on what has been learned, what needs to be learned, and what institutional structures will best serve in the coming decades of this important field.

Introduction: Considering the Future of Teacher Preparation in Light of the Past

1. U.S. Department of Education, Office of Postsecondary Education. Higher Education Act Title II Reporting System (2012).

2. See Linda Darling-Hammond, "Teacher Preparation: Build on What Works," *Education Week*, March 16, 2011; Linda Darling-Hammond, "Constructing 21st-Century Teacher Education, *Journal of Teacher Education*, 57:10 (2006); M. Cochran-Smith et al., *Holding Teacher Preparation Accountable: A Review of Claims and Evidence* (Boulder, CO: National Education Policy Center, 2016), http://nepc.colorado.edu/publication/teacher-prep.

3. For two examples of the levels of hostility involved in the debates about teacher preparation, see Jameson Brewer and Beth Sondel, "Teach for America: Lies, Damned Lies, and Special Contracts," *Huffington Post*, February 10, 2016, updated February 9, 2017, https://www.huffingtonpost.com/t-jameson-brewer/teach-for-america-lies-da_b_9195600.html; Valerie Strauss, "Ravitch: The Problem with Teach for America," and the many comments that followed, *Washington Post*, February 15, 2011, http://voices.washingtonpost.com/answer-sheet/diane-ravitch/ravitch-the-problem-with-teach.html.

4. Kenneth M. Zeichner, *Teacher Education and the Struggle for Social Justice* (New York: Routledge, 2009), 1–2. See also Zeichner's more recent analysis in "Advancing Social Justice and Democracy in Teacher Education: Teacher Preparation 1.0, 2.0, and 3.0," *Kappa Delta Pi Record*, 52:4 (September, 2017), 150–155.

5. See Milton Friedman, "The Role of Government in Education," in *Economics and the Public Interest*, ed. Robert A. Solo (New Brunswick, NJ: Rutgers University Press, 1955). See also Lizabeth Cohen, *A Consumers' Republic: The Politics of Mass Consumption in Postwar America* (New York: Random House, 2003); Daniel Stedman Jones, *Masters of the Universe: Hayek, Friedman, and the Birth of Neoliberal Politics* (Princeton, NJ: Princeton University Press, 2012).

6. Lee S. Shulman, "Autonomy and Obligation: The Remote Control of Teaching and Policy," first published in *Handbook of Teaching and Policy*, ed. Lee S. Shulman and Gary Sykes (Boston: Allyn and Bacon, 1983), and included

in Shulman, *The Wisdom of Practice: Essays on Teaching, Learning, and Learning to Teach* (San Francisco: Jossey-Bass, 2004), 151.

7. Linda Darling-Hammond, Deborah J. Holtzman, Su Jin Gatlin, and Julian Vasquez Heilig, "Does Teacher Preparation Matter? Evidence about Teacher Certification, Teach for America, and Teacher Effectiveness," *Education Policy Analysis Archives* (University of South Florida), 13:42 (October 12, 2005), 20.

8. Doug Lemov, *Teach Like a Champion 2.0: 62 Techniques That Put Students on the Path to College* (San Francisco: Jossey-Bass, 2014). See also Linda Darling-Hammond, "How Teacher Education Matters," *Journal of Teacher Education* 51:3 (May/June 2000), 166–173.

9. Angus Shiva Mungal, "Teach for America, Relay Graduate School, and the Charter School Networks: The Making of a Parallel Education Structure," *Education Policy Analysis Archives* 24:17 (February 8, 2016), 1–26.

10. See Daniel Fallon and James W. Fraser, "Rethinking Teacher Education for the 21st Century: Putting Teaching Front and Center," in *21st Century Education: A Reference Handbook*, vol. 2, ed. Thomas L. Good (New York; Sage, 2008), 58–67.

11. Geraldine Jonçich Clifford and James W. Guthrie, *Ed School: A Brief for Professional Education* (Chicago: University of Chicago Press, 1988), 3.

12. John I. Goodlad, "Connecting the Present to the Past," in *Places Where Teachers Are Taught*, ed. John I. Goodlad, Roger Soder, and Kenneth A. Sirotnik (San Francisco: Jossey-Bass, 1990), 22.

13. In John I. Goodlad, Roger Soder, and Kenneth A. Sirotnik, *Teachers for Our Nation's Schools* (San Francisco: Jossey-Bass, 1990), 228.

14. Judith E. Lanier and Judith Warren Little, "Research on Teacher Education," in *Handbook on Research on Teaching*, ed. Merlin C. Wittrock, 3rd ed. (New York: Macmillan, 1986), 530, cited in David F. Labaree, *The Trouble with Ed Schools* (New Haven, CT: Yale University Press, 2004), 5.

15. Goodlad, "Connecting the Present and the Past," 34.

16. Labaree, *Trouble with Ed Schools*, 2.

17. For a careful look at some of the best teacher preparation programs in the United States, see *Inspiring Teaching: Preparing Teachers to Succeed in Mission-Driven Schools*, ed. Sharon Feiman-Nemser, Eran Tamir, and Karen Hammerness (Cambridge, MA: Harvard Education Press, 2014).

18. See, for example, David Steiner, with Susan D. Rozen, "Preparing Tomorrow's Teachers: An Analysis of Syllabi from a Sample of America's Schools of Education," in *A Qualified Teacher in Every Classroom? Appraising Old Answers and New Ideas*, ed. Frederick M. Hess, Andrew J. Rotherham, and Kate Walsh (Cambridge, MA: Harvard Education Press, 2004), 119–148, especially 129–130.

19. Labaree, *Trouble with Ed Schools*; Labaree, "Progressivism, Schools, and Schools of Education: An American Romance," *Paedagogica Historica*, January 2011.

20. Ellen Lagemann, *An Elusive Science: The Troubling History of Educational Research* (Chicago: University of Chicago Press, 2000).

21. Labaree, *Trouble with Ed Schools*; Labaree, "Progressivism, Schools, and Schools of Education."

22. Ken Zeichner, "Reflections of a University-Based Teacher Educator on the Future of College- and University-Based Teacher Education," *Journal of Teacher Education* 57:3 (May/June, 2006), 326–340. Fraser was one of the three deans sitting in the front row that day.

23. Jesse Solomon, "The Boston Teacher Residency: District-Based Teacher Education," *Journal of Teacher Education* 60:5 (November/December 2009), 478–488, 478.

24. Solomon, "Boston Teacher Residency," 478.

25. See James W. Fraser, *Preparing America's Teachers: A History* (New York: Teachers College Press, 2007).

26. By far the best history of the change from normal schools to state teachers colleges to multipurpose universities is found in Christine A. Ogren, *The American State Normal School: An Instrument of Great Good* (New York: Palgrave-Macmillan, 2005). The National Teachers Corps, founded as part of the Great Society programs of the 1960s, was one significant exception to this story. Designed to offer an end-run around education school programs, this federal effort sought to recruit very able college graduates and move them quickly into needy urban and rural schools. Like many Great Society programs, it was gone by the 1970s.

27. Elizabeth Green, *Building a Better Teacher: How Teaching Works (and How to Teach It to Everyone)* (New York: W. W. Norton, 2014), 27.

28. Arthur Bestor, *Educational Wastelands: The Retreat from Learning in Our Public Schools* (Urbana: University of Illinois Press, 1953), 104–121.

29. James Bryant Conant, *The Education of American Teachers* (New York: McGraw-Hill, 1963), 5; see also 1–8, 209–218. James D. Koerner, *The Miseducation of American Teachers* (Boston: Houghton Mifflin, 1963), 109–110.

30. *A Nation Prepared: Teachers for the 21st Century: The Report of the Task Force on Teaching as a Profession* (New York: Carnegie Forum on Education and the Economy, 1986); *Tomorrow's Teachers: A Report of the Holmes Group* (East Lansing, MI: Holmes Group, 1986).

31. Harry Judge, "Foreword," in Michael Fullan et al., *The Rise and Stall of Teacher Education Reform* (Washington, DC: American Association of Colleges for Teacher Education, 1998), xiii. See also Green, *Building a Better Teacher*, chapter 3, 80–112.

Chapter One: The Emergence of Alternative Routes to Teaching

1. Frederick M. Hess, Andrew J. Rotherham, and Katie Walsh, *A Qualified Teacher in Every Classroom?: Appraising Old Answers and New Ideas* (Cambridge, MA: Harvard Education Press, 2004).

2. Larry Cuban, "Teacher and Community," *Harvard Educational Review* 39:2 (Spring 1969), 253–272.

3. Nick Juravich, "A Classroom Revolution: Community Educators and the Transformation of School and Work in American Cities, 1953–1981" (PhD diss., Columbia University, 2017).

4. Russell Rickford, *We Are an African People: Independent Education, Black Power, and the Radical Imagination* (New York: Oxford University Press, 2016).

5. Lauren Lefty, "Seize the Schools, Que Viva Puerto Rico Libre: Cold War Education Politics in New York and San Juan, 1948–1975" (PhD Diss. in progress, New York University, 2017).

6. Bethany Rogers, "'Better' People, Better Teaching: The Vision of the National Teacher Corps, 1965–68," *History of Education Quarterly* 49:3 (August 2009), 347–372; Rogers, "Voices of the National Teacher Corps: From Liberal Hopes to Radical Dissent," panel presentation entitled "New Migrants, New Movements, and New Teachers in Big City Schools: Educational Dissent in Postwar Urban America," Organization of American Historians Annual Meeting, Washington, DC (April 2006); Dana Goldstein, *The Teacher Wars: A History of America's Most Embattled Profession* (New York: Random House, 2014).

7. Rogers, "'Better' People, Better Teaching," 347.

8. While paraprofessionals, mostly parents of color, often trained alongside Teacher Corps recruits, only the predominantly white university degree holders could legally serve as teachers of record in the city's public schools due to certification laws. They subsequently earned more money and enjoyed greater power within the system.

9. For works that cite the rise of marketization, the publication of *A Nation at Risk*, and neoliberal politics in the 1980s, see Hess et al., *A Qualified Teacher in Every Classroom?*; Pam Grossman and Susanna Loeb, eds., *Alternative Routes to Teaching: Mapping the New Landscape of Teacher Education* (Cambridge, MA: Harvard Education Press, 2008).

10. Milton Friedman, "What's Wrong with Our Schools?," *Free to Choose*, Public Broadcasting Corporation, January 1980.

11. David Tyack and Larry Cuban, *Tinkering toward Utopia: A Century of Public School Reform* (Cambridge, MA: Harvard University Press, 1995), 14.

12. Friedman, "What's Wrong with Our Schools?"

13. *A Nation at Risk: The Imperative for Educational Reform*, The National Commission for Excellence on Education, April 1983, https://files.eric.ed.gov/fulltext/ED226006.pdf, 22.

14. Susan Walton, "States' Reform Efforts Increase as Focus on Issues Shifts," *Education Week*, December 7, 1983.

15. For more on the rise of alternative certification, see Kenneth Zeichner and Elizabeth A. Hutchinson, "The Development of Alternative Certification Policies and Programs in the United States," in *Alternative Routes to Teaching:*

Mapping the New Landscape of Teacher Education, ed. Pam Grossman and Susanna Loeb (Cambridge, MA: Harvard Education Press, 2008), 15–28.

16. Ken Carlson, "The Teacher Certification Struggle in New Jersey," paper prepared for the National Commission for Excellence in Teacher Education, U.S. Department of Education, 1984.

17. See, for example, Frank B. Burray, "Cautions about Common Reforms in Teacher Education" *Journal of Thought*, 22:2 (Summer 1987), 47–55.

18. Edward B. Fiske, "'Tide of Mediocrity' May Not Be Rising As Fast As It Seems," *New York Times*, September 18, 1983, 1; Joseph A. Slobodzian, "NJEA Plan Submitted on Teachers Would Expand Certification," *Philadelphia Inquirer*, November 17, 1983, B1; "Opinion: Proposal for Alternative Route to Teacher Certification Draws Criticism and Applause," *New York Times*, December 4, 1983, A44; Virginia Inman, "Certification of Teachers Lacking Courses in Education Stirs Battles in Several States," *Wall Street Journal*, January 5, 1984, 1.

19. "Alternative Licensing Prevalent," *Education Week*, January 8, 1986, http://secure.edweek.org/ew/articles/1986/01/08/06150003.h05.html.

20. Martin Haberman, "Alternative Teacher Certification Programs," *Actions in Teacher Education*, 8:2 (Summer 2016), 15.

21. Traci Bliss, "Alternative Certification in Connecticut: Reshaping the Profession," *Peabody Journal of Education*, 67:3 (1990), 35–54; Richard Wisniewski, "Alternative Programs and the Reform of Teacher Education," *Action in Teacher Education*, 8:2 (1986), 37–44; Frederick M. Hess, *Tear Down the Wall: The Case for a Radical Overhaul of Teacher Certification* (Washington, DC: Progressive Policy Institute, 2001); Naomi Schaefer, "Traditional and Alternative Teacher Certification: A View From the Trenches," in *Better Teachers, Better Schools*, ed. Marci Kanstorooom and Chester Finn Jr. (Washington, DC: Thomas B. Fordham Foundation, 1999), 137–162.

22. Diane Ravitch, *Reign of Error: The Hoax of the Privatization Movement and the Danger to America's Public Schools* (New York: Vintage, 2014); Megan E. Tompkins-Strange, *Policy Patrons: Philanthropy, Education Reform, and the Politics of Influence* (Cambridge, MA: Harvard Education Press, 2016).

23. Kate Walsh and Sandy Jacobs with a forward by Chester E. Finn Jr. and Michael J. Petrilli, "Alternative Certification Isn't Alternative," Thomas B. Fordham Institute, National Council on Teacher Quality, September 2007.

24. Julie Blair, "Teachers' Union Launches School to Train Teachers," *Education Week*, April 10, 2002, https://www.edweek.org/ew/articles/2002/04/10/30ctu.h21.html.

25. Eric Westervelt and Anya Kamenetz, "Teach For America at 25: With Maturity, New Pressure to Change," *NPREd*, December 1, 2014, http://www.npr.org/sections/ed/2014/12/01/366343324/teach-for-america-at-25-with-maturity-new-pressure-to-change.

26. Linda Darling-Hammond and John Bransford, *Preparing Teachers for a*

Changing World: What Teachers Should Learn and Be Able to Do (New York: John Wiley and Sons, 2007).

27. Doug Lemov, *Teach Like a Champion: 49 Techniques That Put Students on the Path to College* (New York: Jossey-Bass, 2010).

28. U.S. Department of Education, Office of Policy Planning and Innovation, *Meeting the Highly Qualified Teachers Challenge: The Secretary's Second Annual Report on Teacher Quality* (Washington, DC: U.S. Government Printing Office, 2003), https://www2.ed.gov/about/reports/annual/teachprep/2003title-ii-report.pdf. For an updated study, see Melissa A. Clark et al., "The Effectiveness of Secondary Math Teachers from Teach for America and the Teaching Fellows Programs," National Center for Education Evaluation and Regional Assistance, U.S. Department of Education, September 2013, https://ies.ed.gov/ncee/pubs/20134015/.

29. See U.S. Department of Education, *Meeting the Highly Qualified Teachers Challenge*, 30–31; Linda Darling-Hammond, Deborah J. Holtzman, Su Jin Gatlin, and Julian Vasquez Heilig, "Does Teacher Preparation Matter? Evidence about Teacher Certification, Teach for America, and Teacher Effectiveness," *Education Policy Analysis Archives* (University of South Florida), 13:42 (October 12, 2005), 20; and "Response to Recent Linda Darling-Hammond Study: Letter from Abigail Smith, Vice President of Research and Policy," Teach for America, www.tfanewsletter.teachforamerica.org.

30. Paul. T. Decker, Daniel Mayer, and Steven Glazerman, *The Effects of Teach for America on Students: Findings from a National Evaluation* (Washington, DC: Mathematica, 2004).

31. Linda Darling-Hammond, *Educational Opportunity and Alternative Certification: New Evidence and New Questions* (Stanford, CA: Stanford Center for Opportunity Policy in Education, 2009), 3–7.

32. Robert Braun, "Science Teacher Sidelined," *Newark Star-Ledger*, May 29, 1983, quoted in Ken Carlson, "The Teacher Certification Struggle in New Jersey," paper prepared for the National Commission for Excellence in Teacher Education, U.S. Department of Education, 1984.

33. David Stripp, "Up Standards, Drop Some Courses, Add More Time in Classroom—Some Phase-Outs of Degree," *Wall Street Journal*, November 11, 1986.

34. For two narrative accounts of the New Jersey Alternative Certification debates by involved actors from different perspectives, see Leo Klagholz, *Growing Better Teachers in the Garden State: New Jersey's 'Alternate Route' to Teacher Certification* (Washington, DC: Thomas B. Fordham Foundation, 2000), and Carlson, "The Teacher Certification Struggle in New Jersey."

35. Saul Cooperman, "An Alternative Route to Teacher Selection and Professional Quality Assurance: An Analysis of Initial Certification," New Jersey State Department of Education, September 1983.

36. *A Nation at Risk*, 5.

37. *A Nation at Risk.*

38. Sharon Johnson, "The Schools: The Fourth 'R' is for Reform," *New York Times*, April 14, 1985: 17.

39. Johnson, "The Schools," 17.

40. Joseph A. Slobodzian, "Kean Offers Plan to Reform Schools," *Philadelphia Inquirer*, September 7, 1983, 4; Priscilla Van Tassel, "Kean Backs Plan on Licensing of Teachers," *New York Times*, September 18, 1983, 9.

41. Eran Tamir, "Theorizing the Politics of Educational Reform: The Case of New Jersey's Alternate Route to Teacher Certification," *American Journal of Education*, 115 (November 2008), 65–94.

42. Jonna Perillo, *Uncivil Rights: Teachers, Unions and Race in the Battle for School Equity* (Chicago: University of Chicago Press, 2012).

43. Carlson, "Teacher Certification Struggle," 13–15

44. Cooperman, "Alternative Route to Teacher Selection," 1–2.

45. Cooperman, "Alternative Route to Teacher Selection," 6.

46. Quoted in Carlson, "Teacher Certification Struggle," 9.

47. "Former School Chief Still Brimming with Ideas: Saul Cooperman Has Lost None of His Zeal or Controversy," New Jersey Hills Media Group, January 24, 2002, http://www.newjerseyhills.com/former-school-chief-still-brimming-with-ideas-saul-cooperman-has/article_4def5558-e757-577e-8b58-b79b7b1d0f8d.html.

48. Robert Braun, "President Praises State Licensing Plan," *Newark Star-Ledger*, December 9, 1983, 1, 14.

49. Carlson, "Teacher Certification Struggle," 27–28

50. Quoted in Carlson, "Teacher Certification Struggle," 23.

51. Quoted in Carlson, "Teacher Certification Struggle," 22–23. For an overview of dissenting opinions and arguments, see Carlson, "Teacher Certification Struggle"; Joseph Donnelly, "Opinion: Proposal for Alternative Route to Teacher Certification Draws Criticism and Applause," *New York Times*, December 4, 1983, http://www.nytimes.com/1983/12/04/opinion/opinion-proposal-for-alternative-route-teacher-certification-draws-criticism.html?pagewanted=all; Klagholz, *Growing Better Teachers*; Joseph A. Slobodzian, "Critics of Certification Plan Form Coalition," *Philadelphia Inquirer*, November 23, 1983, B04.

52. Priscilla Van Tassel, "State to Name Panel to Explore Teacher Quality," *New York Times*, December 4, 1983, NJ1.

53. Carlson, "Teacher Certification Struggle," 6.

54. For more on the Boyer Panel, see Edward B. Fiske, "'Tide of Mediocrity' May Not Be Rising as Fast as It Seems," *New York Times*, September 18, 1983, E20; Virginia Inman, "Certification of Teachers Lacking Courses in Education Stirs Battles in Several States," *Wall Street Journal*, January 5, 1984, 23; Klagholz, *Growing Better Teachers*; Carlson, "Teacher Certification Struggle," 29–34.

55. Carlson, "Teacher Certification Struggle," 40–49; Klagholz, *Growing Better Teachers*.

56. Carlson, "Teacher Certification Struggle," 50–52

57. Carlson, "Teacher Certification Struggle," 56–59

58. Jonathan Friendly, "New Rules Voted on Teachers' Education in Jersey," *New York Times*, October 4, 1984, B8.

59. Joseph A. Slobodzian, "Teaching Plan Wins Converts: 2 Back Changes in Certification," *Philadelphia Inquirer*, July 15, 1984, B1.

60. Stripp, "Up Standards, Drop Some Courses."

61. Klagholz, *Growing Better Teachers.*

62. Priscilla Van Tassel, "Cooperman Tenure Marked by Unusual Rate of Success," *New York Times*, January 18, 1987, NJ1; Jeanette Rundquist, "Alternative Route to Becoming a Teacher in New Jersey Thrives," *Newark Star-Ledger*, April 12, 2009, http://www.nj.com/news/index.ssf/2009/04/alternate_route_to_becoming_a.html; "Education, New Jersey, in 5 Years, Solves Teacher Shortage: College Graduates Who Did Not Major in Education Are Filling Classrooms," *New York Times*, September 13, 1989, B10.

63. Rundquist, "Alternate Route."

64. As leading examples, see Linda Darling-Hammond, "Who Will Speak for the Children? How 'Teach for America' Hurts Urban Schools and Students," *Phi Delta Kappan* 76:1 (September 1994), 21–34; Elizabeth Duffrin, "Too Quick and Dirty?; Some Pan Alternative Teacher Certification," *Chicago Tribune*, August 8, 2004, 15.

65. Laura Quinn, "When Teachers Are the Experiments: Grades Vary on a N.J. Program to Recruit Educators," *Philadelphia Inquirer*, May 24, 1987, B02.

66. Patricia Alex, "N.J. Improves Its Alternative Teacher Training; New Focus on Running a Classroom," *Record* [Bergen County, NJ], July 7, 2003, A03.

67. See, for example, Marilyn Cochran-Smith and Kenneth M. Zeichner, eds., *Studying Teacher Education: The Report of the AERA Panel on Research and Teacher Education* (New York: Routledge, 2005); Linda Darling-Hammond and John Bransford, *Preparing Teachers for a Changing World: What Teachers Should Learn and Be Able to Do* (New York: John Wiley and Sons, 2007).

68. "Singleton Introduces Innovative Bill Package to Raise the Bar on Public Education in New Jersey," *Burlington County Times*, September 17, 2013, A1; Diane D'Amico, "State Raising the Bar for Teacher Certification," *Press of Atlantic City*, February 5, 2015, http://www.pressofatlanticcity.com/education/state-raising-the-bar-for-teacher-certification/article_6b869c0a-ad83-11e4-83fa-e35dec9eb6b4.html; "Christie Administration Announces Enhancements to Teacher Preparation and Certification," *Targeted News Service*, November 4, 2015, accessed via ProQuest U.S. News Stream.

69. "Christie Administration Announces Enhancements." For the original press release, see "Christie Administration Announces Enhancements to Teacher Preparation and Certification," State of New Jersey Department of Education, November 4, 2015, http://www.state.nj.us/education/news/2015/1104tcp.htm.

For more information on teacher certification in charter schools, see Michelle Exstrom, "Teaching in Charter Schools," National Conference of State Legislatures, http://www.ncsl.org/documents/educ/teachingincharterschools.pdf.

70. Klagholz, *Growing Better Teachers*, 8.

71. Stephanie Simon, "Has Teach for America Betrayed its Mission?," *Reuters*, August 16, 2012, https://www.reuters.com/article/us-usa-education -teachforamerica/has-teach-for-america-betrayed-its-mission-idUSBRE87F05 O20120816. See also Dana Goldstein, "'Big Measurable Goals': A Data-Driven Vision for Millennial Teaching" in *The Teacher Wars: A History of America's Most Embattled Profession* (New York: Doubleday, 2014), 189–230.

72. "About Us: Our History," Teach for America, https://www.teachfor america.org/about-us/our-story/our-history.

73. Wendy Kopp, *One Day All Children: The Unlikely Triumph of Teach for America and What I Learned Along the Way* (New York: Public Affairs, 2003).

74. Donna Foote, *Relentless Pursuit: A Year in the Trenches with Teach for America* (New York: Vintage, 2009).

75. For more on the origin of TFA, see Foote, *Relentless Pursuit*; Dana Goldstein, *Teacher Wars: A History of America's Most Embattled Profession* (New York: Doubleday, 2014), 189–230.

76. Kopp, *One Day All Children*; Foote, *Relentless Pursuit*; Goldstein, *Teacher Wars*.

77. For more on the first institute and the 1990 corps experience, see Bethany Rogers and Megan Blumenreich, "TFA and the Magical Thinking of the 'Best and the Brightest,'" *Education Policy Analysis Archives*, 24:13 (February 8, 2016), http://epaa.asu.edu/ojs/article/view/1926/1723.

78. Nathan Barrett and Douglas Harris, "Significant Changes in the New Orleans Teacher Workforce," policy brief, Education Research Alliance for New Orleans, Tulane University, August 24, 1015, http://educationresearchallian cenola.org/files/publications/ERA-Policy-Brief-Changes-in-the-New-Orleans -Teacher-Workforce.pdf.

79. Rebecca Zukauskas, "Teach for America (TFA) Research Starter," *Salem Press Encyclopedia*, 2016, accessed via EBSCO.

80. "Our History," Teach for America.

81. Rogers and Blumenreich, "TFA and the Magical Thinking," 16.

82. Darling-Hammond, "Who Will Speak for the Children?"

83. Sarah Matsui, *Learning from Counternarratives in Teach for America* (New York: Peter Lang, 2004).

84. Rogers and Blumenreich, "TFA and the Magical Thinking," 23.

85. Rogers and Blumenreich, "TFA and the Magical Thinking," 15.

86. "Alumni Survey and Snapshot," Teach for America, https://www.teach foramerica.org/alumni/community/alumni-survey-snapshot.

87. Quoted in Foote, *Relentless Pursuit*, 37.

88. Foote, *Relentless Pursuit*, 38.

89. "Annual Lobbying for Teach for America," Center for Responsive Politics, data downloaded on April 20, 2015, http://www.opensecrets.org/lobby/clientsum.php?id=D000057438.

90. Kerry Kretchmar, Beth Sondel, and Joseph J. Ferrare, "The Power of the Network: Teach for America's Impact on the Deregulation of Teacher Education," *Educational Policy*, March 23, 2016, accessed via Sage Journals.

91. Stephanie Simon, "TFA Rises as a Political Powerhouse," *Politico*, October 12, 2013, http://www.politico.com/story/2013/10/teach-for-america-rises-as-political-powerhouse-098586.

92. See Kerry Kretchmar, Beth Sondel, and Joseph J. Ferrare, "Mapping the Terrain: Teach for America, Charter School Reform, and Corporate Sponsorship," *Journal of Education Policy* 29:6 (February 2014), 724–759; Chad Sommer, "Teach for America's Pro-Corporate, Union-Busting Agenda," *Salon*, January 13, 2014, http://www.salon.com/2014/01/13/teach_for_americas_pro_corporate_union_busting_agenda_partner/.

93. "About Us," The New Teacher Project, http://tntp.org/about-tntp.

94. Kretchmar et al., "Mapping the Terrain." For more on Teach for All and where they operate, see "Network Partners," Teach for All, November 12, 2017, http://teachforall.org/network-partners.

95. Eric Westervelt and Anya Kamenetz, "Teach for America at 25: With Maturity, New Pressure to Change," National Public Radio, December 1, 2014, http://www.npr.org/sections/ed/2014/12/01/366343324/teach-for-america-at-25-with-maturity-new-pressure-to-change.

96. Westervelt and Kamenetz, "Teach for America at 25."

97. Megan Richmond and Brandon Mendez, "My Year Volunteering as a Teacher Helped Educate a New Generation of Underprivileged Kids vs. Can We Please, Just Once, Have A Real Teacher," *Onion*, July 17, 2012, http://www.theonion.com/multiblogpost/my-year-volunteering-as-a-teacher-helped-educate-a-28803.

98. Catherine Michna, "Why I Stopped Writing Recommendation Letters for Teach for America," *Slate*, October 9, 2013, http://www.slate.com/articles/life/education/2013/10/teach_for_america_recommendations_i_stopped_writing_them_and_my_colleague.html.

99. Valerie Strauss, "#ResistTFA Popular on Twitter," *Washington Post*, February 20, 2014, https://www.washingtonpost.com/news/answer-sheet/wp/2014/02/20/resisttfa-popular-on-twitter/.

100. Jonathon Stith, Hiram Rivera, and Chinyere Tutashinda, "A Vision for Black Lives: Policy Demands for Black Power, Freedom, and Justice: An End to the Privatization of Education and Real Community Control by Parents, Students and Community Members of Schools Including Democratic School Boards and Community Control of Curriculum, Hiring, Firing, and Discipline Policies," Movement for Black Lives, https://policy.m4bl.org/wp-content/uploads/2016/07/Community-Control-of-Schools-Policy-Brief.pdf.

101. Drew Franklin, "Why DeRay Mckesson's Baltimore Campaign Looks Life It Comes Right Out of Teach for America's Playbook," AlterNet, February 20, 2016, http://www.alternet.org/news-amp-politics/why-deray-mckessons -plan-baltimores-schools-looks-it-comes-right-out-teach.

102. Emily Garvey, "Counterpoint: 'My Career as a Real Teacher Helped Education a New Generation,' " *TeacherPop*, July 27, 2012, http://teacherpop .org/2012/07/counterpoint-my-career-as-a-real-teacher-helped-educate-a-new -generation/.

103. Rand Corporation, "Policy Brief: Teach for America Gets Mostly High Marks from Principal Survey," 2015, http://www.rand.org/content/dam/rand /pubs/research_briefs/RB9800/RB9865/RAND_RB9865.pdf.

104. Quoted in Andrew J. Rotherman, "Teach for America: 5 Myths That Persist 20 Years On," *Time*, February 10, 2011, http://content.time.com/time /nation/article/0,8599,2047211,00.html#ixzz22iN9DfLj.

105. Conor P. Williams, "Stop Scapegoating Teach for America," *Daily Beast*, September 24, 2014, http://www.thedailybeast.com/articles/2014/09/24 /stop-scapegoating-teach-for-america.html.

106. Frederick M. Hess, Andrew J. Rotherham, Katie Walsh, eds., *A Qualified Teacher for Every Classroom? Appraising Old Answers and New Ideas* (Cambridge, MA: Harvard Education Press, 2004).

107. See Burnie Bond, Esther Quintero, Leo Casey, and Matthew DiCarlo, "The State of Teacher Diversity in American Education," Albert Shanker Institute, 2015, http://www.shankerinstitute.org/resource/teacherdiversity; Barrett and Harris, "Significant Changes."

108. For more on how TFA has changed, see Westervelt and Kamenetz, "Teach for America at 25"; Kristina Rizga, "Is America's Most Controversial Education Group Changing Its Ways?" *Mother Jones*, February 11, 2016, http:// www.motherjones.com/politics/2016/02/teach-america-most-divisive-education -reform-group.

109. Westervelt and Kamenetz, "Teach for America at 25"; Emma Brown, "Teach for America Celebrates 25th Anniversary at Washington Event," *Washington Post*, February 6, 2016, https://www.washingtonpost.com/local /education/teach-for-america-celebrates-25th-anniversary-at-washington -event/2016/02/06/695d4094-cd0a-11e5-88ff-e2d1b4289c2f_story.html.

110. J.Crew for Teach for America Linen T-shirt, J.Crew, https://www.jcrew .com/p/08414.

111. Alex Zimmerman, "Teach for America's Presence in New York City Hits 11-year Low," *Chalkbeat*, September 13, 2016, http://www.chalkbeat.org /posts/ny/2016/09/13/teach-for-americas-presence-in-new-york-city-hits-11-year -low/#.WA538pMrKSN.

112. Zimmerman, "Teach for America's Presence."

113. "Our Institution," Relay Graduate School of Education, http://www .relay.edu/about/institution.

114. For a snapshot of Relay GSE's enrollment numbers for 2017–2018, see "Impact: Reach," Relay Graduate School of Education, November 12, 2017, https://www.relay.edu/about-us/impact.

115. June Kronholz, "A New Type of Ed School," *Education Next* 12:4 (Fall 2012).

116. Angus Mungal, "Breaking the Monopoly: The Emergence of Relay Graduate School of Education," unpublished paper, 2015.

117. Norman Atkins, "Getting a Kid from Newark to Oberlin: A Pioneer in the Charter-School Movement on What the Best Teachers Are Doing Now," *Wall Street Journal*, October 30, 2010, http://www.wsj.com/articles/SB1000142 405270230328460457558210161442866.

118. Kronholz, "New Type of Ed School."

119. Sharon Otterman, "Ed Schools' Pedagogical Puzzle," *New York Times*, July 21, 2011, http://www.nytimes.com/2011/07/24/education/edlife/edl-24 teacher-t.html.

120. Diane Ravitch, "A Very Bizarre School of Education," *Diane Ravitch's Blog*, July 8, 2012, https://dianeravitch.net/2012/07/08/a-very-bizarre-graduate -school-of-education/; Carol Corbett Burris, "Some Scary Training for Teachers," *Washington Post*, July 26, 2012, http://www.washingtonpost.com/blogs /answer-sheet/post/some-scary-training-for-teachers/2012/07/25/gJQAzXyJAX _blog.html#pagebreak; Otterman, "Ed Schools' Pedagogical Puzzle"; Sarah M. Stitzlein and Craig K. West, "New Forms of Teacher Education: Connections to Charter Schools and Their Approaches," *Democracy & Education* 22:2 (2014), 1–10.

121. Corbett Burris, "Some Scary Training for Teachers."

122. Otterman, "Ed Schools' Pedagogical Puzzle."

123. "Programs," Relay Graduate School of Education, http://www.relay .edu/programs.

124. Relay teacher candidates either enter directly as Relay GSE students or receive training through Relay as TFA corps members, in which case they also qualify for AmeriCorps education award funds. For more on Relay's instructional program, see "Programs," Relay Graduate School of Education, http:// www.relay.edu/programs; Otterman, "Ed Schools' Pedagogical Puzzle"; June Kronholz, "New Type of Ed School"; Mungal, "Breaking the Monopoly."

125. Lauren Anderson and Kenneth Zeichner, as quoted in Valeri Strauss, "The Big Problem with the Obama Administration's New Teacher Education Regulations," *Washington Post*, October 24, 2016, https://www.washingtonpost .com/news/answer-sheet/wp/2016/10/24/the-big-problems-with-obama-adminis trations-new-teacher-education-regulations/.

126. Kenneth Zeichner, "The Re-emergence and Expansion of Independent Teacher Education Programs," June 2016, unpublished article.

127. "Campuses," Relay Graduate School of Education, https://www.relay .edu/campuses.

128. "Norman Atkins: Cofounder, Relay Graduate School of Education," Impact 15, *Forbes.com*, http://www.forbes.com/lists/2012/impact/norman -atkins.html.

129. Angus Shiva Mungal, "Teach for America, Relay Graduate School, and the Charter School Networks: The Making of a Parallel Education Structure," *Education Policy Analysis Archives* 24:17 (February 8, 2016).

130. "Programs," Relay Graduate School of Education, http://www.relay .edu/programs.

131. See "Our Partners," Relay Graduate School of Education, http://www .relay.edu/about/ institution; Mungal, "Breaking the Monopoly."

132. "Education Department Releases Final Teacher Preparation Regulations," U.S. Department of Education, October 12, 2016, https://www.ed.gov /news/press-releases/education-department-releases-final-teacher-preparation -regulations; see also Anderson and Zeichner, as quoted in Strauss, "The Big Problems."

133. Otterman, "Ed Schools' Pedagogical Puzzle."

134. Berkman, Leslie. "New Degree of Interest in Education for Adults," *Los Angeles Times* [Orange County Edition], June 9, 1985, accessed via ProQuest.

135. A. J Angulo, *Diploma Mills: How For-Profit Colleges Stiffed Students, Taxpayers, and the American Dream* (Baltimore: Johns Hopkins University Press, 2016).

136. John Sperling, *Rebel with a Cause: The Entrepreneur Who Created the University of Phoenix and the For-Profit Revolution in Higher Education* (New York: John Wiley & Sons, 2000).

137. Sperling, *Rebel with a Cause*, 3.

138. Exact numbers are notoriously hard to find, in part because the University of Phoenix does not like to share information and in part because many of those who do rank the size of programs count all education programs, whether related to teaching or not. Among the other large teacher preparation programs are Liberty University in Lynchburg, Virginia; Walden University, another online provider; and Teachers College, Columbia University.

139. Quoted in Thomas Bartlett, "Phoenix Risen: How a History Professor Became the Pioneer of the For-Profit Revolution," *Chronicle of Higher Education*, 55:41 (July 10, 2009), A1–A13, https://www.chronicle.com/article/Phoenix -Risen/46988.

140. Sperling, *Rebel with a Cause*, 70.

141. Sperling, *Rebel with a Cause*, 77.

142. Sperling, *Rebel with a Cause,* 91.

143. Berkman, "New Degree of Interest."

144. Jeffrey Leib, "Colleges Mine Adult Learners for Gold," *Denver Post*, August 16, 1992, H1.

145. Steve Stecklow, "Virtual U.: At Phoenix University, Class Can Be Anywhere—Even in Cyberspace—Flexible Schedules Attract Older, Working

Students but School Has Its Critics—Now, a Plan to Go Public," *Wall Street Journal*, September 12, 1994, A1.

146. David Halperin, "The Perfect Lobby: How One Industry Captured Washington, DC," *The Nation*, April 3, 2014, https://www.thenation.com /article/perfect-lobby-how-one-industry-captured-washington-dc/.

147. Quoted in Chris Cuomo, Chris Vlasto, Gerry Wagshcal, Lauren Pearle, and Cleopatra Andreadis, "ABC News Investigates For-Profit Education: Recruiters at the University of Phoenix," *ABC News*, August 19, 2010, http:// abcnews.go.com/TheLaw/profit-education-abc-news-undercover-investigate -recruiters-university/story?id=11411379.

148. Megan Dwyer, "University of Phoenix Under Fire by Government after Deceptive Marketing Tactics," *Fox6.com*, April 23, 2016, http://fox6now .com/2015/04/23/university-of-phoenix-doles-out-financial-settlements-after -misleading-students/.

149. Dwyer, University of Phoenix Under Fire."

150. Eric Kelderman, "Why a Certain $21 Million Is Worth Much More to the U. of Phoenix," *Chronicle of Higher Education* 62:8 (October 23, 2015), 1.

151. Quoted in Halperin, "The Perfect Lobby." See also Kelderman, "Why a Certain $21 Million Is Worth Much More."

152. David Halperin, *Stealing America's Future: How For-Profit Colleges Scam Taxpayers and Ruin Students' Lives* (Washington, DC: RepublicReport .org), 2014.

153. "Consumer Complaints and Reviews: University of Phoenix," Consumer Affairs, https://www.consumeraffairs.com/education/phoenix.html.

154. Goldie Blumenstyk, "HBCUs Aren't Sold on Course Partnerships with U. of Phoenix, *Chronicle of Higher Education*, 62:3 (September 18, 2015), 24.

155. Halperin, *Stealing America's Future*.

156. Aaron Glantz and the Center for Investigative Reporting, "Why the University of Phoenix's Favorite Congressman Killed the GI College Aid Bill," *Daily Beast*, July 24, 2014, http://www.thedailybeast.com/articles/2014/07/24 /why-the-university-of-phoenix-s-favorite-congressman-killed-the-gi-college -aid-bill.html.

157. Sperling, *Rebel with a Cause*, 183

158. Berkman, "New Degree of Interest."

159. Arthur Levine, "Teacher Education Must Respond to Changes in America," *Phi Delta Kappan* 91:6 (October 2010), 19–24.

Chapter Two: Transforming University Programs

1. Bill Keller, "An Industry of Mediocrity," *New York Times*, October 20, 2013, http://www.nytimes.com/2013/10/21/opinion/keller-an-industry-of-medi ocrity.html.

2. "Why Teachers Fail," *Newsweek*, 104:13 (1984), 64–70; Arthur Bestor,

Educational Wastelands: The Retreat from Learning in our Public Schools (Urbana: University of Illinois Press, 1953).

3. See Introduction. See also James Fraser, *Preparing America's Teachers: A History* (New York: Teachers College Press, 2007), 1–40.

4. David Labaree, "An Uneasy Relationship: The History of Teacher Education in the University," in *Handbook of Research on Teacher Education: Enduring Issues in Changing Contexts* (3rd ed.), ed. Marilyn Cochran-Smith, Sharon Feiman Nemser, and John McIntyre (Washington, DC: Association of Teacher Educators, 2008), 295; https://web.stanford.edu/~dlabaree/publications/An_Uneasy_Relationship_Proofs.pdf.

5. Labaree, "An Uneasy Relationship," 304.

6. Fraser, *Preparing America's Teachers.*

7. Labaree, "An Uneasy Relationship."

8. See Christine A. Ogren, *The American State Normal School: "An Instrument of Great Good"* (New York: Palgrave Macmillan, 2005); John I. Goodlad, Roger Sodor, and Kenneth A. Sirotnik, eds., *Places Where Teachers Are Taught* (San Francisco: Jossey-Bass, 1990).

9. For the declining academic quality of the teaching force and its relationship to gender, see W. Timothy Weaver, "Solving the Problem of Teaching Quality, Part I," *Phi Delta Kappan*, 6:2 (October 1984), 108–115.

10. Jeffrey Mirel, "Bridging the Widest Street in the World: Reflections on the History of Teacher Education," *American Educator* (Summer 2011), 6–12.

11. Labaree, "An Uneasy Relationship."

12. Labaree, "An Uneasy Relationship."

13. Thomas Toch, "For Education Schools, a Search for Purpose and Identity," *Education Week*, September 21, 1981.

14. Quoted in James W. Fraser, "Considering the Future of University-Based Teacher Education," prepared for the Woodrow Wilson National Fellowship Foundation, April 2014, http://woodrow.org/wp-content/uploads/2014/04/WoodrowWilson_Fraser_UnivBasedTeacherEd_April2014_FINAL.pdf, 4.

15. Robert Soder and Kenneth A. Sirotnik, "Beyond Reinventing the Past: The Politics of Teacher Education," in *Places Where Teachers Are Taught*, ed. John I. Goodlad, Roger Soder, and Kenneth A. Sirotnik (San Francisco: Jossey-Bass, 1990).

16. Thomas Toch, "For Education Schools: A Search for Purpose and Identity," *Education Week*, September 21, 1981, https://www.edweek.org/ew/articles/1981/09/21/01030075.ho1.html.

17. Arthur Levine, "Educating School Teachers," Education Schools Project, 2005, http://www.edschools.org/pdf/Educating_Teachers_Exec_Summ.pdf.

18. National Council on Teacher Quality, "2014 Teacher Prep Review: A Review of the Nation's Teacher Preparation Programs," 2014, http://www.nctq.org/dmsView/Teacher_Prep_Review_2014_Report.

19. For influential works on teacher education by Linda Darling-Hammond,

see *Preparing Teachers for a Changing World: What Teachers Should Learn and Be Able to Do* (San Francisco, CA: Jossey Bass, 2005), *Teacher Education Around the World: Changing Policies and Practices* (New York: Routledge, 2012), and *Powerful Teacher Education: Lessons from Exemplary Programs* (San Francisco, CA: Jossey Bass, 2013).

20. See, for example, Marilyn Cochran-Smith and Kenneth M. Zeichner, eds., *Studying Teacher Education: The Report of the AERA Panel on Research and Teacher Education* (New York: Routledge, 2005); Cochran-Smith, *Policy, Practice, and Politics in Teacher Education: Editorials from the Journal of Teacher Education* (Thousand Oaks, CA: Corwin Press, 2006); Zeichner, *Studies of Excellence in Teacher Education: Preparation in the Undergraduate Years* (Washington, DC: American Association of Colleges for Teacher Education, National Commission on Teacher Teaching and America's Future, 2000); Zeichner, *Teacher Education and the Struggle for Social Justice* (New York: Routledge, 2009); Zeichner, "Reflections of a University-Based Teacher Educator on the Future of College and University-Based Teacher Education," *Journal of Teacher Education* 57:3 (2006), 326–340.

21. Gloria Ladson-Billings, "Who Will Teach Our Children? Preparing Teachers to Teach African American Learners" in *Teaching Diverse Learners: Formulating a Knowledge Base for Teaching Diverse Populations*, ed. Etta R. Hollins, Joyce E. King, and Warren C. Hayman (Albany: State University of New York Press, 1994), 129–158; Ladson-Billings, "Multicultural Teacher Education: Research, Policy, and Practices" in *Handbook of Research on Multicultural Education*, ed. James A. Banks and Cherry A. McGee Banks (New York: Macmillan, 1995), 747–759; Sonia Nieto, "Placing Equity Front and Center: Some Thoughts on Transforming Teacher Education in a New Century," *Journal of Teacher Education* 51:3 (2000), 180–187.

22. Ted Montgomery, "TeachingWorks Receives $6.8M Grant to Establish Teacher Preparation," *Michigan News*, University of Michigan, November 18, 2015, http://www.ns.umich.edu/new/releases/23306-teachingworks-receives-6-8m-grant-to-establish-teacher-preparation-transformation-center.

23. Quoted in Toch, "For Education Schools."

24. Quoted in Toch, "For Education Schools."

25. Ellen Lagemann, *An Elusive Science: The Troubling History of Education Research* (Chicago: University of Chicago Press, 2000), 1–98.

26. Ethan Bronner, "End of Chicago's Education School Stirs Debate," *New York Times*, September 16, 1997, http://www.nytimes.com/1997/09/17/us/end-of-chicago-s-education-school-stirs-debate.html.

27. "Background on the Department of Education and the Recommendation to Close the Department," Society for the Advancement of Educational Scholarship, 1996, http://web.archive.org/web/19961220160708/http://student-www.uchicago.edu/orgs/eduscholarship/bckgrnd.htm; "Historical Note," University of Chicago, College of Education. Records, Special Collections Research Center,

University of Chicago Library, http://www.lib.uchicago.edu/e/scrc/findingaids /view.php?eadid=ICU.SPCL.EDUCATIONDEPT.

28. For more on the status of educational research within the university setting, see Lagemann, *An Elusive Science*; David Labaree, *The Trouble with Ed Schools* (New Haven, CT: Yale University Press, 2004).

29. Jeanne Ponessa, "U. of Chicago Mulls Axing Ed. Department," *Education Week*, September 18, 1996; Susan Dodge, "U. of C. May Kill Teachers School; Education Program 'Uneven,' Officials Say," *Chicago Sun Times*, August 23, 1996.

30. Ponessa, "U of C Mulls Axing Ed. Department"; Dodge, "U of C May Kill Teachers School;" David J. Bird, "Education Dept. Faces Elimination; Following Comprehensive Review, Dean Recommends Department's Close by 2001," *Chicago Maroon*, August 2, 1996.

31. "Petition to University of Chicago President Hugo Sonnenschein," Society for Educational Scholarship, 1996, http://web.archive.org/web/19961220 160725/http://student-www.uchicago.edu/orgs/eduscholarship/petition.htm; Various authors, "Letters of Support," Society for Educational Scholarship, http://web.archive.org/web/19961220160747/http://student-www.uchicago .edu/orgs/eduscholarship/letsupp.htm.

32. "An Open Letter to the Social Sciences Faculty," *Chicago Maroon*, November 12, 1996, http://web.archive.org/web/19961220160757/http://student -www.uchicago.edu/orgs/eduscholarship/student.htm; Ponessa, "U of C Mulls Axing Ed. Department"; Dodge, "U of C May Kill Teachers School"; Rogers Worthington, "Review Puts U. of C. Education Department In Peril," *Chicago Tribune*, August 24, 1996; John K. Wilson, "A Learning Experience: Will the University of Chicago Destroy the Department of Education?," *University of Chicago Free Press*, November 24, 1996; Steven R. Strahler, "U of C Set to Dismiss Education Department," *Crain's Business News*, August 26, 1996.

33. "National Academy of Education: Statement of Concern," Society of Educational Scholarship, October 25, 1996, http://web.archive.org/web/1996 1220023507/http://student-www.uchicago.edu/orgs/eduscholarship/nae.htm; "Letter from the President of the American Educational Research Association," Society of Educational Scholarship, November 10, 1996, http://web.archive.org /web/19991104060443/http://student-www.uchicago.edu/orgs/eduscholarship /aera.htm; Geoff Fischer, "National Groups Fight to Keep Education Department Open," *Chicago Maroon*, November 8, 1996.

34. "National Academy of Education."

35. "The Department of Education's Report," Society for Educational Scholarship, 1996, http://web.archive.org/web/19970616053813/http://www .uchicago.edu/u.scholarly/education/report.html; "An Open Letter to the Social Sciences Faculty"; Wilson, "A Learning Experience"; Alan Gewirth, "Don't Cut Education Quite Yet," *Chicago Maroon*, November 12, 1996.

36. Editorial Board, "Let's Learn from the Ed. Dept," *Chicago Maroon*, November 12, 1996.

37. Dan Steinberg, "Education Rally Airs Issues to Small Crowd," *Chicago Maroon*, October 29, 1996.

38. Jonathan Bassett, "The University of Chicago's Education School Will Not Be Missed," *Education Week Online*, November 12, 1997.

39. Bronner, "End of Chicago's Education School Stirs Debate"; Bird, "Education Dept. Faces Elimination"; Dodge, "U of C May Kill Teachers School."

40. Dan Steinberg, "Faculty Votes to Dissolve Ed Department," *Chicago Maroon*, November 15, 1996.

41. Bronner, "End of Chicago's Education School Stirs Debate."

42. See "Students," University of Chicago Urban Teacher Education Program, University of Chicago, https://utep.uchicago.edu/page/students; "Partner Spotlight: Chicago UTEP," Urban Teacher Residency United, http://www.utrunited.org/blog/entry/partner-spotlight-chicago-utep/; Michael Haederle, "Chicago Charter Schools Aim to Lift Urban Education," August 23, 2011, *Pacific Standard Magazine*, http://www.psmag.com/books-and-culture/chicago-charter-schools-aim-to-lift-urban-education-34328.

43. Haederle, "Chicago Charter Schools Aim"; Karen Hammerness, "What Keeps Good Teachers Teaching?" *Washington Post*, July 23, 2013, http://www.washingtonpost.com/blogs/answer-sheet/wp/2013/07/23/what-keeps-good-teachers-teaching/; "UTEP," https://utep.uchicago.edu/.

44. Michael Liplin, "Cabinet Members Praise University's Pragmatic Work at D.C. Forum," *Chicago Maroon*, September 11, 2009, http://chicagomaroon.com/2009/09/11/cabinet-members-praise-university-s-pragmatic-work-at-d-c-forum/.

45. Program Overview," University of Chicago Urban Teacher Education Program, https://utep.uchicago.edu/page/program-overview; Justin Snider, "Preparing Teachers for a Lifetime in the Classroom," *Huffington Post*, August 30, 2011, http://www.huffingtonpost.com/justin-snider/preparing-teachers-for-a-_b_887995.html; Hammerness, "What Keeps Good Teachers Teaching?"

46. Haederle, "Chicago Charter Schools Aim"

47. Abby Seiff, "Social Sciences Division Creates a New Committee on Education," *Chicago Maroon*, February 21, 2006, http://chicagomaroon.com/2006/02/21/social-sciences-division-creates-new-committee-on-education/.

48. For more on the history of education research and teacher preparation at Stanford, see "Graduate School of Education Timeline," Stanford University, https://ed.stanford.edu/about/history; Geraldine Jonçich Clifford and James W. Guthrie, *Ed School: A Brief for Professional Education* (Chicago: University of Chicago Press, 1988), 202–258.

49. As quoted in Clifford and Guthrie, *Ed School*, 229.

50. Clifford and Guthrie, *Ed School*, 228–231.

51. "College Presidents Push for Public School Support," *The Stanford Daily*, August 19, 1983, http://stanforddailyarchive.com/cgi-bin/stanford?a=d&d=stanford19830819-01.1.1&e=-------en-20--1--txt-txIN-------#.

52. Associated Press, "37 College Presidents Call for Better Teaching," *New York Times*, September 19, 1987, http://www.nytimes.com/1987/09/19/us/37-college-presidents-call-for-better-teaching.html; Barbara Vobejda, "Colleges Urged to Face Education Crisis,' *Washington Post*, September 19, 1987, http://www.washingtonpost.com/pb/archive/politics/1987/09/19/colleges-urged-to-face-education-crisis/28430af7-a836-4eb8-af06-0ce306e16b02/?resType=accessibility; Clifford and Guthrie, *Ed School*, 231.

53. Lee Shulman, *The Wisdom of Practice, Essays on Teaching, Learning, and Learning to Teach* (San Francisco: Jossey-Bass, 2004), 203.

54. "Faculty Meetings, 1981–1983," Stanford Graduate School of Education, October 6, 1987, http://sul-derivatives.stanford.edu/derivative?CSNID=00002411&mediaType=application/pdf.

55. "Faculty Evaluation Report, 1997–1998," Stanford Graduate School of Education, 1998.

56. Mark West, "Op-Ed: Valuing Teacher Education," *Stanford Daily*, October 30, 2008.

57. "Faculty Meetings, 1981–1983," Stanford Graduate School of Education, October 6, 1987, http://sul-derivatives.stanford.edu/derivative?CSNID=00002411&mediaType=application/pdf.

58. "Faculty Evaluation Report, 1997–1998."

59. "Faculty Evaluation Report, 1997–1998."

60. Linda Darling-Hammond and Joan Baratz-Snowden, *A Good Teacher in Every Classroom: Preparing the Highly Qualified Teachers Our Children Deserve* (New York: Jossey-Bass, 2007).

61. "Faculty Evaluation Report, 1997–1998."

62. Barnett Berry, "Stanford University and Preparing Teachers for a New Era: A Critical Review with Considerations for the Future," Center for Teaching Quality, July 2008.

63. Lisa Trei, "'Cosby on Campus' Raises $1 Million for Teacher Education," *Stanford News*, May 26, 2004, http://news.stanford.edu/news/2004/may26/cosby-526.html.

64. "New $20 Million Loan-Forgiveness Program to Encourage Stanford Graduates to Become K–12 Teachers," *Stanford News,* October 3, 2006, http://news.stanford.edu/pr/2006/pr-steploan-100406.html.

65. Adam Gorlick, "Education Minor Offered to Undergraduates," *Stanford News*, October 2, 2009, http://news.stanford.edu/news/2009/september28/undergrad-edu-minor-100209.html.

66. Jonathan Rabinovitz, "Nine Top Teaching Fellowships Awarded to STEP," *Stanford News*, June 13, 2013, https://ed.stanford.edu/news/nine-top-teaching-fellowships-awarded-step.

67. F. Andre Favat, "Factions Clash as the Ed School Grows; One-Year Students and Ph.D. Candidates Stimulate Curriculum Changes but Feel a Mutual Distrust," *Harvard Crimson*, May 18, 1966.

68. Quoted in Eleanor Barkhorn, "Why Isn't Harvard Training More Teachers?," *Atlantic*, November 13, 2013, http://www.theatlantic.com/education/archive/2013/11/why-isnt-harvard-training-more-teachers/281432/.

69. See Rediet T. Abebe and Linda Zhang, "Teaching Programs Attract Students," *Harvard Crimson*, September 16, 2010; Lory Hough, "A Look at the Growing Interest in Education and Teaching Among Harvard College Students," *Harvard Ed. Magazine*, September 5, 2014, http://www.gse.harvard.edu/news/ed/14/09/welcome-undergrads.

70. Dev A. Patel, "Ed School to Launch Teacher Fellows Program for College Seniors; Forty Seniors from Class of '16 Will Inaugurate TFA Alternative," *Harvard Crimson*, November 3, 2014, http://www.thecrimson.com/article/2014/11/3/teacher-fellows-program-announce/.

71. For more on the field of education at Harvard, see Arthur G. Powell, *The Uncertain Profession: Harvard and the Search for Educational Authority* (Cambridge, MA: Harvard University Press, 1980); "History of HGSE," Harvard Graduate School of Education, https://www.gse.harvard.edu/about/history; Geraldine Jonçich Clifford and James W. Guthrie, *Ed School: A Brief for Professional Education* (Chicago: University of Chicago Press, 1990); Patricia A. Graham, "Education at the Ed School," *Harvard Crimson*, October, 26, 1983.

72. Fred M. Hechinger, "Heads of Six Universities Vow to Improve Schools," *New York Times*, August 17, 1983.

73. Clifford and Guthrie, *Ed School*, 216

74. Graham, "Education at the Ed School."

75. Graham, "Education at the Ed School."

76. David J. Baron, "A Different Sort of Preprofessionalism," *Harvard Crimson*, March 7, 1986, http://www.thecrimson.com/article/1986/3/7/a-different-sort-of-pre-professionalism-pbubsually/.

77. See Abebe and Zhang, "Teaching Programs Attract Students"; Barkhorn, "Why Isn't Harvard Training More Teachers?"; Hough, "A Look at the Growing Interest."

78. Eric P. Newcomer, "TFA Sees Growth in Applicant Pool," *Harvard Crimson*, April 23, 2010, http://www.thecrimson.com/article/2010/4/23/tfa-harvard-baichorova-year/.

79. "HGSE Timeline," Harvard Graduate School of Education, https://www.gse.harvard.edu/about/history/timeline; Daniel P. Mosteller, "Ed School Dean Murphey to Step Down Next June," June 6, 2000, http://www.thecrimson.com/article/2000/6/6/ed-school-dean-murphy-to-step/?page=3; Claire A. Pasternack, "Repolishing the Red Apple," *Harvard Crimson*, June 5, 2003, http://www.thecrimson.com/article/2003/6/5/repolishing-the-red-apple-university-president/.

80. Quoted in Laura L. Krug, "Dean: Ed Schools Need Research Reforms," *Harvard Crimson*, October 17, 2002, http://www.thecrimson.com/article/2002/10/17/dean-ed-schools-need-research-reforms/. See also Claire A. Pasternack, "GSE Dean Stressed Teacher Training," *Harvard Crimson*, Septem-

ber 20, 2002, http://www.thecrimson.com/article/2002/9/20/gse-dean-stresses
-teacher-training-by/.

81. Quoted in Patel, "Ed School to Launch Teacher Fellows Program,"
http://www.thecrimson.com/article/2014/9/25/office-hours-merseth/.

82. Quoted in Christina Pazzanese, "A New Lesson Plan: HGSE Program
to Prepare College Seniors for Teaching Careers," *Harvard Crimson*, November
10, 2014, http://www.thecrimson.com/article/1983/10/26/education-at-the-ed
-school-pmany/.

83. Pazzanese, "New Lesson Plan."

84. Quoted in Mariela A. Klein, "Student Activist Group Calls on Faust
to Sever Ties with TFA," *Harvard Crimson*, September 28, 2014, http://www
.thecrimson.com/article/2014/9/28/student-labor-action-tfa-letter/.

85. Hough, "A Look at the Growing Interest."

86. "Teacher Education Program," Harvard Graduate School of Education,
https://www.gse.harvard.edu/masters/tep.

87. Quoted in Barbara McKenna, "Teacher Education Mixes It Up with
High Schools," *AFT On Campus, Education Digest*, April 1, 1999.

88. Jonathan Friendly, "Jersey Colleges Criticize Study on Teacher Testing,"
New York Times, November 17, 1985.

89. "History," Montclair State University, https://www.montclair.edu/provost
/faculty-handbook/history/, accessed April 18, 2017; James B. Conant, *The Education of American Teachers* (New York: McGraw Hill, 1963).

90. McKenna, "Teacher Education Mixes It Up," 54.

91. Michelli, interviewed in McKenna, "Teacher Education Mixes It Up," 55.

92. Harry Judge, "Foreword" in *The Rise and Stall of Teacher Education
Reform*, ed. Michael Fullan, Gary Galluzzo, Patricia Morris, and Nancy Watson
(Washington DC: AACTE Publications, 1998), xiii.

93. Nicholas M. Michelli, Robert Pines, and Wendy Oxman-Michelli, "Collaboration for Critical Thinking in Teacher Education: The Montclair State
College Model," *Resource Publication* 3:3, Montclair State College, Institution
for Critical Thinking, Upper Montclair, NJ, 1990, 4.

94. Michelli et al., "Collaboration for Critical Thinking," 10.

95. Academy for Educational Development, "Montclair State University:
Documentation of the Teachers for a New Era Learning Network," ERIC: Education Resources Information Center, April 2009.

96. Velma L. Cobb, "Professional Development Schools as Educational Reform," *Journal of Education for Teaching* 20:4 (1994): 58–60.

97. Howard Gregory, "'Everyone's a Learner'; Show of Class; Dumont High
School Forces Ties with College," *The Record* (Bergen County, NJ), February 3,
1998.

98. Academy for Educational Development, "Montclair State University."

99. Quoted in McKenna, "Teacher Education Mixes It Up."

100. "On Campus," *Record* [Bergen County, NJ], January 9, 2000; Jean

Rimbach and Robert Gebeloff, "Wanted: Minority Teachers; A New Challenge for School Diversity," *Record,* July 2, 2000.

101. Caitlin Rose Daily, Eric Watts, Ivan Charner, and Robin White, "Partnering to Prepare Tomorrow's Teachers: Examples from Practice," Teachers for a New Era Learning Network and FHI 360, April 2009, https://www.montclair.edu/media/montclairedu/cehs/documents/cop/Partnering_to_Prepare_Tomorrow_s_Teachers.pdf.

102. "Findings," National Council on Teacher Quality, http://www.nctq.org/teacherPrep/2016/findings/home.do, accessed May 3, 2017.

103. "Teacher Education Program," College of Education and Human Services, Montclair State University, https://www.montclair.edu/cehs/academics/cop/teacher/; "Edutopia Names 10 Schools of Education That Will Change the Way We Teach," *Newswire,* November 28, 2007.

104. McKenna, "Teacher Education Mixes It Up."

105. Anya Kamenetz, "For Teacher, Many Paths into the Classroom . . . Some Say Too Many," NPR Now, WGBH Radio, September 12, 2014, http://www.npr.org/sections/ed/2014/09/12/347375798/for-teachers-many-paths-into-the-classroom.

106. Chelsea Schneider, "Indiana Gets Low Marks in Attracting Teachers," *Indianapolis Star,* September 16, 2016.

107. Quoted in Sarah Butrymowicz, "Indiana Seeks to Reform Teacher Training," *Indiana Star,* and the Hechinger Report, March 15, 2012, http://hechingerreport.org/indiana-seeks-to-reform-teacher-training/.

108. "UIndy's History and Mission," University of Indianapolis, http://www.uindy.edu/about-uindy/history-and-mission.

109. "Undergraduate Programs," University of Indianapolis School of Education, http://www.uindy.edu/education/teaching.

110. Information on the UIndy undergraduate and master's programs comes from a research paper by Amber Joseph for Jim Fraser's Spring 2014 graduate seminar "Public Problems: Education and Social Policy-Teacher Education" at New York University, as well as conversations with UIndy School of Education faculty.

111. New "Entrance to Program" requirements began in the 2013–2014 academic year. Because of historical difficulties placing teacher candidates with a GPA lower than 2.75 at student-teaching sites, the School of Education required a minimum 2.75 GPA. A teacher candidate can demonstrate basic skills competency through the Pearson CASA Core Assessment in Reading, Writing, and Math; a SAT composite score of 1100; or an ACT score of 24. See University of Indianapolis School of Education Department of Teacher Education, "Undergraduate Handbook 2012–2013," 19.

112. University of Indianapolis School of Education Department of Teacher Education, "Undergraduate Handbook 2012–2013," 20

113. "Undergraduate Programs," University of Indianapolis Elementary and Secondary Education, http://uindy.edu/education/teaching.

114. University of Indianapolis School of Education Department of Teacher Education, "Undergraduate Handbook 2012–2013," 20.

115. Interview with Kathryn Moran, conducted by Amber Joseph, April 8, 2014.

116. University of Indianapolis School of Education Department of Teacher Education, "Undergraduate Handbook 2012–2013," 21.

117. Jennifer Drake, Kathryn Moran, Deb Sachs, Azure Dee Smiley Angelov, and Lynn Wheeler, "The University of Indianapolis Woodrow Wilson Indiana Teaching Fellowship Program: Reviewing the Policy Implications of University-Based Urban Clinical Residency Programs in STEM Teacher Preparation," *Planning and Changing* 42:3–4 (2011), 316–333.

118. Charlotte Danielson, *Enhancing Professional Practice: A Framework for Teaching*, 2nd ed. (Alexandria, VA: Association for Supervision & Curriculum Development, 2007).

119. "University of Indianapolis Woodrow Wilson Indiana Teaching Fellowship (WWITF) Program: Clinical Immersion Overview," University of Indianapolis School of Education; "University of Indianapolis Woodrow Wilson Teaching Fellowship Program Handbook, 2015–2016," University of Indianapolis School of Education.

120. Deborah W. Balogh, "U of I Preparing Teachers in Crucial Disciplines," *Indianapolis Star*, November 14, 2011.

121. The (STEM)³ program is a full-time, one-year UIndy clinical residency for college graduates with a degree in mathematics, science, technology, or engineering. Its curriculum is unique in that it is presented in a project-based-learning format. "About Teach (STEM)³," University of Indianapolis School of Education, http://uindy.edu/education/teaching-fellowship/about.

122. "Grant Supports STEM Teaching Collaboration," *UIndy 360*, February 25, 2014, https://news.uindy.edu/2014/02/25/grant-supports-stem-teaching-collaboration/.

123. Drake et al., "University of Indianapolis Woodrow Wilson Indiana Teaching Fellowship Program."

124. Linda Darling-Hammond et al., *Empowered Educators: How High-Performing Systems Shape Teaching Quality around the World* (New York: Jossey-Bass, 2017).

125. Schneider, "Indiana Gets Low Marks in Attracting Teachers."

126. Schneider, "Indiana Gets Low Marks in Attracting Teachers."

127. Genevieve Anton, "Virtual University Is a Virtual Reality, Governors Say," *Colorado Springs Gazette*, June 25, 1996; Kevin Kinser, "Innovation in Higher Education: A Case Study of the Western Governors University," *New Directions for Higher Education* 137 (Spring 2007), 15–25; Katrina A. Myer, "Western Governors University," *New Directions in Higher Education* 146 (Summer 2009), 35–43. This and later material has greatly benefitted from an interview by James W. Fraser with WGU founding president Robert Mendenhall, Salt Lake City, Utah, May 18, 2016.

128. Quoted in Julie Titone, "WGU: 13 States, No Buildings 'Virtual University' Aims to Bring Education to Most Remote Regions," *Spokesman Review* (Spokane, WA), November 10, 1996.

129. Quoted in Anton, "Virtual University."

130. Titone, "WGU: 13 States, No Buildings."

131. Quoted in Titone, "WGU: 13 States, No Buildings."

132. The Chronicle of Higher Education alone published 189 stories about the project between 1995 and 2008, though many of the articles were critical.

133. Robert Mendenhall, president emeritus, interviewed by James W. Fraser, Western Governors University, May 18, 2016.

134. Kinser, "Innovation in Higher Education"; Interview with Robert Mendenhall, May 18, 2016.

135. Vaishali Honawar, "Accreditation Makes Virtual Teachers College 'Real Thing,'" *Education Week* 26:14 (December 6, 2006), http://www.wgu.edu/wgu files/ed-week-article-12-6-06.

136. "Program Guidebook: Bachelor of Arts in Teaching, Mathematics (5–12)," Western Governors University, 2017.

137. Anya Kamenetz, "Who Is a College Teacher, Anyway? Audit of Online University Raises Questions," *National Public Radio*, September 28, 2017, http://www.npr.org/sections/ed/2017/09/28/553753020/who-is-a-college -teacher-anyway-audit-of-online-university-raises-questions.

138. Information on WGU's academic program comes from the Western Governors University website, http://www.wgu.edu/education/online_teaching _degree; Meredith Liu, "Disrupting Teacher Education," *Education Next*, 13:3 (Summer 2013), http://educationnext.org/disrupting-teacher-education/.

139. Quoted in Betsy Hammond, "Nation's No. 1-ranked Teacher Prep Program Operates in Oregon," *Oregonian/Oregon Live*, June 19, 2014, http:// www.oregonlive.com/education/index.ssf/2014/06/nations_no_1-ranked _teacher_pr.html.

140. "Tuition and Financial Aid," Western Governors University, http:// www.wgu.edu/tuition_financial_aid/overview.

141. Philip A. Schmidt, "Assessment at Western Governors University and the NCATE Accreditation Process," *Assessment Update* 20:1 (January 2008), 11–15.

142. Hammond, "Nation's No. 1-ranked Teacher Prep Program."

143. For more on challenges related to principal ratings as part of program evaluation, see Cochran-Smith and Zeichner, *Studying Teacher Education.*

144. Degrees and Programs: Teachers College," Western Governors University, https://www.wgu.edu/education/teacher_certification_elementary_program.

145. Quoted in Paul Fain, "Federal Audit Challenges Faculty Role at WGU," *Inside Higher Ed*, September 22, 2017, https://www.insidehighered.com/news /2017/09/22/education-depts-inspector-general-calls-western-governors-repay -713-million-federal.

146. Quoted in Fain, "Federal Audit Challenges Faculty Role at WGU."

147. Quoted in Fain, "Federal Audit Challenges Faculty Role at WGU."

148. Kamenetz, "Who Is a College Teacher, Anyway?"

149. For a review of the literature regarding online and distance learning, see S. E. Eaton, R. Dressler, D. Gereluk, and S. Becker, "A Review of the Literature on Rural and Remote Pre-Service Teacher Preparation with a Focus on Blended and Learning Models," University of Calgary, June 2015, http://hdl.handle.net/1880/50497.

150. Johann N. Neem, "A University without Intellectuals: Western Governors University and the Academy's Future," *Thought & Action* 28 (Fall 2012), 63–79.

151. Liu, "Disrupting Teacher Education."

152. Harry Judge, "Foreword," in *The Rise and Stall of Teacher Education Reform,* ed. Michael Fullan et al. (Washington, DC: American Association of Colleges for Teacher Preparation, 1998), xiii. See also Elizabeth Green, *Building a Better Teacher: How Teaching Works (and How to Teach It to Everyone)* (New York: Norton, 2014), chapter 3, 80–112.

153. Arthur Levine, *Educating School Teachers,* Education Schools Project, 2006, http://edschools.org/pdf/Final313.pdf, 5.

154. Arthur Levine, *Educating Researchers* (New York: Education Schools Project, 2007), 6.

155. Linda Darling-Hammond, "How Teacher Education Matters," *Journal of Teacher Education* 51:3 (May/June 2000), 166. See also Darling-Hammond, Ruth Chung Wei, and Alethea Andree, "How High-Achieving Countries Develop Great Teachers," research brief, Stanford Center for Opportunity Policy in Education, August 2010.

156. Darling-Hammond, "How Teacher Education Matters," 166.

Chapter Three: The New Hybrids

1. Jackie Mader, "The Promise of Teacher-Residency Programs," *The Atlantic,* April, 15, 2016, http://www.theatlantic.com/education/archive/2016/04/what-happens-when-teachers-spend-more-time-in-a-classroombefore-teaching/478359/.

2. Kenneth Zeichner, "Improving Teacher Education in the United States," June 2011, essay invited by the American Educational Research Association, posted on the AERA website in conjunction with the 2012 annual meeting in Vancouver, http://www.aera.net/Portals/38/docs/Annual_Meeting/Zeichner_AERA_essay-1b.pdf.

3. U.S. House of Representatives, Subcommittee on Early Childhood, Elementary and Secondary Education, Committee on Education and the Workforce, *Education Reforms: Discussing the Value of Alternative Teacher Certification Programs,* 112th Congress, Second Session, Washington, DC, July 24, 2012, http://www.gpoaccess.gov/congress/house/education/index.html.

4. The Bill & Melinda Gates Foundation, "Gates Foundation Awards over $34 Million in Grants to Help Improve Teacher Preparation Programs," press release, November 18, 2015, https://www.gatesfoundation.org/Media-Center /Press-Releases/2015/11/Teacher-Prep-Grants.

5. "About BTR," Boston Teacher Residency, http://www.bostonteacher residency.org/about/; Office of the White House Press Secretary, "Background on the President's Trip to TechBoston Academy," March 8, 2011, https://www .whitehouse.gov/the-press-office/2011/03/08/background-president-s-trip-tech boston-academy.

6. Linda Darling-Hammond, "A Future Worthy of Teaching for America," *Phi Delta Kappan*, June 1, 2008, https://edpolicy.stanford.edu/publications /pubs/1198.

7. Stephen Sawchuk, "Teacher 'Residencies' Get Federal Funding to Augment Training," *Education Week*, October 9, 2009; Vaishali Honawar, "Boston, Chicago Teacher 'Residencies' Gaining Notice," *Education Week*, September 11, 2008, https://www.edweek.org/ew/articles/2008/09/10/04residencies.html.

8. Jesse Solomon, "The Boston Teacher Residency: District-Based Teacher Education," *Journal of Teacher Education* 60:5 (November/December 2009), 478–488.

9. "Teacher Quality Partnership Grant Program: Awards, 2009–2016," U.S. Department of Education, https://www2.ed.gov/programs/tqpartnership /awards.html.

10. "Teacher Quality Partnership Grant Program."

11. "Boston Reinvents Teacher Training," *Administrators Magazine,* March/ April 2009, http://www.scholastic.com/browse/article.jsp?id=3751490.

12. Tamara Azar and Sudipti Kumar, "Investing Up Front: The School-Based Approach to Teacher Prep," *Huffington Post*, October 5, 2015, http://www.huff ingtonpost.com/tamara-azar/investing-up-front-the-school_b_8223662.html.

13. "Teacher Quality Partnership Grants, Funding: FY18 Update," American Association of Colleges for Teacher Education, https://aacte.org/policy-and -advocacy/federal-policy-and-legislation/435-teacher-quality-partnership-grants.

14. Lillian Mongeau, "In Search of High Quality Teachers, Charter Network Trains Its Own," *Hechinger Report*, http://hechingerreport.org/in-search -of-high-quality-teachers-charter-network-trains-its-own/; Jenn Hatfield and Ian Lindquist, "How to Solve Charter Schools' Biggest Challenge," *U.S. News & World Report*, May 6, 2016, http://www.usnews.com/opinion/articles/2016 -05-06/charter-schools-biggest-challenge-is-recruiting-and-training-good-teachers.

15. For more information on the role of academies in the Every Student Succeeds Act, see U.S. Department of Education Press Office, "Education Department Releases Final Teacher Preparation Regulations," October 12, 2016, https://www.ed.gov/news/press-releases/education-department-releases-final -teacher-preparation-regulations; Stephen Sawchuk, "ESEA-Rewrite Bill Includes Controversial New Teacher Prep Provisions," *Education Week,* December

8, 2015, http://blogs.edweek.org/edweek/teacherbeat/2015/12/teacher-prep_pro
visions_in_ess.html; Valerie Strauss, "The Big Problem with the Obama Administration's New Teacher Education Regulations," *Washington Post*, October 24,
2016, https://www.washingtonpost.com/news/answer-sheet/wp/2016/10/24/the
-big-problems-with-obama-administrations-new-teacher-education-regulations/;
American Federation of Teachers, "Teacher Prep in the Every Student Succeeds
Act," http://www.aft.org/sites/default/files/essa_teacher-prep.pdf.

16. Pete Fishman, "Learning to Teach . . . Better," *New Schools Venture
Fund*, December 20, 2010, http://www.newschools.org/news/learning-to-teach
-better/.

17. This meeting also encouraged participants to create new entities committed to improving teacher education. For example, the Deans for Impact group,
an organization that brings twenty-seven deans of schools of education from
around the country together to share ideas and work together to improve the
nature of teacher preparation in the United States, originated from this conversation. TeacherSquared became another product of the umbrella organization,
a teacher education innovation hub that links alternative programs like Relay
GSE, Sposato GSE, and Alder GSE (an alternative provider that trains teachers
from YES Prep, KIPP, and some Texas school districts). See "Home" and "What
We Do," TeacherSquared, https://www.teachersquared.org/ and "About Us" and
"Our Work," Deans for Impact, https://deansforimpact.org/.

18. "Great Teachers and Principals Act," *Education Week*, http://www.ed
week.org/media/greatactbackground-blog.pdf.

19. Lauren Anderson and Ken Zeichner, quoted in Strauss, "The Big Problem."

20. Jonathan Zimmerman, "Why Is American Teaching So Bad?" *New York
Review of Books*, December 4, 2014.

21. Quoted in Anya Kamenetz, "For Teachers, Many Paths into the classroom
. . . Some Say Too Many," *NPR*, September 12, 2014, http://npr.org/sections/ed
/2014/09/12/347375798/for-teachers-many-paths-into-the-classroom.

22. Quoted in "Boston Reinvents Teacher Training."

23. "Boston Reinvents Teacher Training."

24. "Boston Reinvents Teacher Training."

25. For more on the creation of BTR, see Solomon, "Boston Teacher Residency"; Honawar, "Boston, Chicago Teacher 'Residencies' "; "Boston Reinvents
Teacher Training."

26. Solomon, "Boston Teacher Residency."

27. "BPE Teaching Academies," Boston Teacher Residency, http://www.bpe
.org/schools/newschools.

28. Grace Rubenstein, "Boston Teacher Residency: Real-World Training and
Cost Incentives Keep Teachers Teaching," *Edutopia*, November 19, 2007, http://
www.edutopia.org/schools-of-education-boston.

29. "BTR Impact," http://www.bostonteacherresidency.org/btr-impact/.

30. The Alliance for Education is a Seattle non-profit developed in 1995 as

an independent organization to raise funds from private donors, businesses, and philanthropies to directly serve initiatives in Seattle public schools.

31. John Higgins, "Starting Seattle Teachers Learn Alongside Kids in New Apprentice Program," *Seattle Times*, November 12, 2013, http://old.seattletimes .com/html/education/2022245271_teacherresidencyxml.html.

32. For information on the Seattle Teacher Residency program, see "Program" and "Curriculum," Seattle Teacher Residency, http://www.seattleteacher residency.org/program/what-is-seattle-teacher-residency/. Information was also gathered through an oral interview between James W. Fraser and STR director Marissa Bier on July 24, 2017.

33. "Seattle Teacher Residency Releases Teacher Retention, Diversity, Student Achievement Data," press release, Seattle Teacher Residency, April 5, 2017.

34. Seattle School Board of Education, "Proposed Action Report," October 9, 2015, http://www.seattleschools.org/UserFiles/Servers/Server_543/File/Dis trict/Departments/School%20Board/15-16agendas/102115agenda/20151021 _Action_Report_SPS_AllianceforEd_Packet.pdf.

35. For more on the Alliance, see "History," Alliance for Education, http:// www.alliance4ed.org/who-we-are/history/; Sarah Gonser, "This May Be the Best Way to Train Teachers, But Can We Afford It?," *Huffington Post*, May 5, 2016, http://www.huffingtonpost.com/entry/seattle-teacher-residency_us_572ba231 e4b0bc9cb0461eba.

36. Ann Dornfield, "Nonprofit Brings Support—and Pressure—to Seattle Schools," KUOW.org, January 22, 2013, http://kuow.org/post/nonprofit-brings -support-and-pressure-seattle-schools.

37. Dornfield, "Nonprofit Brings Support."

38. Gonser, "This May Be the Best Way."

39. Seattle Board of Education, "Proposed Action Report."

40. Gosner, "This May Be the Best Way."

41. Seattle Times Editorial Board, "Seattle Public Schools, Alliance for Education Should Salvage Their Relationship," *Seattle Times*, November 3, 2015.

42. For the Alliance perspective, see Jon Bridge and Sara Morris, "Mend Relations between Seattle Public Schools and Alliance for Education," *Seattle Times*, October 21, 2015, http://www.seattletimes.com/opinion/mend-relations -between-seattle-public-schools-and-alliance-for-education/; for UW's position, see Kenneth Zeichner, "Successful Mentoring Program for Teachers Still Needs Seattle's Support," *Crosscut*, January 27, 2016.

43. Gosner, "This May Be the Best Way."

44. "Clinically Oriented Teacher Preparation," research report, National Center for Teacher Residencies, June 2015, https://nctresidencies.org/wp-con tent/uploads/2016/01/COTP_Report_Singlepgs_Final.compressed.pdf.

45. Neal Morton, "Innovative Training Program Places More Teachers of Color in Seattle's Public Schools," *Seattle Times*, April 5, 2017, http://www

.seattletimes.com/education-lab/innovative-training-program-places-more
-minority-teachers-in-seattles-public-schools/.

46. Morton, "Innovative Training Program."

47. Mader, "Promise of Teacher-Residency Programs."

48. "Overview," Woodrow Wilson Academy of Teaching and Learning, 2015.

49. Arthur Levine, "Educating School Teachers," The Education Schools Project, 2006, http://www.edschools.org/pdf/Educating_Teachers_Report.pdf.

50. Levine, "Educating School Teachers," 109.

51. Claudio Sanchez, "A Vision for Teacher Training at MIT: West Point Meets Bell Labs," *NPR Morning Edition*, June 17, 2015; "MIT and Woodrow Wilson National Fellowship Foundation Collaborate to Transform Teaching in the Digital Age," *MIT News*, June 16, 2015.

52. Sanchez, Vision for Teacher Training at MIT."

53. Caroline Porter, "Teacher-Training Initiative Aims to Reinvigorate Profession," *Wall Street Journal*, June 16, 2015.

54. Michael Blanding, "How Should We Teach the Teachers?" *MIT Technology Review*, June 21, 2016, https://www.technologyreview.com/s/601547/how -should-we-teach-the-teachers/.

55. "Institute-wide Task Force on the Future of MIT Education, Final Report," July 28, 2014, http://web.mit.edu/future-report/TaskForceFinal_July28 .pdf.

56. Grace Rubenstein, "Learning at High Tech High," *Edutopia*, December 3, 2008, https://www.edutopia.org/collaboration-age-technology-high-tech.

57. Rob Riordan and Larry Rosenstock, "Changing the Subject," program materials presented on a school tour, Winter 2017.

58. Riordan and Rosenstock, "Changing the Subject."

59. "Our Approach," High Tech High Graduate School of Education, http:// gse.hightechhigh.org/ourApproach.php.

60. Victoria Murphy, "Where Everyone Can Overachieve," *Forbes*, October 11, 2004, https://www.forbes.com/forbes/2004/1011/080.html.

61. Data are from the 2014–2015 school year. "High Tech High: Student Body," *U.S. News & World Report*, https://www.usnews.com/education/best -high-schools/california/districts/san-diego-unified-school-district/high-tech -high-3217/student-body; Jean Fluver and Larry Rosenstock, "Choice and Diversity: Irreconcilable Differences?," *Principal Leadership*, April 2003, 12–18. See also "SARC Report for High Tech High," High Teach High, https://www .hightechhigh.org/wp-content/uploads/2016/06/HTH-SARC-2017.pdf.

62. "Adult Learning: HTH District Intern Program," High Tech High Graduate School of Education, https://www.hightechhigh.org/adult-learning/hth-dis trict-intern-program/.

63. "Programs of Study," High Tech High Graduate School of Education, https://www.hightechhigh.org/adult-learning/hth-district-intern-program/.

64. Jean Hatfield and Ian Lindquist, "How to Solve Charter Schools' Biggest Challenge," *U.S. News & World Report,* May 6, 2016, https://www.aei.org/publication/how-to-solve-charter-schools-biggest-challenge/.

65. "Larry Rosenstock, Responses," program materials presented on a school tour, Winter 2017.

66. "Larry Rosenstock, Responses."

67. U.S. Department of Education, "Beginning Teacher Attrition and Mobility: Results From the First Through Third Waves of the 2007–08 Beginning Teacher Longitudinal Study," as referenced in Mongeau, "In Search of High Quality Teachers."

68. Kenneth Zeichner and César Peña-Sandoval, "Venture Philanthropy and Teacher Education Policy in the U.S: The Role of the New Schools Venture Fund," *Teachers College Record* 117:5 (2015), 1–44.

69. "About High Tech High," www.hightechhigh.org/about-us/; "Five California Public Charter Networks Receive $60 million to Promote Effective Teaching and Prepare More Students to Succeed in College," press release, Bill & Melinda Gates Foundation, http://www.gatesfoundation.org/Media-Center/Press-Releases/2009/11/Five-California-Public-Charter-Networks-Receive-$60-Million-to-Promote-Effective-Teaching.

70. For critiques, see Sarah Marla Stitzlein and Craig K. West, "New Forms of Teacher Education: Connections to Charter Schools and Their Approaches," *Democracy and Education* 22:2, 2014, http://democracyeducationjournal.org/home/vol22/iss2/2/; Barrett A. Smith, "If You Cannot Live by Our Rules, If You Cannot Adapt to This Place, I Can Show You the Back Door," *Democracy and Education* 22:2, 2014, http://democracyeducationjournal.org/home/vol23/iss1/13/; Diane Ravitch, "Laura Chapman: ESSA and the Degradation of Teacher Preparation," Diane Ravitch Blog, July 8, 2016, https://dianeravitch.net/?s=Success+Academy+Teacher+Residency.

71. Andre Carnovsky, "How Teens Move from Innovative K–12 to College," *U.S. News and World Report* and *Hechinger Report,* August 11, 2015, https://www.usnews.com/news/articles/2015/08/11/how-teens-move-from-innovative-k-12-to-college?int=news-rec.

72. Quoted in Carnovsky, "How Teens Move."

73. "Our Approach," High Tech High Graduate School of Education, http://gse.hightechhigh.org/ourApproach.php.

74. Rob Riordan, personal communication, June 27, 2017.

Conclusion: Lessons Learned

1. For examples of just two of the best such calls for reform, see Arthur Levine, *Educating School Teachers* (New York: The Education Schools Project, 2006), and Marilyn Cochran-Smith and Kenneth M. Zeichner, *Studying Teacher Education: The Report of the AERA Panel on Research and Teacher Education*

(Washington, DC: American Educational Research Association and Mahway, NJ: Lawrence Erlbaum Associates, 2005).

2. Harry Judge, "Foreword: A Beginning or An End?," in Michael Fullan, Gary Galluzzo, Patricia Morris, and Nancy Watson, *The Rise and Stall of Teacher Education Reform* (Washington, DC: American Association of Colleges for Teacher Education, 1998), xiii.

3. "A Pivot toward Clinical Practice, Its Lexicon, and the Renewal of Educator Preparation," report of the AACTE Clinical Practice Commission (American Association of Colleges for Teacher Education, 2018), http://aacte.link/cpc-press.

4. Frederick M. Hess, Andrew J. Rotherham, and Kate Walsh, "Introduction," in *A Qualified Teacher in Every Classroom: Appraising Old Answers and New Ideas* (Cambridge, MA: Harvard Education Press, 2004), 1.

5. Cochran-Smith and Zeichner, *Studying Teacher Education*, 43.

6. There are multiple case studies of excellent university-based teacher preparation programs beyond those included in this volume. See, for example, Linda Darling-Hammond, *Powerful Teacher Education: Lessons from Exemplary Programs* (San Francisco: Jossey-Bass, 2006). To fail to acknowledge the existence of such excellent programs is to significantly misread the current state of the field. On the other hand, to assume, as some defenders of the university model do, that these exemplary programs represent the norm in teacher preparation is to make an equally inexcusable mistake.

7. Harvey Kantor and Robert Lowe, "Bureaucracy Left and Right: Thinking about the One Best System," in *Reconstructing the Common Good in Education: Coping with Intractable American Dilemmas*, eds. Larry Cuban and D. Ships (Stanford: Stanford University Press, 2000), 130–131.

8. Fraser expanded this argument in "Notes toward a New Progressive Politics of Teacher Education," *Journal of Teacher Education*, 56:3 (May/June 2005), 279–284.

9. James Bryant Conant, *The Education of American Teachers* (New York: McGraw-Hill, 1963), 5, see also 1–8.

10. Michael J. Feuer, Robert E. Floden, Naomi Chudowsky, and Judie Ahn, *Evaluation of Teacher Preparation Programs: Purposes, Methods, and Policy Options* (Washington, DC: National Academy of Education, 2013), 1, 10.

11. Lee S. Shulman, "Reconstructing Educational Research," in *Review of Educational Research* (Washington, DC: American Educational Research Association, 1970), reprinted in Shulman, *The Wisdom of Practice: Essays on Teaching, Learning, and Learning to Teach* (San Francisco: Jossey-Bass, 2004), 18.

12. Linda Darling-Hammond and Joan Baratz-Snowden, eds., *A Good Teacher in Every Classroom: Preparing the Highly Qualified Teachers Our Children Deserve* (San Francisco: Jossey-Bass, 2005). See also Linda Darling-Hammond, John D. Bransford, P. LePage, Karen Hammerness, and H. Duffey, eds., *Preparing Teachers for a Changing World: What Teachers Should Learn*

and Be Able to Do (San Francisco: Jossey-Bass, 2005); Linda Darling-Hammond, *Studies of Excellence in Teacher Education*, 3 vols. (Washington, DC: American Association of Colleges for Teacher Education, 2005); and Linda Darling-Hammond and Deborah L. Ball, *Teaching for High Standards: What Policymakers Need to Know and Be Able to Do* (Philadelphia: Consortium for Policy Research in Education, 1998).

13. Education Commission of the States, *What Does Research Say About How to Prepare Quality Teachers* (Denver, CO: Education Commission of the States, 2003); Dale Ballou and Michael Podgursky, "Teacher Training and Licensing: A Layman's Guide," in *Better Teachers, Better Schools*, ed. Checker Fin and M. Kanstoroom (Washington, DC: Fordham Foundation, 1999); Hess et al., "Introduction," 6–7.

14. Cochran-Smith and Zeichner, *Studying Teacher Education*, 29.

15. S. Paul Wright and William. L. Sanders, "Teacher and Classroom Context Effect on Student Achievement: Implications for Teacher Evaluation," *Journal of Personnel Evaluation in Education*, 11:1 (April, 1997), 57–67.

16. See, for example, the National Research Council's publication, John D. Bransford, Ann L. Brown, and Rodney R. Cocking, eds., *How People Learn: Brain, Mind, Experience, and School* (Washington, DC: National Academies Press, 2000).

17. Franklin D. Roosevelt, Address at Oglethorpe University, Atlanta, Georgia, May 22, 1932.

18. Frederick M. Hess, "Tear Down This Wall: The Case for a Radical Overhaul of Teacher Certification," *Educational Horizons*, 80:4, (Summer 2002), 169–183.

19. Fraser developed the argument in these two paragraphs in more detail in an earlier article, "Notes toward a New Progressive Politics of Teacher Education," *Journal of Teacher Education*, 56:3 (May/June 2005), 279–284.

20. Council for the Accreditation of Educator Preparation, 2013 CAEP Standards, http://caepnet.org/~/media/Files/caep/standards/caep-standards-one-pager-061716.pdf?la=en.

21. George S. Counts, *Dare the School Build a New Social Order* (New York: the John Day Company, 1932).

22. National Education Association, "English Language Learners Face Unique Challenges," policy brief, http://www.nea.org/assets/docs/HE/ELL_Policy_Brief_Fall_08_(2).pdf.

23. For a survey of research on the importance of preparing teachers to teach students with varying needs, including those with learning disabilities, English language learners, low-income students, students in rural and urban areas, and so on, see Etta R. Hollins, "Research for Preparing Teachers for Diverse Populations" and Maria Smith et al., "Teaching Diverse Learners," both in Darling-Hammond et al., *Preparing Teachers for a Changing World*.

24. H. Y. Sebastian Cherng and Peter F. Halpin, "The Importance of Minor-

ity Teachers: Student Perceptions of Minority Versus White Teachers," *Educational Researcher* 45:7 (2016), 407–420.

25. Kenneth Zeichner, *Teacher Education and the Struggle for Social Justice* (New York: Routledge, 2009), 27–28.

26. For more on recruiting a diverse pool of students, see Laura Elizabeth Boles et al., "Moving toward Excellence in Teacher Preparation," white paper, Woodrow Wilson National Fellowship Foundation, 2017.

27. See, for example, Jameson T. Brewer and Kathleen deMarrais, eds., *Teach for America Counter-Narratives: Alumni Speak Up and Speak Out* (New York: Peter Lang, 2015).

28. Peter C. Murrell, Jr., *The Community Teacher: A New Framework for Effective Urban Teaching* (New York: Teachers College Press, 2001).

29. Kenneth Zeichner, Katherina Payne, and Kate Brayko Gence, "Democratizing Teacher Education," *Journal of Teacher Education*, 66:2 (March/April, 2015), 122–135; see also, Ellen Condliffe Lagemann, *An Elusive Science: The Troubling History of Education Research* (Chicago: University of Chicago Press, 2000).

30. See Cynthia Onore and Bonnie L. Gildin, "A Community-University Partnership to Develop Urban Teachers as Public Professionals," in *Moving Teacher Education into Urban Schools and Communities*, ed. Jane Noel (New York: Routledge, 2013), 152–168; Dennis Shirley et al., "Bringing the Community Back In: Change, Accommodation, and Contestation in a School and University Partnership," *Equity and Excellence in Education* 39 (2006), 27–36; Christine E. Sleeter and Marilynne Boyle-Baise, "Community Service Learning for Multicultural Teacher Education," *Educational Foundations* 14:2 (2000), 33–50; Kenneth M. Zeichner, *Teacher Education and the Struggle for Social Justice* (New York: Routledge, 2009); Kenneth M. Zeichner and Susan Melnick, "The Role of Community Field Experiences in Preparing Teachers for Cultural Diversity," in *Currents of Reform in Preservice Teacher Education*, ed. Kenneth Zeichner, Susan Melnick, and Mary Louise Gomez (New York: Teachers College Press, 1996), 176–198.

31. Quoted in "What Made Me the Teacher I Am Today?" a white paper, Woodrow Wilson National Fellowship Foundation, May 2016.

32. Boles et al., "Moving toward Excellence"; see also James W. Fraser, *Preparing America's Teachers: A History* (New York: Teachers College Press, 2007), 216–219.

33. Lee S. Shulman has discussed and described the term "pedagogical content knowledge" many times. For an example, see his American Educational Research Association presidential address, "Those Who Understand: Knowledge Growth in Teaching," originally published in *Educational Researcher* 15:2 (February 1986), 4–14.

34. Shulman, "Those Who Understand."

35. See James W. Fraser and Audra M. Watson, "Why Clinical Experience

and Mentoring Are Replacing Student Teaching on the Best Campuses," white paper, Woodrow Wilson National Fellowship Foundation, November 2014. See also, "A Pivot toward Clinical Practice, Its Lexicon, and the Renewal of Educator Preparation," report of the AACTE Clinical Practice Commission (Washington, DC: American Association of Colleges for Teacher Education, 2018).

36. For further discussion of this issue and examples of places that address the cost problem, see Boles et al., "Moving toward Excellence."

37. *A Nation Prepared: Teachers for the 21st Century: The Report of the Task Force on Teaching as a Profession* (New York: Carnegie Forum on Education and the Economy, 1986); *Tomorrow's Teachers: A Report of the Holmes Group* (East Lansing, MI: Holmes Group, 1986).

38. Albert Shanker, "Reflections on Forty Years in the Profession," https://www.educationevolving.org/pdf/Shanker-Forty_Years_in_the_Profession.pdf.

39. Lee S. Shulman, "Calm Seas, Auspicious Gales," originally published as the conclusion to *Detachment and Concern: Conversations in the Philosophy of Teaching and Teacher Education*, ed. Margaret Buchmann and Robert E. Floden (New York: Teachers College Press, 1993), reprinted in *The Wisdom of Practice*, 437–438.